Volume 23 / 2024

REAL WOMEN WRITE

The Power of Friendship

FOREWORD BY

Helen (Len) Leatherwood

EDITED BY

Shelley Johnson Carey

**SHARING STORIES, SHARING LIVES
IN PROSE AND POETRY FROM
STORY CIRCLE NETWORK**

Story Circle
NETWORK
...by, for, and about women.

A Publication of Story Circle Network

Real Women Write: The Power of Friendship
Volume 23, 2024

Foreword by Helen (Len) Leatherwood
Edited by Shelley Johnson Carey
Cover image, interior design, and technical support by Sherry Wachter

ISBN: 979-8-9861302-1-7

Story Circle Network
723 W University Avenue #300-234
Georgetown TX 78626

https://www.storycircle.org

Story Circle Network is a nonprofit—501(c)(3)—organization dedicated to helping women share the stories of their lives and to raising public awareness of the importance of women's personal histories. We carry out that mission through publications, websites, classes, workshops, writing and reading circles, and woman-focused programs. SCN activities empower women to tell their stories, discover their identities through their stories, and choose to be the authors of their own lives.

Story Circle Network's 2024 anthology of members' writing, *Real Women Write,* has taken up the topic of friendship, a subject that informs every aspect of our lives today. Contributors explore *The Power of Friendship,* including how strong social connections reduce stress, and how friendships improve mental and physical health, and enhance overall well-being. This theme speaks to SCN's goal of supporting writing women of all ages, sexual orientations, gender identities, races, religions, and ethnicities.

"We should always have three friends in our lives—one who walks ahead, who we look up to and follow; one who walks beside us, who is with us every step of our journey; and then, one who we reach back for and bring along after we've cleared the way."

— MICHELLE OBAMA

CONTENTS

TRIBUTE

F – Fiction   L – Lifewriting   P – Poetry

FRIENDS FROM THE PAST

SERENDIPITOUS FRIENDSHIPS

FRIENDS—GONE BUT NOT FORGOTTEN

ENDURING FRIENDSHIPS

FOREWORD

Helen (Len) Leatherwood

Friendship. That word conjures up a myriad of emotions all on its own—happiness, connection, solidarity, openness, and honesty. Friendship allows each of us to feel seen, valued, and cherished, whether for a moment, a day, a week, or a lifetime. Friendship is not limited to people. Dogs, cats, horses, physical locations, bikes, and even pain can become a friend. Friendship can also be nurtured within oneself, which offers a fertile training ground for lessons in forgiveness, acceptance, and the power of grace. Sadly, friendship has the potential to be bittersweet, if or when that close connection shifts, or time, attention, or access changes that once trusting dynamic. And then there is the dark side to friendship, when there is hurt, danger, or betrayal, which produces necessary self-protection from that once trusted friend. Finally, deep friendship holds the possibility of profound grief if our beloved confidante dies. In short, friendship is a mixed bag, which requires risk and vulnerability.

The essays, memoir pieces, poems, and fictional stories in this anthology reveal the multilayered aspects of friendship—the joy, pain, ambivalence, and love that friendship brings, whether in the past, the present, or the hoped-for future. Within these pages, you will recognize your own experiences, empathize with those who chronicle painful outcomes, and laugh with those who describe the lighter, more joyful moments of friendship. Mostly, you will feel a connection with these writers because of their willingness to open up their hearts to share the nuanced experiences they have had or can conjure in their minds related to this highly charged word: friendship.

I am in a unique position as I read these stories in the anthology. In my role as Story Circle Network's Education Coordinator, I directly know or have made the acquaintance of many of the women whose stories fill this volume. Many of them are, in fact, my friends and I have heard first draft readings of some of these pieces in our shared writing communities, such as the online classes, webinars, e-groups, and online writing workshops. I must say that it is thrilling to see the transformation of these stories and poems from first draft to polished submissions, and I have been deeply touched by the depth, breadth, and authenticity of every piece I've read, whether from a friend or someone I've not yet met. Story Circle Network is at its core a community of women writers who navigate their writing life with the help of the friendships they nurture as members of this highly supportive organization. The trust that the authors have displayed on the page aptly demonstrates their sense of safety among like-minded writing sisters.

Here are just a few examples of the trust that graces the pages of this anthology:

> "I have no regrets. I'm grateful that the Pied Piper, who had the spirit of Puck, took me by the hand and showed me a whole other world...I had to leave Fred, or I would have died with him. However, I still treasure the gifts."
>
> —from *Fred, Drugs, and Rock 'n' Roll*

> "Most of the time I just sat, stunned by grief and bewildered as to what my life would look like going forward. The dogs never left my side, snuggling as close to me as possible...I was glad to have them."
>
> —from *My Girls Got Me Through*

> "After closing and locking the door, she sat in her favorite upholstered chair next to the telephone table. She picked up the receiver and dialed the familiar number. Mildred will just die when she hears this! Lucille smiled slyly as she waited for her friend to answer."
>
> —from *Holy Rivalry*

> "Magic happens in the alchemy of collaboration—taking the best each has to offer and combining it to make something neither of us could have created alone, in our books, in our lives, in our very selves."
>
> —from *Friendship, Collaboration, and Magic*

In my own life, I can truthfully say that writing has been one of my closest friends. I can sit for hours pouring my hurts, thoughts, and dreams onto the page. I confide intimate secrets and pray no human knows where to find them to read. I chuckle at funny lines my characters (or I) say and cry without shame when writing about events, factual or fictional, that touch me on a deeper level. My writing is like having a cozy spot on the front porch where it's an everyday routine to sit, share, and confide with my deeper self while laughing out loud at downright silly events that add spice to life. Writing is a trusted friend, a willing confidante, and a co-conspirator when pushing past the familiar and forging into the unknown. Writing also can be fickle. Just when I need to quickly get something on the page to meet a deadline, I can almost hear my muse mumbling, "Don't rush me," and there I sit, waiting impatiently as I stare at the blank page. Writing brings comfort and solace as well as a deep sense of satisfaction when the words shift and change before aligning into just the right order, creating sentences I am proud to have produced. Writing, like a good friend, also requires positive thinking and dedication, which offers the opportunity to live a focused and uplifting life.

In a recent poem for my grandchildren, I wrote:
>Dedicate yourself to a passion, a cause, a belief
>Open up your world
>Meet like-minded people
>Pursue what is healthy and good for you
>Encourage others to do what is good for them

Writing is my passion, and my writing mentors, students, and friends are those like-minded people of whom I speak. Engaging in a positive activity gives me a clear direction to aim, and interacting with others—my writing friends—has provided a support system to help me realize my dreams. I am proud to say that I have just released my first novel, *Hope in the Time of Dying*, and I am working on my second. I write daily to produce fiction, nonfiction, or poetry to share on my blog and submit for publication. Not only do I write often, but as a writing teacher, I have the chance to help others write often, too. As a result, I have stretched and grown and, hopefully, helped my students to do the same. Story Circle Network has been my primary source of friendships over the last twelve years. I am grateful for the camaraderie I've found and look forward to meeting friends I have yet to make. Sharing a passion makes for close and enduring connections.

As you read this anthology, you will find stories that explore the many facets of friendship. Read slowly and savor each story, essay, or poem. Each will offer you the opportunity to reflect on your own friendships, good and bad, easy and difficult, lost and found, and will help you remember that we humans all share a common need: to be seen, heard, and loved, flaws and all. In exchange, we are happy to return the favor.

Wishing you, dear reader, many pleasant hours of discovering the honesty, wisdom, and insight you'll find within these pages. You might even chuckle here and there, which, as we all know, is another key ingredient of friendship.

Helen (Len) Leatherwood is a past president of Story Circle Network. Please see her bio in the Contributors section.

FROM THE EDITOR

Shelley Johnson Carey

A friendship that lasts through the ages,
Must evolve with our many stages.
From youth's joyful treasures
To life's pain and pleasures,
A friendship through time all engages.

The theme of friendship has always held a special place in my writing, but I found myself reflecting upon it deeply when one of my dearest friends was diagnosed with laryngeal cancer. After 35 years of friendship, it became clear that a relationship that I had hoped would continue through our golden years would soon be coming to an end. One day, the above poem flowed out of me about our time together—the days when we'd laughed for hours with each other and the bumpy times when misunderstanding threatened to end our alliance. Though my friend succumbed too soon, and I still grieve that loss, I also am grateful for the chance to have had such camaraderie and closeness. As my work on this anthology began, memories of that treasured relationship and others that have been like sparkling charms on my bracelet of life inspired me to champion the topic of friendship for this edition of *Real Women Write*.

Navigating friendships is often tricky—they operate without written contracts or instruction manuals. And yet these relationships are essential for our well-being. They are beautiful, complex, essential elements of life that we must learn about through experience. In the 2024 edition of *Real Women Write, The Power of Friendship*, 65 Story Circle writing sisters generously share their experiences traversing the terrain of friendship. This collection of 64 prose pieces and 16 poems—some heart wrenching, others humorous—will surely bring to mind the joys and sorrows you have found in similar relationships.

Helen (Len) Leatherwood, former Story Circle Network president and gifted writer and teacher, contributed the Foreword to this volume. Len shares the following thoughts about the range of selections found in this anthology: "Within these pages, you will recognize your own experiences, empathize with those who chronicle painful outcomes, and laugh with those who describe the lighter, more joyful moments of friendship. Mostly, you will feel a connection with these writers because of their willingness to open up their hearts to share the nuanced experiences they have had or can conjure in their minds related to this highly charged word: friendship."

Though friendship is difficult to define and classify, the creative works in this anthology have been placed into seven groups—Friends from the Past, Friends in Need, Unexpected Friendships, Family Friends, Serendipitous Friendships, Friends—Gone Not Forgotten, and Enduring Friendships. These groupings are simply organizational—each story is so multifaceted that it could fit into more than one of these categories. These sections are merely lenses through which your reading can begin. I'm certain you will find yourself returning to read and appreciate each piece more than once. Also included among the other selections is Jeanne Guy's special tribute to beloved Story Circle Network member and writer, Judy Alter.

My first year editing *Real Women Write* has been a wonderful experience that found me smiling and weeping as I reviewed and edited scores of remarkable submissions. I am grateful for the extraordinary women of Story Circle Network who work with me to create this annual member showcase. Among them are Susan Wittig Albert, SCN founder, mentor, and steadfast advisor; Susan Schoch, president of SCN, previous anthology editor, and my mentor who guided me through this process with her generous support; Teresa Lynn, vital technical manager of submission processes and website pages; Liz Beaty, who keeps finances and program goals in sight; the Board of Directors, who continue to support this member opportunity; Sherry Wachter, for superlative cover art, book design, and technical formatting. We all have great appreciation for the thoughtful contribution of Helen (Len) Leatherwood, author of our Foreword. Her timely and important writing continues to inform and inspire many women. And all of us are thankful to the SCN members who submit their work to the anthology each year. The creativity, self-awareness, and perception of these women have made meaningful contributions to preserving twenty-first-century herstory.

Shelley Johnson Carey is a retired publications professional and author of *Thin Mint Memories: Scouting for Empowerment through the Girl Scout Cookie Program*. She is the current secretary and publications coordinator for the SCN Board of Directors.

ABOUT STORY CIRCLE NETWORK

Susan Schoch

In its 27 years as a nonprofit organization, Story Circle Network has grown from a handful of motivated women to an international group that has touched thousands. We remain devoted to our mission of helping women share the stories of their lives through writing, and to raising public awareness of the importance of women's personal histories.

This edition of our annual anthology is devoted to the Power of Friendship, and that power is evident in our group of writing women. We support and encourage women to find and use their authentic voices in the form that works for them, be it fiction, memoir, nonfiction, or poetry. By helping them grow their writing skills and share their work, SCN builds confidence and demonstrates the value of women's experience in moving all of us forward. We also build connections and develop friendships that are deeply meaningful.

Story Circle Network carries out our mission through publication opportunities in our annual anthology, *Real Women Write*, in our quarterly *Journal*, and in two blogs. Our website details our services—https://www.storycircle.org—including a range of online classes, national and international workshops and conferences, ongoing writing and reading circles, work-in-progress groups and other woman-focused programs. We consistently explore new technologies and methods for creative expression, most recently on the Substack platform—https://storycirclenetwork.substack.com/

We proudly sponsor Story Circle Book Reviews, the oldest and largest women's book review site on the internet. SCN also honors excellent women writers with the annual Sarton and Gilda Book Awards. Named for beloved comedienne Gilda Radner, the Gilda recognizes writing about women's experience using humor. The Sarton Awards are named for the brilliant writer May Sarton, and recognize excellence in the categories of Memoir, Nonfiction, Contemporary Fiction, Historical Fiction, and Young Adult Fiction. SCN also encourages high-quality work with lifewriting, essay, and poetry contests. All of these activities empower women to discover their identities through their stories, and to choose to be the authors of their own lives.

Story Circle Network sustains a community of women who recognize and appreciate the bravery of writing down our truths, and welcomes writers at every level, novice to professional. This community is open to all women and has always been committed to diversity and inclusion. We actively work to expand equality in our programs.

Sustained by the time, energy, and expertise of a large group of dedicated volunteers and a small paid staff, our revenues are generated primarily from annual membership dues, program fees, and generous donations from grants and supporters. All of us offer our passion and commitment to lift up the lives of all women through the healing force of story, and to continue our exploration of what it means to be a woman in this ever-changing world. We hope that you will join us in this labor of creativity and friendship.

Susan Schoch is a freelance writer and editor specializing in personal history. Among her works is *The Clay Connection*, a biography of ceramic artists Jim and Nan McKinnell. She is also a reviewer for Story Circle Book Reviews, the editor of six SCN anthologies, and the current president of Story Circle Network.

CONTRIBUTORS

Kathie Arcide – Bellevue, WA

Kathie Arcide is a Psychotherapist/Professional "Mom," in private practice for 50 years, but more important, I am my father's daughter. My calling is to pass on his creative, and often covert childhood lessons for me and my sisters, the most valuable one being the ability we all have to choose how we see or experience a person, place or thing. Teaching people how to find many different perspectives is my lifelong mission. My blog is https://chosenperspectives.com/.

Carol J. Wechsler Blatter – Tucson, AZ

Mrs. Blatter is a recently retired psychotherapist. She has published stories in Birren Center Collection, The Gift of Long Life, Chaleur Press, Jewish Writing Project, Jewish Literary Journal, Writing it Real anthologies, prose poems in Story Circle Network's anthologies, and Covenant of the Generations by the Women of Reform Judaism. Mrs. Blatter is a wife, mother, and grandmother. Her granddaughter is a bright, interesting, and lovable little girl with a wonderful future. And she is an avid reader.

Sue Boggio – Albuquerque, NM

Sue Boggio is the co-author with Mare Pearl of four novels (*Sunlight and Shadow, A Growing Season, Long Night Moon, Hungry Shoes*) published by the University of New Mexico Press. She has presented fiction writing workshops at Southwest Writers Workshop, UNM Writers Conference, Women Writing the West national conference, and the Tony Hillerman Writer's Conference. Learn more at our website: www.boggioandpearl.com.

Amy J. Bostelman – Leander, TX

Amy lives in the Texas Hill Country outside of Austin. She lives with her husband of 29 years and her young adult daughter. She enjoys writing poetry, creative nonfiction, essays, and prose. She's participated as a judge on the Sarton and Gilda Awards for Story Circle.

Lorinda Boyer – Bellingham, WA
Lorinda Boyer is a multi-award-winning author, and published poet. She lives with her wife, Sandy, and pup, Mollie, in the Pacific Northwest. She enjoys writing, reading, running, and drinking far too much coffee.

Lin Marshall Brummels – Winside, NE
Lin Marshall Brummels earned a BS from University of Nebraska and MS from Syracuse University. Her poem, "Jerry's Hands" was selected as an Honorable Mention poem, 2021 Nebraska Poetry Society's poetry contest. Brummels has published poems in *Poet Lore*, *San Pedro River Review*, *Concho River Review*, *Oakwood*, *Plainsong*, *Nebraska Life*, and others. Chapbooks are *Cottonwood Strong* and *Hard Times*, a 2016 Nebraska Book Award winner. Latest book, *A Quilted Landscape*, Scurfpea Publishing. Forthcoming, *The Last Yellow Rose*, Sandhills Press.

Judy Burman – Roseburg, OR
For many of you I am not a stranger. I have been writing with Story Circle since I retired in 2001. I am 84 years old and a newlywed (3 years). My husband of 60 years passed away in 2018. When I worked, I was a Cost Accountant for an electronic manufacturing company. In October 2023, I became a great-great grandmother. I love being busy and I teach a line-dance class in my neighborhood.

Claire Butler – Cincinnati, OH
Claire Butler lives in Cincinnati, Ohio. She is the author of *Conversations with the Tuesday Night Girls*, a collection of humorous short stories about her girlfriends. She is the first-place winner for Story Circle Network's 2023 LifeWriting Contest, and she has contributed to Story Circle Network's yearly anthologies and other short story sites. Her memoir is currently in revision. She is also a professional artist painting in oil. Learn more at Claire-Butler.com.

Donna Cameron – Brier, WA
Donna Cameron is the author of the Nautilus award-winning book *A Year of Living Kindly*. Her work has been featured in *The Washington Post*, *Writer's Digest*, *Dorothy Parker's Ashes*, *Thanatos*, *Eclectica*, and many other publications. She lives in the Pacific Northwest. Visit her website: https://ayearoflivingkindly.com.

Joan L. Connor – Kerrville, TX

Joan lives in Kerrville, Texas, and also in her travel trailer as she, her husband, and their dog, Ava, spend weeks traveling the USA. She is completing a Peace Corps (Mongolia 2011-2013) memoir, part of which constituted her thesis for her MFA, Lindenwood University. When not tapping the computer keys, Joan spends hours as a novice fiddler, lifelong pianist, amateur weaver, sunflower admirer and still thinking she should be bicycling along the Guadalupe River.

Patricia Daly – Largo, FL

Patricia Daly is a *USA Today* bestselling author and writer of narrative nonfiction and spirituality. She has been published by Leaders Press, Story Circle Network, *The Sun*, Medium.com and *Reiki News Magazine*. She has indie-published, *The Women in His Life*, *Indelible Imprint*, and *The Deliberate Thinker*, all available on Amazon. She is retired and lives in Largo, Florida. Connect with her at www.PatriciaDalyWrites.com.

Cynthia F. Davidson – Hope Valley, RI

A member of SCN for over a dozen years, Cynthia F. Davidson is now a member of the board and on the faculty. A long-time expatriate and former CBS News journalist, she spent two decades as a pioneer in the global management field. She credits SCN membership with the support and skill development required to publish her first memoir, *The Importance of Paris*. SCN also inspired her to start facilitating workshops and writing groups that capture women's lived wisdom.

Debra Dolan – West Vancouver, BC

Debra Dolan lives on the west coast of Canada, is a long time (50+ years) private journal writer, and an avid reader of women's memoir. She has been a member of Story Circle Network since 2009 and is a self-described pluviophile. Debra enjoys intimate conversations over red wine and candlelight, solo nature walks, and has completed two book projects, "Writings and Reflections: 1958 to 2018" and "Writings and Reflections: Turning 50 in 2008" (*Walking the Camino de Santiago*).

MaryAnn Easley – Laguna Niguel, CA

MaryAnn Easley is an award-winning author of over a dozen books for young adults and teaches journaling, memoir writing, and poetry in Laguna Niguel, California. She has been published nationally and regionally and actively supports aspiring writers in accomplishing their creative goals through salons, workshops, and events. She received the Junior Library Guild Selection Award for her first novel, *I Am the Ice Worm*, and the Career Achievement Award from the University of Redlands.

Sara Etgen-Baker – Anna, TX

After retiring from teaching, Sara began writing memoirs and personal essays many of which have been published in anthologies and magazines including *Good Old Days Magazine, Chicken Soup for the Soul, Guideposts, Times They Were A Changing*, and *Wisdom Has a Voice*. She's currently compiling her collection into a book titled *Shoebox Stories*. She recently finished writing her first novel, *Secrets at Dillehay Crossing*. She hopes to publish both books sometime in 2025.

Sarah Fine – Toronto, ON

I am a mostly unpublished writer and poet, born and raised in Canada from Colonizer and Indigenous ancestry, living most of my life in Toronto on the shores of Lake Ontario, an environmentalist and a lover of trees, a Baby Boomer mother of three adult children, a wife for 40 years, a retired introvert and an optimist.

Carolyn Foland – Sacramento, CA

I am retired from work in the health and welfare field. With degrees in both journalism and public administration, I created public information and education programs in mental health and later worked in program monitoring, contract development, and facility management in health and welfare. I enjoy travel, writing, reading, plays, and lectures.

B. Lynn Goodwin – Danville, CA

Writer and editor B. Lynn Goodwin owns Writer Advice, www.writeradvice.com. She's written three award-winning books—two YAs, *Talent* and *Disrupted,* and a memoir titled *Never Too Late: From Wannabe to Wife at 62.* Her flash fiction is published in *Flashquake, Nebo, Cabinet of Heed, Murmur of Words, 100-Word Stories, Ariel's Dream,* and *Writing in a Woman's Voice.* She's also a book reviewer and teacher at Story Circle Network.

Jeanne Guy – Langley, WA

Jeanne, SCN's 2018-2020 president, is a speaker and veteran self-awareness reflective writing teacher. She's the multi-award-winning author of *You'll Never Find Us: A Memoir,* the story of how her children were stolen from her and how she stole them back (She Writes Press 2021), co-author of *Seeing Me: A Guide to Reframing the Way You See Yourself,* and author of numerous anthology essays. Details about this avid walker, slow reader, and irreverent blogger are on her website, www.jeanneguy.com.

Christine Hassing – Bloomingdale, MI

Christine is a writer, published author, life and leadership mentor / trainer, adjunct professor, an advocate of cold noses as healers, and a champion of unconditional listening and hope. To find her additional writings: "Good News" a monthly Michigan newspaper publication, books via Amazon, blogs at https://Christinehassing.com, and previous SCN anthologies. When Christine is not joyously writing, teaching, and mentoring, she immerses herself in time with her other great loves: her husband, their two cold noses (dogs), Nature, friendships, and family.

Kathryn Haueisen – Reynoldsburg, Ohio

My books cover life's little and not-so-little challenges including relocation, natural disasters, changing marital status, and the tragedies and triumphs of the people we call the Pilgrims. I blog regularly to promote good people doing great things and publish articles and books when I can. Published books: *Married & Mobile, A Ready Hope, 40-Day Journey with Kathleen Norris, Asunder, Mayflower Chronicles: The Tale of Two Cultures* and *Mary Brewster's Love Life: Matriarch of the Mayflower.* More information at HowWiseThen.com.

Linda Healy – Dayton, OH

Linda Healy was a hospice nurse. In retirement she writes legacy pieces and poetry. She also enjoys doing color pencil drawing and Zentangles. Other activities include hiking, pets, travel, movies and books. Her favorite pastime is spending time with her grandchildren. Linda has stories published in two *Chicken Soup for the Soul* books. She was published in Story Circle's 2022 and 2023 *Real Women Write* anthologies and nominated for a Pushcart Prize for her story, "Will Work for Food."

Patricia Roop Hollinger – Westminster, MD

"Pat" was raised on a farm, thus developed an imagination pondering the nature of the universe as plants emerged from seeds the size of a grain of salt. Words held the magic of stories. She sings words to her own accompaniment on the piano or organ. She is a retired Chaplain/Pastoral Counselor/Licensed Clinical Professional Counselor who lives in a retirement community with her husband and their cat "Spunky."

Marion Hunt – Berkeley, CA

I enjoyed 25 years as an elementary school teacher successfully feeding young developing minds with courage, excitement for exploration, discovery, and mastery, while continuously advancing my knowledge of the field. My first love was writing, and I am pleased that some of my students are working as writers and editors. I am proud to have helped craft their professional adult lives. I write mostly for friends, family, SCN, and myself, and have one article that was published in *WOODWORK* magazine.

Teresa H. Janssen – Port Townsend, WA

Teresa H. Janssen's essays and short fiction have appeared in a variety of anthologies and journals, including *Zyzzyva, Parabola, Notre Dame Magazine,* and *Los Angeles Review.* Her debut historical novel, *The Ways of Water* (2023), inspired by family lore, won the Best Book Award in western fiction and the Western Heritage Wrangler Award. Teresa writes from her home in Port Townsend, WA where she hikes, bikes, and tends a small orchard.

Deb Johnson, MPA – Laguna Niguel, CA

Deb earned her master's degree in public administration from Columbia University and has spoken at numerous conferences, been a regular guest on Southern California PBS television, published over a dozen articles in *Western Banking* and *The Findley Reports*, SAG member, a former elected official and featured in the *Los Angeles Times*, *OC Register*, *Voice of OC*, and *OC Radio*. Find her at www.keepwalkingyounglady.com

Cindy Jones – Columbia, MD

Cindy Jones is a retired librarian and co-owned a yarn shop with another mother of a daughter with special needs. She has a BA in Psychology from University of Maryland Baltimore County and an MLS. from Texas Woman's University. She's currently writing a memoir about adopting her daughter from a Bulgarian orphanage and historical fiction. Her piece, "Uncharted," was published in the 2023 *Real Women Write* anthology and nominated for a Pushcart Prize.

Barbara Rady Kazdan – Los Angeles, CA

The author of creative nonfiction, Barbara draws inspiration from personal experience and reflections on contemporary life. The works, *Oh. I'm a Widow*, chronicles her journey from bereavement to a full new life. Recently relocated to Los Angeles, she Zooms into her longtime memoir group in Silver Spring, Maryland. Enjoy her work at https://www.achievingchangetogether.com/published-essays.

Kimberly Krantz – Laguna Niguel, CA

Kim is a published author, editor, teacher, and an award-winning writer. She enjoys the creative process of building poems and stories from prompts and real-life experiences. Kim works with teens and adults to help them gain confidence in their storytelling abilities through journaling and creating poetry. She is an avid community volunteer, supporting our active military, their families and veterans. She and her husband live in Southern California with their rescue dogs.

Sue Kusch – White Salmon, WA

In theory, I am retired. I live on a five-acre homestead in the foothills of Washington State's Cascade Mountains. My summers are spent growing food, herbs, and flowers. I chase native wildflower blooms in spring and tent camp in the fall. In winter, I knit, read, and shovel snow. I write year-round for my Substack site (suekusch.substack.com) about the journey of aging and my relationship with nature.

Denise Larson – San Francisco, CA

Denise Larson is the author of *Anarchy in High Heels*, a memoir of her adventures in Les Nickelettes, and a 2022 IPPY Awards Silver Winner in Women's Issues. After graduating from San Francisco State University with a BA degree in Theater, Denise founded Les Nickelettes: A feminist satirical musical comedy troupe. For thirteen years she guided the group as its Artistic Director in addition to taking on the roles of actress, playwright, producer, and stage director. https://anarchyinhighheels.com.

Shawn LaTorre – Austin, TX

Shawn, a star book reviewer for Story Circle Network and a member of a local Story Circle book group, retired from secondary education after 25 years of teaching English. She used to spend summers sailing the Great Lakes aboard HMS Juicy Fruit. Now she delights in traveling, volunteering, quilting, and spinning tales. You can visit her blog at shawnlatorre.com or follow her educational tweets as MizLaTee on Twitter. You can enjoy her latest book, *Footfalls to the Alamo*.

Helen (Len) Leatherwood – Ojai, CA

Len Leatherwood, the Program Coordinator for SCN's Online Classes program and past president of Story Circle Network, has been teaching writing privately to students in Southern California for the past 24 years. She is a nationally recognized writing coach and award-winning author. Len has published work in flash fiction and nonfiction and has been nominated for two Pushcart Prizes. Her blog, 20 Minutes a Day, can be found at lenleatherwood.com.

Susan Marsh – Jackson, WY

Susan Marsh lives in Jackson, Wyoming, where she is grateful to find wild nature, from forests to feeder birds, at her door. Published books include her Sarton Award-winning novel, *War Creek*, ten nonfiction books, and a poetry chapbook, *This Earth Has Been Too Generous*. She writes a monthly column, "Back to Nature," for *Mountain Journal*.

Beth Mattheus – Naples, FL

Beth's writing has come full circle. Initially, told fantasy stories to her seven younger siblings and later did professional writing for social work agencies in the New York City area. After moving to Southwest Florida 29 years ago, she wrote newsletters and reports as a volunteer for organizations in the arts and politics. For the last seven years, she has returned to writing flash memoir, poetry, and is now writing flash fiction.

Julie Ryan McGue – Michigan City, IN

Julie Ryan McGue is an American writer, a domestic adoptee, and an identical twin. In her writing, she explores finding out who you are, where you belong and making sense of it. She is the author of two award-winning books: *Twice a Daughter: A Search for Identity, Family, and Belonging*, and *Belonging Matters: Conversations on Adoption, Family, and Kinship*. Her third book, *Twice the Family: A Memoir of Love, Loss, and Sisterhood* releases in February 2025.

Merimee Moffitt – Albuquerque, NM

Merimee has been a teacher grades 8-12 and community college. She was faculty at SCN after her retirement and several times a judge in the annual contests. She has published five books since 2013 (two reviewed in SCN). She has participated in workshops and teaching here and there in Albuquerque, a city with a high per capita of poets and happy roadrunners enjoying the lack of traffic. She is currently working on her sixth book: a collection of poems.

Lisa Nackan – Thornhill, Ontario

"Making the invisible visible" is a theme inspiring everything I do. As an Art Therapist and Registered Psychotherapist, I strive to help others find voice. My passions are writing, painting and mosaic, photography, rock collecting, and spending time with my three grown up kids. I live, work, and create in Thornhill, Ontario with my husband, three dogs, and a parrot who can't talk.

Ellen Notbohm – Portland, OR

Ellen Notbohm's work touches millions in more than 25 languages. She is author of the acclaimed novel *The River by Starlight* (2018 Sarton Women's Book Award winner for historical fiction), the nonfiction classic *Ten Things Every Child with Autism Wishes You Knew*, and numerous short prose pieces appearing in literary journals, magazines, and anthologies in the US and abroad.

Joy Packard-Higgins – Downers Grove, IL

I began my writing journey at the age of six with an informative report on cows. As an adolescent, I wrote angst-filled poetry. I have been a teacher, an elementary school principal, and a college professor. Since retiring, I've been honored to have work published in the *Story Circle Journal*, *Real Women Write*, and *Matter*. I write flash fiction, memoir, and poetry. I live in Downers Grove, Illinois, with my husband.

Lucy Painter – Willow Street, PA

I live just outside Lancaster, PA, where my husband and I retired to live closer to family. I write every day I can and am working on poetry and flash fiction, both a challenge for me.

Stacy Ann Parish – Appleton, WI

Stacy is an award-winning storyteller, producer, and educator who's been honing her craft for almost 30 years. What began as a career in professional broadcasting has evolved onto performing stages across the nation. She has been professionally involved in education and communication for decades—spending the last decade creating and presenting self-empowerment workshops and programs using the arts as her vehicle.

Christy Piszkiewicz – Spring Valley, OH

Christy Piszkiewicz grew up in Chicago and raised her three children in its suburb of Des Plaines. Moving to Ohio (2014) to be near her two grandchildren, she and her husband, Paul, reside on a "Hobby Farm." Being a Beekeeper, she enjoys making fruit jams (some fresh-picked!) and exploring nature. Storytelling, writing down, and making up stories with her grandkids is her passion. Sharing her love for God, she has taught parish religious education for more than 40 years.

Martina Reaves – Berkeley, CA

I grew up in a Navy family and lived in thirty-four places before I finally settled in my current home in Berkeley with my wife and son. As a mediator, I worked with divorcing couples and neighbors with disputes. In 2007, I began writing. My memoir, *I'm Still Here*, published in April 2020, received numerous awards. My second book, *Pistachios, Ashes, & Pruning Wisteria*, is just finished and looking for a home. Website: www.martinareaves.com.

Terry A. Repak – Seattle, WA

Terry A. Repak's memoir, *Circling Home: What I Learned By Living Elsewhere*, (published in 2023) details the adventures and challenges of finding home in African countries and Europe. While her husband did AIDS work, she wrote and raised their children. She has a PhD in Women's Studies and has published two other nonfiction books, travel articles and essays (see links at her author website https://www.terryrepak.com/). She lives in Seattle where she writes, teaches English to Language Learners, gardens, hikes and swims.

Christina Ryan – St. Louis, MO

Christina Ryan grew up in Massachusetts, and St Louis is now her home. An early childhood educator and classically trained flutist, she teaches preschool music and volunteers in community organizations. She has been writing forever but would only recently call herself a Writer. She finds inspiration in motherhood, memories, relationships, and identity. In addition to her family (and poetry!), reading, walking, cooking, travel, yoga, music, watercolor painting, and her basset hound all bring her joy.

Eileen Harrison Sanchez – South Plainfield, NJ

Eileen Harrison Sanchez is retired after a forty-year career in education. She is a devoted reader, writer, and a perennial—a person with a no-age mindset. Family and friends are the most important parts of her life, followed by traveling and bird watching from her gazebo. Her debut, *Freedom Lessons - A Novel,* was a 2020 Sarton Award Finalist for Historical Fiction. Her work has also appeared in *Real Women Write: Living in COVID Time* and *Kitchen Table Stories 2022.*

Laura Santos-Farry – Austin, TX

Laura is a retired school district administrator, who lives in Austin, Texas, with her husband and two beloved cats. Laura is an aspiring writer who is close to finishing her memoir. When Laura is not writing, she spends her time volunteering with Family Eldercare delivering fans to the elderly and disabled and with Circle Up where she facilitates groups in women's prisons. Laura also loves to make art and to take long walks.

Nancilynn Saylor – Austin, TX

Nancilynn lives and writes from Austin, Texas. She lives as simple a life as she can, gardening, reading, and being out in nature. This influences her poetry. She's been in Story Circle Network since 2007 and writes in several Circle online groups. She primarily writes poetry and participates annually in a Poetry Postcard challenge.

Monique Susanna Simón – Binghamton, NY

Born in Antigua, Caribbean and raised between St. Thomas, USVI, and Antigua, Ms. Simón is an award-winning writer of fiction, creative nonfiction and poetry. After the life-altering diagnosis of ME/CFS, she was compelled to retire from life as a college professor and educational programs developer. With many adjustments to her sense of active time and down time, she has returned to her life as a writer, with a bit more humor and a lot more faith.

Esti Skloot – Kensington, CA

Esti Skloot was born in England to Jewish-German refugees. She grew up in Israel where she graduated from the Teachers' Seminary in Jerusalem. Esti immigrated to the United States, taught Hebrew language at the University of San Francisco, received her BA in music from Sonoma State University, and her MFA in creative writing from USF. In September 2019 Esti published a book titled *Uprooted, A Memoir of a Marriage*.

Irena Smith – Palo Alto, CA

Irena Smith is the author of Story Circle Network's Gilda Prize-winning memoir, *The Golden Ticket: A Life in College Admissions Essays*. When not searching for the perfect pair of overalls, she can be found on her Substack, Personal Statements, where she writes about life, literature, parents, children, and creative nonfiction *about* parents and children. She is currently at work on her second book.

Lee Ann Stevens – Port St. Lucie, FL

Lee Ann Stevens writes fiction and creative nonfiction. Publication credits include *Straylight Literary Magazine*, *Good Old Days Magazine*, *BoomSpeak*, *The Journal of Expressive Writing*, *Story Circle Journal*, and Story Circle Network publications. Currently working on her memoir, she is exploring ways to blend the lessons of the natural world with her lived experience. She also has a special interest in writing about women's strengths and stories of survival at every stage of life.

Barbara Wolf Terao – Freeland, WA

From Northfield, Minnesota, and Evanston, Illinois, Barbara Wolf Terao, Ed.D., moved to Whidbey Island, Washington, in 2016. Her memoir, *Reconfigured*, tells her story of falling in love with the Pacific Northwest and was a finalist for the Sarton Award and won first place for the Journey Award. Barbara's writing has appeared in *The Seattle Times*, *Orion*, *Writer's Digest*, *Realize*, ihadcancer website, and in the anthology *Art in the Time of Unbearable Crisis*. Her essays are available at barbaraterao.substack.com/p/quote-and-tote.

Marie Unini – Pearblossom, CA

Marie is a writer and ICF-certified Wayfinder Life Coach, and recovering urban animal. She lives in Juniper Hills, California, a rural high-desert mountain community in North Los Angeles County with artist husband Robert Le Clair; Calypso, the mellow gelding; and Miss Piggy, the voracious mare. She has published short pieces in anthologies with University of Texas Press, and Tulip Tree Publishing, and authored a one-act play produced in festival with Antelope Valley College. Find her at marieunini.com.

Jo-Ann Vega – Millsboro, DE

Published author and dynamic speaker with 30 years of experience presenting to academic, business, and community groups. Recent works include *Moments in Flight: A Memoir [2021] Bronze Medal for Memoir Classics, Reader Views Reviewer's Choice Awards, 2023-2024*, and *Wolf Woman & Other Poems [2022]* awarded a *Bronze Medal* in *Reader Views Reviewer's Choice Awards, 2021-2022*. A devotee of journaling, I live with my life partner and canine companion.

Jo Virgil – Austin, TX

Jo Virgil lives in Austin, Texas, and retired from a career in journalism and community relations. She has a Master of Journalism degree with a minor in Environmental Science, reflecting her love of writing and appreciation of nature, and has had stories and poetry published in various books, newspapers, and magazines, including Story Circle Network's publications. She lives by words she learned from one of her journalism professors: "Stories are what make us matter."

Danna Walker – Kensington, MD

Danna Walker has published pieces in *The Washington Post, Months to Years, American Journalism Review, Sixty and Me*, and other publications, and been featured on NPR's "Tell Me More" and in other venues. She has studied with memoirists Amanda Montei and Stacy Pershall, poet Marcelo Hernandez Castillo and author Beth Kanter through The Writer's Center, Gotham Writers Workshop, and Electric Literature. She teaches at the university level after having graduated 24th grade. Find additional writing at https://rustedcadillac.substack.com/.

Jude Walsh – Dayton, OH

Jude Walsh writes personal essays, self-help, and romance. As a Creativity Coach and the author of *Post-Divorce Bliss: Ending Us and Finding Me*, she helps women find their superpowers and create a life to match. She is published in numerous anthologies and literary magazines. A Story Circle member since 2005 and a current board member, she credits SCN with lighting the spark that inspired her to become a full-time writer. www.secondbloomcoaching.com.

Mary Jo West – San Clemente, CA

I am eighty-four years old and have been married for sixty-six years. I reside in San Clemente, California, and have three daughters and nine grandchildren. I started writing when I was seventy-two and during that time, I have published my memoir, *No Reservations*, and a recipe book of my Italian American family's favorites that have been handed down for generations. I continue to write free verse poetry and short stories.

Charlotte Wlodkowski – Pittsburgh, PA

I feel a responsibility to express experiences of living my life through written essays. It is also my pleasure to create places and characters that provide exciting reading.

Terilee Wunderman – Miami, FL

With doctoral degrees in Counseling Psychology and Spiritual Science, Teri enjoys writing with love through memoir and in reports advocating for children in foster care. A professor for counseling graduate students and a psychologist in private practice specializing in healing from trauma and loss, Teri is the author of *Wonder Walking: Enjoying the Wonders of Walking Outdoors*, a sweet, inspiring book for enjoying the blessings of gentle exercise in nature.

Jeanne Zeeb-Schecter – Valley Village, CA

I have been a homeopathic doctor for the past 28 years. During this pandemic I retired. I belong to a local poetry class, a writing class, and I teach a Life Writing class. I joined SCN five years ago. Currently, I am writing a nonfiction book on Homeopathy and Grief as well as a historical novel about a healer. I am blessed to be married to a wonderful man, have a daughter, four granddaughters and eight great grandchildren.

Carol Ziel – St. Louis, MO

Carol is SCN's eCircle coordinator. She took on this role with a desire to give others some of the confidence she gained from SCN in crafting her own life story. Caroline's commitment to women's stories springs from her 45 years as a clinical social worker, and her own story of trauma, mental health issues, and a tenacious desire to be emotionally healthy. In addition to her work with the eCircle, Caroline assists with our conferences and the Sarton Award.

Ariela L. Zucker – Auburn, ME

Ariela was born in Jerusalem. In September 2001, she and her husband left Israel and start a new chapter in Maine. They were soon joined by three of their daughters. They ran a mom-and-pop motel near Acadia National Park, welcoming guests for sixteen memorable years. Now retired, Ariela finds time to indulge in her lifelong passion for writing, weaving her experiences into nonfiction and poetry, her favorite genres.

TRIBUTE

REMEMBERING JUDY ALTER

(July 22, 1938 - July 13, 2024)

Jeanne Guy

I went to Healing Circles Langley this morning to grieve the sudden death of author/friend, Judy Alter, a Story Circle Network (SCN) "sister" who died just shy of her 86th birthday. Healing Circles is a gathering place, a safe and accepting environment here on Whidbey Island where people can connect, explore their healing, and enjoy the wonderful benefits of community. We sat in a fourteen-person circle—six men, eight women—and, after listening to a poem by author Vicki Robin about aging and mortality, one by one we deeply shared a piece of ourselves, our stories.

With Judy on my mind, the rawness of her passing, I could not hold back the tears. My weeping and the recognition of my own mortality were received and lovingly held. I had found out just the night before that Judy had died. Though we knew she had recently been diagnosed with cancer, we were left shocked and bereft at her quick passing.

Jude Whelley broke the news to our SCN longstanding Work-in-Progress writers' email support group. "I am devastated by the Facebook post by Judy's family that she passed away on Saturday morning. What a loss for us all. … I simply can't believe it. I thought we'd have her forever." She later added, "I will always remember Judy's tenacious embrace of living, how constant she was with her writing and devotion to her family, and her fire about politics. What a warrior! I just loved her. She was a rare gem and I am better for knowing her."

For those of you who didn't know her, Judy was the mother of four, grandmother of seven, and spent almost 30 years with TCU Press, 20 of them as director before becoming a prolific author, penning more than 40 books (some say upwards of 100+). A novelist and author of both fiction and nonfiction for adults and young adults, she wrote primarily about the history and literature of Texas and the American West, especially the experiences of women in the nineteenth century.

She also delighted in writing contemporary cozy mysteries (and cookbooks), writing several series: Kelly O'Connell Mysteries, Blue Plate Café Mysteries, and Oak Grove Mysteries. *Saving Irene* and *Irene in Danger* were the first two titles in her Irene in Chicago Culinary Mysteries. *Irene in a Ghost Kitchen* was released the day before she died.

"Judy was always supportive of everyone," said Linda Wisniewski, "A true 'big sister' to women writers. I am shocked, probably because she was such a lively, constant presence in this group. Generous, wise and direct, honest and ... oh, I could go on. I'm glad to know about the ways she will be honored by SCN. Life is so precious and fleeting."

Life is fragile. Impermanent. Judy knew that and lived accordingly. However, I too thought we'd have her forever. A writing matriarch in so many worlds, she was beloved by those of us, about 15 in number, who shared space with her weekly as members of the aforementioned

"Work-in-Progress" writers chat/support email group. I "met" Judy when she joined in 2018. She handled "Wednesday's Bookmark," providing us with a platform of shared good reads and excellent reviews. I was always in awe of how many books that woman could digest in a week's time.

We all looked up to her though she steered clear of praise in spite of the boatload of awards she'd received over the years. Judy's western fiction has been recognized with awards from the Western Writers of America, the Texas Institute of Letters, and the National Cowboy Museum and Hall of Fame. She has been honored with the Owen Wister Award for Lifetime Achievement by WWA and inducted into the Texas Literary Hall of Fame at the Fort Worth Public Library. And the list goes on.

"What mattered is that she cared about stories, knew where to look for them, and how to share them with the rest of us," said Susan Albert, SCN's founder, president-emeritus, and creator of the WIP group.

And Judy cared about us. Everyone spoke in terms of her welcoming ways and her willingness to help and guide other writers on their own paths.

Stephanie Raffelock felt the pain, especially because she had lunch with Judy in Austin in 2021 and at her famous cottage in Ft. Worth, Texas in 2022. "Judy made Kristina Hall (from Lone Star Literary) and me the most amazing lunch. Again, I was left feeling special, because I sat in the presence of a great and good woman, a woman of decency and purpose. I aspire to be like her—to write up to the edges of where my life bleeds into the vast unknown. She was always writing her blog, a book or her neighborhood newsletter. She lived fully and loved well. Her heart was open and welcoming to everyone; she was the consummate professor, teacher, mentor, and friend."

Member Marilea Rabasa said, "Hard to imagine her not being here with all her kindness, wisdom, and fiery determination to make the world better. She was such a force, full of energy and love for us all." She admitted, "This has taken me by surprise. I had no idea she was that sick. I was hoping the therapy was working. It all seems so sudden. And I'm so sad."

It felt like that. Diagnosed only weeks earlier and then poof, she was gone. Gone from our lives.

SCN President Susan Schoch shared her pain by saying, "What a grievous loss! I will miss Judy enormously. She had a tremendously kind soul and encouraged me many times. In this group, her absence will be enormous."

Former President Len Leatherwood expressed her shock and sadness by saying, "I loved Judy through and through. May light perpetual shine upon dear Judy. May her memory be a comfort to us all." For Len's beautiful tribute to Judy, go here: <u>https://lenleatherwood.</u> <u>com/2024/07/15/judy-alter-rest-in-peace/</u>.

Susan Albert, heartsick over the sad news, said, "She was such an energetic spirit! Loving and loved." She reminisced, "I met Judy in the early 2000s, at a dinner during a conference of the Texas Institute of Letters, to which we both belong. I already knew of her writing (so prolific!) and had read and enjoyed several of her books. But I wasn't prepared for her instant friendliness, her quick, easy smile, her sense of humor—and her energy! My god, that woman just didn't quit! Everyone there knew her or had worked with her (in her editorial career), and she was deeply respected and admired, as a writer and as a person."

"I'm smiling as I write this," Susan added, "remembering my feeling that I had found a sister I didn't know I had. She was so very, very special."

Longtime SCN member Pat Bean said, "Judy's online presence was almost always inspiring. I will miss her voice."

Christina M. Wells agreed, "I wish I had met her in person, but her voice in this space was always distinctive and clear. And of course, there are also all the voices she gave her characters… I appreciated her candor so much. She was very kind to me and also had the ability to spell out a truth. I remember her saying that she thought my cancer treatment was harder than I was letting on. She had a way of getting through the B.S. to the heart of things. I will miss hearing from her, and I will miss getting to see where she might have sent [her protagonist] Irene next. … I think she lived on her own terms, and that's the best way."

Susan Tweit reflected, "I had the immense good fortune to finally meet her in person when her family came out to Santa Fe and rented a house only a few miles from where I live. She invited me to join them one evening, and I am so glad I went. What a bright and wise and steady light she shone in this world. I know her family is grieving; it was so obvious during that evening I spent with them how loved she was."

Longtime friend Babette Fraser Hale thanked Judy. "Judy brought me into this group awhile back. What a woman she was! What a great friend! I met her years ago at the A&M Press Consortium Meetings and I was in awe of her. She knew her mind so clearly and quickly."

Babette continued, "When I became reacquainted with her a few years ago I was astonished by the expanse and generosity of her heart. She was a wonderful mentor on my recently published memoir, but most of all a friend. She understood the nuances, the ribbons of feeling and connection that trail from the concept of friend. A complete friend, and not by any means only to me. She leaves such a vacancy in our world."

Marilea Rabasa remarked that Judy was "a bright light of kindness to all of us in any kind of distress—always the first to offer encouragement and guidance…she had so much love and wisdom to pass on to us."

I was a recipient of that love and wisdom. Here's what Judy had to say when my sister died in January 2024.

Jeanne, I can add nothing to the words of others except what a blessing you have Len's [writing] class to help you with this grief. Yours is an eloquent tribute to your sister, made more meaningful to this circle by what we know of your recent history with Joanne, both good and not so good. Grief is bold, not sneaky, and wallops us when we think we're prepared. I know that from experience. Sending a virtual hug and holding you in my heart.

B. Lynn Goodwin spoke for all of us when she said, "Judy was prolific and wise. Nobody knows how long any of us have. She will be missed, I know, but maybe she's creating a whole new series of mysteries somewhere on the other side, or maybe she's discovered that heaven is the place where you can read whatever you want. The whole thing makes me want to hold all of you a little closer."

Judy, we send you virtual hugs and will hold you always in our hearts a little closer. You have left a legacy for so many writers who will forever be indebted to you for your encouragement, your many talents, and your loving, caring ways.

For details about this amazing woman's life: https://judyalter.com/about-judy/ and https://en.wikipedia.org/wiki/Judy_Alter.

REAL WOMEN WRITE: THE POWER OF FRIENDSHIP

FRIENDS FROM THE PAST

RED ARMY SKIRT

Ariela L. Zucker

When I finished high school, in 1967, I made some life changing decisions. I got rid of the glasses I wore since I was three years old, shed some of my religious habits, and decided to join the army. I was only 17, shy, and a little overweight with a head full of curls.

My religious high school did not encourage girls to go to the Army. The two preferred options were to accept the deferment the army routinely gave girls from religious background or volunteer to work in an agriculture settlement.

Only one girl, a few years ahead of me, took the army route, and I did not know her well enough to talk to her. My best girlfriend, Naomi, and a few other students from my class were planning to go the volunteer route. Everything was already set up, including the kibbutz located above the Lake of Galilee, where we were supposed to be, and visited several times.

All during our senior high school year while preparing ourselves for this move, I felt it was not what I wanted to do but said nothing. So, my change of plans was unexpected, and I had much explaining to do. I had to do even more explaining when I tried to convince the army recruiting office to enlist me, even though I was not 18 yet, the formal age to be drafted.

I spent that last summer writing back and forth to different army offices and having long into the night, heart-to-heart talks with Naomi. At the beginning of September, I turned seventeen and a half and that same month the army consented to draft me.

The first day in the Army had the usual frenzy of the drafting routine. Hundreds of confused, over-stressed girls and very blunt, short-tempered army personnel. We stood in one line after another, receiving uniforms, getting shots, and filling in papers. Being ushered from one building to another until late in the afternoon. Exhausted and overwhelmed, we finally arrived at the base and had to stand in yet another line to get our "sleeping gear"—three gray wool folded army blankets, sheets, and pillows. It was the first time in that long and exhausting day I realized the extent of my decision. I also realized another thing, none of the other girls were talking to me.

The why soon became apparent. Most of the girls assigned to my group were from my hometown—Jerusalem. Only they came from two prestigious private schools, schools that traditionally accepted kids from very influential and high-class families. There was a long-going rivalry between these schools, which were secular, and my school. And so, I was treated as if I were not even present.

From that first lonely night, away from home, I have one vivid memory I carried and never forgot. When we were getting ready for lights off, the girl next to me, a stranger until that moment, took off her dark green, khaki skirt, and with a secretive smile revealed a bright, shiny, smooth, red under-liner.

"My mother made it," she whispered, "so I will have something colorful, and cheery to look at."

"Yael," she introduced herself, still whispering.

In the years to come in times of uncertainty, I often thought about my six weeks of "basic training." How extremely challenging and intimidating it is to make a life change. Leaving behind the known and struggling with the unknown made me feel, for a while, as if I was hanging in midair without a steady support and nothing but my senses to guide me. Slowly the new terrain became familiar and my steps steadier. I could breathe with greater ease, and raise my eyes, until then focused on the trail in front of me, to see the new scenery.

And then I think of Yael. I never saw her again. After basic training, we separated ways. I still feel sorry that I never told her how impressed I was with her red skirt. How the thought of it made me smile every time I encountered a challenge, and how her friendship lightened my burden. I can recall the exact shade of red of her under-liner's smooth satin, but not her face, hair color, or last name.

My daughter's name is Yael too, and whenever she got sad, I told her the story about the whimsical skirt, it always helped to cheer her up.

FRED, DRUGS, AND ROCK 'N' ROLL
Carol Ziel

Fred was my best friend and favorite ex-husband. He mentored me in beer, marijuana, and sniffing nitrate while dancing. He took an ex-convent girl who grew up on Gregorian chant and show tunes and introduced me to Fleetwood Mac, Tina Turner, Donna Summers, the blues, and bluegrass. Although I had lived in a convent for five years, my most intense spiritual experiences didn't happen until I was in smoke filled blues halls in the deep inner city and disco halls hung with mirrored silver balls. Fred was a kind of high priest of rock 'n' roll and made me his high priestess. He worshiped music and dance and me. Like a pied piper, he led me into dark places where those mysteries lived. Gratefully, ecstatically I followed.

I grew up in a community that was essentially Beaver Clever land. Absolutely no diversity. Suddenly rubbing elbows with drag queens, and being the only woman in gay bars was a weekly occurrence. He took me to strip clubs where I sat at the edge of the stage, trying to memorize the dancers' movements. I had grown up with strict rules about not touching or looking at my body. I was in mourning for the woman I had not been allowed to be. I hoped that by osmosis I could learn what it was to look like and be a woman. I thought that the pole that they danced with could be my salvation. It would be something I could hold onto that would make me a "real woman," and keep me anchored to my essential self, whoever that was.

Fred taught me about bluegrass music and blue highways. He considered modern highways to be the bane of civilization. The original highways that wound through corn fields and hamlets had history, character, and stories. And why pay for a campsite when we could pull over and throw out our sleeping bags? Speaking of campsites, bluegrass festivals, where we didn't even need tents, were transformational. We threw out our sleeping bags, lit a fire, and melted into the music for days.

Canoeing down the Black River with a case of beer in the bow was ecstasy. He taught me to cast my Catholic prudishness to the winds by skinny dipping. I did. The freedom of breaking the shackles of my upbringing was extraordinary—until we were arrested for what the local sheriff considered lewd and lascivious behavior. My children were with us and were nearly put in foster care until we could post bond. That should have been my wake-up call. Speaking of wake-up calls, his friends kept telling me that he was frequently seen at the "Baths," a pick-up place for gays. Of course he denied it. I still had a galaxy of stardust in my eyes, even when I contracted multiple venereal diseases and had surgery to remove the damage.

Fred was the son of Orthodox Jews and would absolutely crow about getting drunk on his bar mitzvah wine. He carried a banner that said he would drink and use drugs until the day he died. He did. He pulled me through the looking glass into a world where life was fun and magical—until it wasn't. I had to leave my best friend behind.

But before I left, I learned how to grow marijuana in between tomato plants in summer and under the basement steps with grow lights in winter. We were considered the United Way of St Louis due to our generosity in sharing all that we grew.

I learned that I was still basically a nice ex-convent girl from a small Midwestern town, but I had been sown with the seeds of adventure and misadventure.

I have no regrets. I'm grateful that the Pied Piper, who had the spirit of Puck, took me by the hand and showed me a whole other world. The scales dropped from my eyes and life became multicolored and multidimensional. I had to leave Fred, or I would have died with him. However, I still treasure the gifts.

A MEMORABLE KISS

Terilee Wunderman

The first boy I really liked kissed me once. It was in the spring of 1998. I was 41, some 30 years after I'd first met Charles. I was chaperoning my son's fifth grade field trip to the Miami Beach Holocaust Memorial, not expecting to see Charles nor receive his sweet kiss.

As I stood behind the ten-year-olds, the children sat on a stone floor under a low ceiling designed to give us the claustrophobic sense of concentration camp barracks. Plain beige concrete walls with small rectangular openings up high provided little air or light. A warm breeze wafted through narrow doorways. The yellow six-pointed stained-glass Star of David centered in the ceiling projected a soft beam of sunlight onto our group. The word "Jude" in the middle of the star spread its blackness across the children's heads and shoulders as they raised their hands to ask inquisitive, heartfelt questions of the Memorial docent, a petite grandmotherly volunteer.

The docent stood in front of us, sharing with the riveted youngsters about falling in love with her teenage beau in Poland, their abductions by Nazis, surviving concentration camps, and then finding one another by surprise in their elder years in South Florida. Both widowed, they married. Her beloved was a Memorial docent too.

"Such insightful children!" The survivor clasped her hands and smiled. "How wonderful you want to understand. Your questions warm my heart!" She patted her flowered blouse.

The children, in matching royal blue polo shirts, sat up tall, beaming with pride. They had read *Number the Stars* and studied about the Holocaust through the sensitive direction of their public school teachers. With my School Volunteer button pinned to my white top, I felt proud as well.

Although I had no formal Jewish education, I studied on my own since first reading a picture book, *Bible for Jewish Children*. I found spirituality and religion deeply meaningful, intriguing, and comforting, and even took "The Bible as Literature" as a high school English elective. I read extensively about the Holocaust, starting in junior high with my treasured copy of *The Diary of Anne Frank*. During the field trip, children, teachers, and moms came to me with poignant questions. I realized I knew more about the Holocaust and Memorial than anyone on the trip. I felt honored and grateful to share what I knew.

As the docent continued her tender, inspiring story, six adults in business suits walked in, interrupting our sacred space. I recognized Florida's Lieutenant Governor, who was running for Governor at the time. He wore a black yarmulke, although he was not Jewish—his visit an apparent attempt to "Get the Jewish vote."

My heart leapt as I spotted Charles walking close behind the politician, whispering to him. His fair balding head peeked out from under his white yarmulke, strands of gray hair brushing his light blue shirt collar. He wore round, wire-rimmed glasses. He seemed absorbed in his mission with the group.

I knew Charles had been involved with the Memorial's production. His father, a successful architect in Miami and a leader in the Jewish community, was the designer. Charles, also an architect, worked with him. I had followed the Memorial's development from afar, learning of Charles's contributions through newspapers, magazines, and local television news stories. From the beautiful book chronicling the saga of the Memorial, which I had bought as soon as it was published, I knew in-depth about its years of intricate planning, construction, and ultimate dedication in 1990.

I first met Charles in 1968 during junior high school band practice. I was 11, and he was 12. I liked him so very much with his sandy brown hair and light blue eyes behind awkward Clark Kent glasses. He was a gentle boy, smart and thoughtful. For an hour a day over the next two years, we sat beside one another, playing our trombones, alternating first chair, commiserating about sore gums from our instrument mouthpieces pressing against our metal braces. We strived to master the music, eager to contribute our best. We had other classes together through the years and got along well but never outside of school, as much as I wished we would.

Charles came from a prominent family. He sat at the popular kids' lunch table and got elected to student council. I ate with my two close girlfriends and volunteered in the band library. I heard Charles had a big bar mitzvah and went to Jewish summer camps out of state. I attended public summer school for creative writing and typing. Still, we had those special times we connected and harmonized, and my fondness for him endured.

The Memorial docent paused as the Lieutenant Governor waved to the class. Then his entourage ventured outside toward the lily-pad-covered reflecting pool. A peaceful circle of water surrounded the heart-wrenching sculpture of men, women, and children, struggling to climb up one 40-foot-tall hand reaching toward the open sky. I watched Charles head out with the group. Then he stopped, letting the group go on without him.

My heart skipped a beat as Charles turned and walked towards me, navigating around the seated youngsters. I stepped forward, and he smiled, extending his right hand, which I took in mine, cherishing its warmth and soft strength. Then he bent down and kissed my cheek, our hands still clasped together. I kissed him back in sweet joy and ageless gratitude.

As we let go, our eyes met. We nodded in sacred silence. Then Charles headed back to tend to his group. My eyes filled as I watched my beloved old friend until I could no longer see him. I turned back to the children and the survivor, and I sighed, knowing our hearts never forget.

ALL THINGS FELICIA

Jude Walsh

Remember photo albums? From the quaint old times when we used a camera, with film, to take black and white pictures? The pictures were small, with white wavy borders, and came in a little booklet with a bright yellow Kodak cover. We saved the good shots in an envelope in a drawer. When I married, my mother made a photo album for me with pictures from my baptism right up to my marriage. Included were a few of those precious photos from the 1950s. One really resonated, taking me down memory lane.

There we were in all our black and white glory, Felicia and I, standing on the steps of Lee Park Elementary, on the first day of school. We're about the same height and have braids. She's blond and I have dark hair. She's as Polish as I'm Irish. We're wearing dresses. I remember mine well because my mother sewed it, special for the first day, red plaid. I know it's second grade because Felicia and I didn't meet and become inseparable until first. She'd gone to morning kindergarten and I'd gone to afternoon. Kindergarten was only a half day in 1955. Her mother had a camera and must have taken some first-day pictures and given one to my family.

We did all the fun things you do in elementary school. We held hands in line. We played jump rope, single and double dutch. Spring was hopscotch time. Having a good piece of chalk was important and Felicia always did. We'd scratch out the blocks and number them, then write "This hopscotch belongs to Felicia and Judy." We "owned" that hopscotch until the rain washed it out. It wasn't exclusive, we let anyone who wanted to play join in. It was just thrilling to see our names on the pavement. In fourth grade, we discovered Chinese Jump Rope. We collected brown rubber bands and hooked them one inside the other, making a chain long enough to wrap around the legs of two girls standing five feet apart. I'm not sure how we learned to do this and the rules that ordered the jumping and stretching of the bands, but it was a real phenomenon for a while.

As we got older, we moved into ball bouncing games, first with pink hard rubber balls bought for a dime at the corner store and later golf balls. I had to save to buy my pink one, in the meantime, Felicia let me use hers when it was my turn. In sixth grade we abandoned games and stood around in clutches, watching the boys show off as they chased each other. Some of us got training bras that year and there were episodes of the boys sneaking up to snap them from the back, followed by the girl stomping at the boy in mock outrage. I felt sorry for the late bloomers as they missed this. When we moved to the junior high in seventh grade the boys were over bra snapping.

We were different in many ways. My family and I lived in an old, shabby rented double block, my grandmother and aunt lived on the other side. It had a fenced yard and two big trees that shaded the front porch, a perfect spot for reading. I now know we were kind of poor, but I never felt that way. My dad was a coal miner and after second grade, my mom worked in a sewing factory. Felicia's dad was a social worker, and her mom was an elementary teacher but didn't work while her daughters were young.

The first time I saw their house, I was dazzled. It was NEW, it had shiny wood floors, and an open staircase so wide you could go to either the living or dining room. Felicia and her sister had their own rooms. There were TWO bathrooms upstairs, plus something they called a powder room on the first floor. They had a screened porch, overlooking a big yard with a garden. Most magical of all? My friend's bedroom had a window seat, every little book-loving girl's dream. I was impressed but not jealous. I loved my house and my family and found hers different, not better.

When Felicia and I moved to junior high, our closeness continued. My parents were old-fashioned. I was never allowed to spend the night at anyone's house, so no pajama parties for me. We went to our first dance. Her mom drove us. My mom didn't have a car, and my dad was not up for anything like that. Felicia's mom drove us everywhere, to the movies, to dances, to parties.

In 8th grade, my dad got sick, had surgery, and was hospitalized for five weeks. He was very ill—cancer—but I didn't know that. I only knew I was allowed to spend the night at Felicia's. JOY! It was during Lent, and we were fasting. In 8th grade that meant "giving up" something. We'd given up french fries. The weekly dances were canceled during Lent, so we spent Saturday nights at home. Her dad informed us that we did not have to fast on Sundays. This was news to me, but he was a grown-up and therefore was right. Not only was he a grownup, he was a cool grownup. He stayed up until midnight on Saturday, got out his deep fryer, and made us the most delicious french fries. Looking back, I can see that my being with them on weekends gave my mother a break and spared me the worst of my Dad's illness.

Felicia and I remained close until I transferred to a different high school. We reconnected when we went to college but were both in committed relationships with our prospective husbands so only saw one another in shared classes. She hadn't changed much, no braids but gorgeous long white-blond hair. She still had her beautiful smile and generous spirit.

After graduation, we got teaching jobs in the same elementary school. Now we were sharing lesson plans, parent conferences, and classroom management tips. Felicia didn't have a car, but I did. I was already married, and she was planning her wedding while still living with her parents. I picked her up every day at that magical house. I loved going inside and being flooded with wonderful memories. Her parents bought lots near the house they built, one for each daughter. Felicia still lives in the home she built there.

Felicia was my first close friend. We were together for most of our formative years. Her mom and dad always made me feel good about myself. And that house? It's still there but is painted blue as opposed to the white it was then. That house has appeared in my dreams throughout my adult life. I believe it represents Felicia and her family, the closeness and acceptance I experienced there, the beauty and the power of a nest that nurtured the friendship between two young girls. That one photo brought me back, to the friendship, to the family, to the house, to school—and to how life alters us as we grow, pulling us together, then apart, then sometimes together again. I know I'm better because of it and I'm grateful.

STICK-SHIFT SISTERHOOD
Danna Walker

Whenever we were bored, which was all the time, we got in the car. In the car, my friends and I cussed, drank, smoked, and outraced anyone on our tails. We ate onion rings from the KoKoMo Drive-in, honked at each other's houses and headed out on Highway 1 on Sunday afternoons. The two-lane road connected Shreveport in northwest Louisiana—more akin to East Texas in culture—to the roughneck oil fields of the Gulf Coast, 360 miles south.

The car served as a haven, every one of us able to drive a stick. Driving a stick is a lost art (just 2 percent of new US cars had manual transmissions in 2020), and "art" doesn't overstate it. It's like we were on an elite team in an obscure sport only we understood.

Sherry liked to tease second gear until it screamed while she sped down narrow residential streets, her peripheral vision and motor response bionic. "Where'd you get that blue-green shade of eyeshadow you're wearing?" she asked one day, peering over at me from the driver's seat while her long blonde hair swirled around her shoulders. One hand rested on the bottom of the wheel like a monkey bar and the other dangled leisurely outside while she floored it, side mirrors on parked cars whooshing by my head.

Caroline was the safe, reliable one and Mary served as team captain, fostering a sense of unity and camaraderie when she, for example, engineered an undercover pot drop at a neighborhood mailbox and arranged for us to sunbathe as (non-paying) "guests" at a hotel pool. Her steady hand at the stick made me feel safe enough to flout rules and break laws.

But nobody could baby a clutch like Danielle. Sometimes she picked me up in her father's lumbering Chevy Biscayne. It had "three on the tree," meaning you shifted from the steering column and looked like a one-armed orchestra conductor while getting from first to third. We made fun of its fuddy-duddy bench seats that sent you sliding, especially if you didn't feel like downshifting to make a corner, which Danielle never did. (The first seat belt law went into effect in the United States in 1968 but was largely ignored.)

The Biscayne may have been a brute, but Danielle's long, slender limbs moving effortlessly at the controls meant it glided through the neighborhood, down the new Interstate 20 and through life more elegantly than it deserved to, a rumpled middle-class salesman transformed into Don Draper at cocktail hour. It was her brother's 1960 vintage VW, though, that really allowed Danielle to shine. The bohemian Beetle, with its pared down dignity, fit her like the perfect Indian-print halter dress. Sitting in the passenger seat, I watched admiringly one day while she drew on a Marlboro, drank a Coke through a straw, effortlessly shifted into second and flung her leg over to my side to release the reserve fuel tank with her foot. (The Beetle didn't get a gas gauge until 1962; look it up.)

"You're a badass," I told her.

"Why?" she asked, not realizing her feat—the car sputtered for a second from lack of fuel but never lost a rotation—which made her even more of a badass.

That was the difference with a stick shift; it wasn't about the car so much as about the talent, grace and humble self-possession of the driver—virtually non-existent variables in an automatic where what counts are the make and model, cost and miles to the gallon or kilowatt hour.

Automatics were the muscle cars my high school boyfriend spit-shined and vacuumed before we went out on weekend nights. The insides were clean and close, our domain for the night's drinking, socializing and making out—clothes on, mostly.

Firebirds, Chargers, Mustangs, Chevelles, Camaros and Javelins— "gear selector" on the floor, between the bucket seats—me, the passenger, my body ferried through space and time in a sleek metal box. But as a driver, the car provided a room of my own in which to live my own narrative. Even in the sexist South, there were no restrictions against women getting driver's licenses like there were for obtaining credit or an abortion or winning an argument with my father.

I took pride in my ability to provide a smooth ride despite the need to let off the gas to push in the clutch and shift into gear. Give me a hill with a stop light at the top, and if you were a passenger, you would *never* find yourself rolling into the car behind you.

I was taught how to drive a stick one summer on a classic Triumph owned by my aunt's boyfriend. Just a little older than me, she balked and played helpless, but I wanted to learn.

In the complex symphony of gears and cogs, the clutch, located to the left of the brake, disengages the engine from the transmission, creating a pause in which the operator can tap into the surge. Finding that sweet spot put me at the helm of a machine I could tame into submission, engaging in conversation with the car and showing it what I needed. Like getting up on water skis at Cross Lake in summer, once you do it, you know you've got it.

The stick wasn't about showing off but about potency and control. It was something long haulers, James Bond in his Aston Martin, and I had in common. I didn't brag about it. I held my ability until it was needed like the torque from second to third gear. I wasn't a symbol on a mud flap but a disruptor of male domination, and sometimes men took notice.

Once in college, I ferried a guy to his friend's house in a complicated switching of vehicles and rides to a party or football game. I drove out of necessity because no one else could handle a standard. As he sat in the passenger seat, I could feel him watching my body move with the car as I gripped the gear shift with confidence but a gentle ease, my legs pumping expertly between the clutch, brake and gas.

Mid-trip, I heard him clear his throat. "Sorry I'm not saying much," he said, his voice husky. "I'm watching you drive. You're good at it."

Being in the driver's seat, literally, lent us a level of agency and general badassery before we knew much consciously about systemic discrimination, sexual harassment or any of the other challenges ahead.

Our stick-shift sisterhood helped us feel for a moment that the way we saw the world had merit and together we might have a chance against its dings, dents and downright defeats. That became clear at the funeral of the mother of our friend, Lynn. Norma Jean had the best bright blonde bouffant that she often wore in a French twist. Gazing into her coffin, I knew Norma Jean wouldn't be happy with her outfit. Morticians had made the only one of our friends' mothers who talked to us about boys and friendships into a matron with garish red lips.

As Mary drove to the cemetery, the stick shift rocked us in a soothing cradle. We parked and sat in silence, wondering how we would survive in the same way we had before.

"Look, isn't that the woman from the funeral?" Sherry asked, pointing to *that* woman, the one who yelled out 'how-are-you' and generally made the event about herself, as we all mourned. She was walking alone in heels across the damp grass, arm waving high, voice raised to get someone's attention.

I wished she would die instead of Norma Jean. And then she fell. Flat on her face. Suddenly, our laughter seemed to strain the glass windows. The woman looked up as we glanced away, pretending to be straight-faced while bathed in redemption.

I continued to drive a manual transmission long after. I didn't want to let go of the small prize I had earned. I gave up my last one, in a Honda, in the early 2000s when city traffic far from Shreveport taxed my patience. I know I need to practice because to this day I have a recurring dream in which my escape route is only accessible by a car with a manual transmission.

"Who can drive a standard?" someone yells.

"I can!" I respond, jumping in and grabbing the stick.

DEATH OF A FRIENDSHIP

Nancilynn Saylor

"Soul mate"
"I love her"
"I know you'll understand"
"Please understand"
"Don't leave"

The pain of this remembering is bizarre
Because when I lost him
I lost all of my friends, his friends were my friends.
Did I become someone else?
Did it get to "the point
where I was no fun anymore"
Thanks to Crosby, Stills and Nash whose
"Suite Judy Blue Eyes" never suffered
More than Cat-Nap Nan with Green eyes-
Green-eyed lady of the lowlands maybe…
I find myself strangling again
Strangling on the words you said through tears,
Tears, I am not sure from where,
Strangling on the sound of goodbye.
Not forever, but forever was so close that
eternity was even closer.
Death would have been a blessing
So many days
And so many more
nights.
For whom?
For me?
For you?

You left us crushed and broken on the bedroom floor that night,
just as surely as I laid to waste
My friendship with her when
my hand struck her cheek in rage!
The pain,

The betrayal,
The loss
I cried tears for you and for me
I cried for years
My soul mate, my life… gone.
All gone….

ROBIN

Lorinda Boyer

The first time you fall in love, it will change your life forever, and no matter how hard you try, the feeling never goes away.
—FROM *RUBYFRUIT JUNGLE,* RITA MAE BROWN

Perched atop a stack of book-filled boxes, as far out of sight of my coworkers as possible, I covered my face with my hands and cried. At 23 years old I'd already been married for five years to my high school boyfriend, Chet, and was now expecting our first baby. Life was going exactly according to plan, and I couldn't have been more devastated. My mother-in-law, Jo, who was also the head of the department I worked in, had spent all morning spreading the good news. The library was abuzz with delighted middle-aged women anxious to share their advice, good wishes and of course, their own labor stories. Their joy, as appropriate as it was, only sharpened the contrast between how I knew I should feel and how I felt.

Ten days after graduating from high school, Chet and I were married. I wasn't knocked up, but we had slept together and in my straight and narrow fundamental Christian upbringing, this was reason enough to tie the knot. So, we had. I had wanted to wait at least five years before having a baby and nearly to the day, we had done that also. What I hadn't banked on, what I never in a million years could have imagined, was meeting and falling in love with a woman.

Robin came from the city library to work for the county library as a delivery driver. Her job was to load and unload boxes of books pulled from the twelve library branches' shelves and shuffle them between the libraries. This was how we ensured the twelve county branches' collections remained varied. Our previous driver had been male and in the early nineteen-nineties in our conservative small town, hiring a woman was still uncommon. There were doubts amongst the ranks that a woman would be suited for such a strenuous job. I remember pushing paperbacks aside, peering through bookshelves at the new delivery driver as she came through the library door for the first time. Her stocky build, short, spiked, brown hair, the confidence in her swagger; she was not like any woman I'd ever met. Jo made the rounds with Robin and eventually introduced her to me. Robin held her hand out.

"Howdy darlin'." She cocked her head to the side, smiled.

I took her hand. Her skin was softer than I'd expected. I tried to reply but suddenly my tongue had turned to stone in my mouth. My legs felt a bit wobbly; I squeezed her hand to steady myself. She squeezed back and I quickly let go. I couldn't explain the feeling I had that day; I didn't yet have the vocabulary. But something stirred inside of me, my fledgling sexuality was aroused.

Love for me was conditional. In the hierarchy of my existence Jesus took top rung. Below Jesus were my parents until I married, and then they moved below my husband. Quite literally every move I made, or thought I dared think, was measured first and foremost against the will of Jesus. Would my actions glorify him? If the answer was no, then I was sinning. Life was just that black and white, there was no room for gray. This was the primary reason for marrying in the first place. Once we'd had sex out of marriage we were already tarnished and therefore unsuitable for marriage to anyone else. I never thought to question whether I loved Chet or not. I liked him. We had fun together. As teenagers this seemed sufficient, and it was, until I met Robin.

Excluding the hours she was on the road traveling between libraries, Robin and I worked side-by-side. We had desks on the same wall where we ate our lunches and took our breaks together, but the bulk of our time was spent packing boxes and loading and unloading the van. She loved to sing, and she could dance, too. She knew every word to Tracy Chapman's "Give Me One Reason" and she belted it out, swinging me around the shipping room. Up until then I'd mostly listened to Christian radio. I'd never heard of Tracy Chapman or Melissa Etheridge or any of the artists she sang along to. But it wasn't just the music, she read extensively, traveled around the United States, and even drank espresso. She described the places she'd lived, the jobs she'd worked, the people she'd met, and I hung on to her every word. She was only five years my senior but to an isolated small-time-country-girl, she seemed a woman of the world to me. After nearly a year together, I could no longer remember my life before Robin, nor did I want to. I couldn't wait to see her every day and I missed her every night. Nothing physical occurred between us but I was conscious enough to realize that my feelings for her were stronger than friendship. In my youthful naivety, I felt no urgency to question this, I was content to go on as we were. But that all changed the day I found out I was pregnant. Babies were the next step on my preordained life schedule, this was what Jesus would want. Why then did I feel as if I was suffocating?

My first thought was for Robin. What would she think? What would she say? I felt as if I'd betrayed her and yet, that was, of course, ridiculous. These were the fears that shook my young soul and not the larger question of why I even cared in the first place. Conflicted and confused by the tangle of feelings churning inside of me, I hid in the library garage. When Robin burst through the doors cheerfully singing out my name, I froze. I couldn't bear to face her, but she rounded the corner and spotted me right away.

"Congratulations!" her voice rang out joyfully then faded as she took in my obvious despair. Without another word, she rushed over and enveloped me in a hug. I buried my tear-stained face into her shoulder. I inhaled the lingering scent of lavender soap on her skin mingled with coffee on her breath and I sobbed. I wept for what I stood to lose, for a love I'd yet to experience, for an ache I could not yet name but would spend the next 20 years searching for.

"You will be okay," Robin whispered into my ear, pulling me even tighter. And then as if she knew, and of course she did, she tenderly brushed my cheek with her lips.

STOP SIGNS

Monique Susanna Simón

"There is no tomorrow
This is the end of the road,
    right here," I said
To my friend
As she begged me to stop

STOP
In bright white
Marked on a red sign
Shaped in an octagon
Is what I wanted for her

For her
To stop drinking
Stop dying

Stop dying
Here
In this place
Leaving me
To watch

To watch
The clock tick down
For hours

For ours—our friendship
There is no tomorrow
This is the end of the road
As she slips
Into stupor
Into oblivion

Besides the oversized
Bottle of vodka
Bottled in plastic
So it wouldn't break

But this plastic breaks
My heart
While it states
In a triangle
By way of a number
That it is
Recyclable

That it is possible
It will come back
To break
Another…

Maybe tomorrow
At the end
Of the road
With a red-signed, white-
    knuckled–
STOP!!!

Out of time

There is no tomorrow

NANDO

Esti Skloot

In the summer of 1960, at the age of nineteen, I listened to the call of wanderlust which beckoned to me to get out of my small country, Israel, and explore the wide world. I landed in Venice. While waiting for a *vaporetto* to take me to a youth hostel not far from piazza San Marco, I met a tall, handsome Italian. His official name was Ferdinando Di Mariano, but he went by his nickname, Nando. He had wavy black hair, velvety dark-brown eyes, and an aquiline Roman nose.

It was a beautiful balmy night; a full orange moon cast a soft glow on the canal, in which a golden strip of dancing lights rippled upon the water. My heartbeat racing, I stood in line behind him. He must have felt me watching him, for he turned around and with a warm smile addressed me.

"*Buonasera, signorina!*"

I felt the blood rush to my face. With the little Italian I knew, I responded, "*Non parlo bene Italiano, tu parli Inglese?*"

"*Un poco.*" He spread his thumb and forefinger about two inches apart, "a *little.*"

"*Va bene,*" I giggled.

It was the beginning of a lifelong friendship. I fell in love with anything Italian: the language, villages, Fellini movies, Sophia Loren, Marcello Mastroianni, Neapolitan chansons and pop songs such as *Ciao, Ciao Bambino* and *Di mi Quando tu Verai.*

I had to return to Israel, so at the time I didn't get to see much more of Nando. However, he invited me to visit him in his hometown Palermo in Sicily. The following year after hitchhiking through Europe, I took a train from Roma to Palermo. The young Italian men sharing the train compartment with me were overjoyed. They got to ogle and chat with this blond, blue-eyed tourist wearing a blue, flowery summer dress and a ready smile. I enjoyed their attention and was happy to practice my Italian.

I arrived in Palermo on a bright, sunny morning. Nando, my gallant friend, was waiting for me at the train station. Dressed in a long-sleeved white shirt, black suit with patent leather shoes, a cigarette dangling between his middle and forefinger, he embodied my movie-star dream. I wondered what he thought about my casual dress and floppy sandals.

To my delight, he took my backpack and summoned a horse and buggy. I climbed up to my seat next to my *amico,* the driver clicked his tongue and off we went, the queen riding into her new kingdom.

Nando put me up in an *albergo,* a small hotel which turned out to be a room in a family's home. We spent the days together, hand in hand, viewing churches, palaces and strolling in public parks. I loved the feeling of his warm hand with slender fingers enveloping mine. Every evening, at nine o'clock, my *amico* promptly deposited me at the family's home. Perplexed, I asked him:

"Why can't we stay out a bit later?"

His voice was somber, "In my country we are Catholics..." He paused. "Young men and women aren't supposed to be together after dark."

In the *albergo* I was bored stiff. The older couple sat every evening in their small living room glued to the television watching Italian soap operas. Luckily, after a week, Nando transferred me to a youth hostel a couple of miles out of town. I guess he ran out of money, and as a true Sicilian gentleman, wouldn't let me pay a penny. I loved staying at the hostel where I met young people from all over the world.

Nando and I never made love; you had to be married first. Yet I was his *amica,* his girlfriend, so he was possessive of me. We had an arrangement in which I took the bus every morning from the hostel to the center of Palermo. Nando would meet me at the bus station, and we'd spend the rest of the day together. On one occasion a young man at the hostel offered me a ride which I happily accepted. He dropped me off at the bus stop where Nando was waiting. Upon seeing me, he narrowed his eyes.

"Why didn't you come by bus?" His voice had a hard edge.

"I was offered a ride. What's wrong with that?"

"It's very wrong," he pursed his lips," It's not proper to go in another man's car."

'I'm sorry," I replied in a timid voice. "I had no idea." In Israel I hitchhiked all the time.

On another occasion Nando invited me to join his family for lunch. We walked in the mid-day heat, the sun glaring down, until we reached his parents' house, a white-washed, two-story, stucco building. When we got to the front door, Nando stopped. I expected him to open the door, but he just stood there. I eyed him.

"Nobody's at home?"

"No," was his curt reply.

Perspiration trickled down my armpits. More than anything I wanted to go in. "Don't you have a key to enter?"

"I do, but we're not supposed to go in."

"Why?" My voice rose. "What's wrong?"

He shook his head as if to chase away a buzzing insect. "If we're not married, we're not allowed to be alone in the house."

I stared at him in disbelief.

Our lives and ways of seeing the world were so different. Yet we were attracted to each other. Over the years we corresponded, sending each other love letters in which we carefully placed dried flowers. When I wrote Nando that I had married an American, he was heartbroken. He wrote me: *I wanted to marry you, but couldn't propose before I had a job or a house to offer you.*

Nando, my dear Sicilian friend, always the gentleman, wanted to act the proper way. I visited him ten years ago before he died of cancer. When there's a full moon, I look up wistfully, my throat choking, and whisper: *Ti amo Nando. Ti voglio bene.*

IN THE SHADOW OF HER BLOOM

Christina Ryan

A blossom seeks the sun
as a brittle brown leaf releases from her stem,
falling softly in the shadow of her bloom.
She is strengthened, lengthened, tended, in part,
because of this fallen friend.
Once so integral to her flourishing
she no longer finds every leaf nourishing
so she observes some go into the earth below.

As a sprout, she didn't—couldn't—know the leaves that
    would help her soak up the sun,
survive the seasons, strive through storms, thrive in joyful
    sunshine,
the ones who would grow deep green over years of cheer
    and fears and tears,
veined with trust,
robust from basking in shared experiences.

And she didn't—couldn't—know the leaves that would
    fall,
that would separate progressively or shear off
    distressingly.
"Am I worthy of long-lasting leaves? Why do leaves leave
    me?" she wonders.
In the shadow of her bloom, they whisper:
We grew in different directions.
I served you well and moved on.
I loved you, for a while.
YOU hurt ME.
I'm sorry I had to die.
I'm dealing with my own pain.
I don't know.
Their replies often go unheard above the heavy hum of
    her own heartache.

As she blossoms anew, which leaves will remain, sustain,
    constrain?
What new fronds will befriend or arrive at their end?
Each one a pleasure, a treasure, a sustenance source of
    which she is, of course, deserving.

And yet—

The leaves that fall land tenderly in the shadow of her
    bloom,
surrender in soft soil rooms amid roots,
decomposing to nourish and still persevering
to partake in her creation and formation and fruits.

JOAN

Martina Reaves

When I first met her, Joan had the shortest hair and the longest legs of any woman I'd ever met. Think Twiggy. If you're too young to know who she is, check Google. It was September 1967: move-in day at Pomona College, Claremont, California.

I spied Joan across the hallway, talking to her mother, whom she called "B.J." B.J. was big, bold, and bossy. The two of them hauled things into Joan's dorm room all day long. When they finally left, mentioning to us that they'd return the next day with more items, my new roommate Malinda and I sneaked across the hallway, turned Joan's doorknob, opened the door, and peeked in.

We gasped! It was wondrous: A shocking pink shag rug covered the floor; psychedelic posters hung on the walls; fancy furniture replaced generic dorm fixtures; trendy clothing and knee-high boots stuffed the closet. A room straight from *Seventeen* magazine.

Malinda had one item in our room: a yellow trunk with psychedelic designs. I had three small, well-used suitcases.

The next day, after Joan and B.J. finished unloading their treasures, B.J. left, and Joan emerged. Even though she was everything I wasn't—flamboyant, flashy, well-dressed, wealthy, skinny, and gloriously entertaining—I couldn't help but love her.

B.J. decided Joan should be a doctor.

Joan decided she should party.

And party she did.

But she had a formidable brain. She could cram what she needed to learn just before exams, managing even organic chemistry. When exams were over, Joan would be in a stupor from pulling all-nighters, and she'd sleep for days to recover.

I didn't understand why Joan liked me. I wasn't cool. Perhaps she thought I was a good listener. Perhaps I was more grounded and helped her stay tethered. Perhaps I was just as weird as she was, though in a different way, and we resonated weirdness together. She was a free-spirit and did what she wanted to do, not what she "should" do.

When I first arrived at Pomona, my boyfriend was a Marine on the front lines in Vietnam. I watched the news on our dorm TV every night. Every day but Sunday, I waited for the mail, hoping to glimpse Dale's blue, tissue-paper mailgrams.

One day, a friend called. "I heard Dale died. Do you know anything?"
I slid to the floor, unable to speak.
I called his mother. She'd heard nothing.
I called my father to check the Pentagon.
I waited.

Meanwhile, Joan hovered, then typed a poem she'd written and gently handed it to me.

Epistle to Marti
By Joan Jones

Will I read organic or western civ?
Organic, of course, western civ always loses.
Don't tell me reaves rates a phone call....

Instantaneously
Her soul full of love
> *cracks,*
>> *splinters,*
>>> *and shatters*
and the faculties of reason and rationalization
can't inhibit
the explosion.

As she tries
to reassemble
the s c a t t e r e d fragments
> *that*
>> *are*
>>> *her,*
the masses invade with their all too harmful sympathy.
Through the mist of my own mind,
I see flashes of soap-operas,
but what can I do to distinguish myself as a friend:
> *fawn*
>> *and*
>>> *cater*
>>>> *as the daughters of King Lear?*

as I ponder the impact of a nuclear explosion of the mind,
I find myself
> *void,*
>> *without expression.*
there is only unutterable compassion.

a vigil begins—
> *first at the phone booth,*
> *then in her room.*
as I can find no role to assume
I escape to my psychically applicable poster.
the atmosphere
> *is saturated*
>> *with tension:*
a hope for rumor
a fear of truth.

the tension is broken.
each returns to her world
but
the memory of the hell is still there
and
> *deserves*
>> *to remain.*

Joan was the only person who knew just what to do.

Hours later, I learned that Dale was alive.

When he returned in the spring, he looked exactly the same on the outside, but he wasn't the same inside, and neither was I. We ended things by doing nothing: we just stopped calling each other.

Following my depressing second year, I left Pomona to move to San Francisco and transfer to Cal. Joan graduated—she'd been a junior transferee when she'd arrived. Soon, she got involved with a playwright named Jeff. B.J. was not thrilled by their marriage, but oh, did she throw a fabulous party for her Hollywood friends and Joan's and Jeff's counter-culture friends, all under an enormous tent in B.J.'s luxurious Hollywood backyard.

I'd never experienced anything like it: piles of food, live music, abundant flowers, champagne. I don't remember anything about the ceremony, but I remember the strawberries—big, plump, juicy red—piled high beside a crystal bowl of rich, melted dark chocolate.

Strawberry juice and chocolate slurped down our chins.

I dropped out after my first week at Cal when my advisor refused to let me take a painting class. l got a job, joined a commune with my streetcar driver, and took classes in painting and sociology. A year later, my streetcar driver and I got married. I went on to finish college, graduated from law school, and after ten years, got divorced. In the early 1980s, I came out and now live happily in Berkeley with my wife, Tanya. We've been together 44 years.

After rebelling against her mother for a decade—during which time she got a teaching credential at Claremont College and a Master of Social Work from Columbia, graduating first in her class—Joan got divorced and finally decided to become a doctor. She married John, a scientist, and they've been together over forty years. When Joan retired recently, she'd been the Director of Anatomic Pathology at Weill Cornell Medicine.

What a completely unexpected friendship. Joan remains the only friend from my Pomona days. Over the years, we connected sporadically through phone calls and a handful of visits. In the early 1990s, seven years after our son Cooper was born, Joan was in San Francisco for a conference, and we had dinner at a Japanese restaurant near Union Square. She was still tall, slender, and stylish; I was still shorter, rounder, and decidedly unstylish. I always felt like a country bumpkin in San Francisco when Cooper was young, and I was a Berkeley mom and divorce mediator. Joan was peaking in her career, living in New York, and frenzied with work, John, adult children, and B.J. I was frenzied with two sets of parents nearby, Cooper, and my practice.

In 2008, when Joan called, I had to tell her that I was recuperating from tongue cancer. "You should see the six-inch gash across my neck. But I'm OK." I didn't yet know that I would be told I had only months to live, a diagnosis that came a year later. Of course, Joan must have known that my prognosis was terrible: after all, my cancer had metastasized, and Joan was a pathologist.

She told me that she was also having surgery: cosmetic eyelid surgery to eliminate droopy eyes!

I laughed aloud.

Time passed. We didn't connect. Nor did I think about it. I was busy trying not to die—despite my prognosis—and then failing to die—a glorious miracle. She called again in 2020 during the pandemic.

"I read your memoir," she said. "I was noodling around online and found it. I can't believe you wrote a book!" I wondered if she'd Googled me to see if I'd died from cancer and called when she figured I hadn't. We talked about my unlikely recovery, our kids, our retirements, Covid.

In October 2022—approximately 55 years from the day I met her, I saw "Joan" scroll across the screen of my muted phone. Why not? I thought.

"Hey Joanie!"

"IT'S YOU!" Joan yelled, laughing, "OH MY GOD, YOU ANSWERED!"

She knows I rarely answer the phone.

For an hour, we blabbed about Covid life.

"Can you believe I have a kid who's 50?" she asked. Joan's very close to John's children. "Peaches was 50 in March."

"Cooper's almost 37."

More blabbing about aging and how much it sucks. I asked her what prompted her phone call in 2020. She wasn't looking for my obituary! She was reminded by seeing an old card I'd sent.

As we said goodbye, Joan said, "I love you."

"I love you, too," I said.

It was the first time we'd ever uttered those words to each other. And they felt so true.

A PACKAGE DEAL

Carol Ziel

I wasn't looking for love
But there you were
Holding your small son's hand.
Calling each mother in the group "Friend"
I wasn't looking for blue highways
Camping under the stars
Skinny dipping in the Little Piney
Bluegrass and honky tonk
I wasn't looking for drugs
Beer, wine, brandy, gin
But there they were
You were a package deal.
I wasn't expecting to lose myself
I did
And then you were gone

Leaving me alone in emptiness.

PROCRASTINATION

Kathie Arcide

It would not surprise any of the people close to me how much I still miss her. My realization today is just how much. She was my best friend from the 1970s through the end of the century.

I try not to think about her, or even talk about her. It's still painful, but every now and then, in our professional worlds, she and I still cross paths, and it all floods back. So many years ago now, but I'll never forget it. Our friendship was so easy, so equal. I always felt as important to her as she was to me. That's hard to find.

Though she and I had occasional problems, as friendships do, the most wonderful thing we had for so long was daily contact…someone to check in with or be checked on by. I have never found that again.

I know it was partly because of our ages and stages of life way back then. Our living proximity, including together for a while, and all our common problems, were like friendship food. We were super-glued together over ex-husbands, money, school, new loves, and single moming, etc. These topics simply required daily updates.

I couldn't tell you what happened to our friendship, but our "sisterhood" ended, in my memory now, rather abruptly, the severing complete.

In the ensuing 25 years, I've never come close to replacing that connection.

Since then, I've made a few gentle overtures toward her, and her response has always been gracious and kind, but also brief and singular, no follow-up. My biggest secret is just how often I imagine making grand gestures, resulting in an emotional reunion, which would have been more congruent for our early years as friends. I play out these scenes in my head a couple times a year…or any time I drive by her house.

During the peak of the Pandemic Years, like many, I contemplated my life, and my mortality, creating a whopper of an existential crisis, accompanied by a profound sense of panic. If I have unfinished business, I'd better hurry up!!

The list was long but what often rose to the surface was our friendship.

I hadn't seen her for years, but it was Grand Gesture time. Dramatic I know, but hey, contemplating your remaining days is dramatic. I absolutely had to reach out to my old best friend/sister just to tell her how lucky I was to have her in my life, even if just for those early years.

So, in the throes of that emotion, I drove toward her street. As I got closer, I panicked, pulled into a parking lot, and sat for ten minutes, thinking, getting grounded, psyching myself up. I rehearsed my speech, making sure it was loving and hopefully, unconditional. And then I resolutely decided to proceed.

Knowing it was a long shot that she would even be there, I drove straight to her home. This is what I found.

Her beautiful classic older house was gone. The lovely side yard where she got married was gone. The picnic table that we sat at for barbecues, or to have hours of important conversations, gone. The quaint living room where we had Christmas mornings, all gone. Even the trees and all her flowers…

In place of all these visual reminders, the proof of our wonderful friendship, there was nothing…except a barrier of hay bales, and the final piece of heavy machinery, a Track Hoe, probably used to level out the land where our history as friends once stood.

I had no idea what it meant, where my dear former friend was, or if she was even alive. It was a very hard lesson to learn.

Procrastination is a risky game!

LETTER TO AN OLD FRIEND

Judy Burman

As the years go by, my mind wanders to the people I wished I could have said goodbye to and the people who made me the person that I am today.

You were my first boss. I was 35 when I entered the workforce, and I started there as a temp from the Manpower Agency. I had a 10th grade education and that was 20 years in the past. Those years were spent as a wife and mother. My only knowledge of the outside world came from my husband, the TV and children. I was shy and introverted. I had no idea of how people should dress for jobs or act in public, I had not changed much over the years, I wore no make-up, and my hair and clothing were out of date and what I could afford. I was afraid of the challenge, but very excited to have my first job.

It was at my first performance review that you told me that I had the worst grammar that you had ever heard. I broke down and cried like a baby. As you tried to calm me down, you explained that when I was ready, I would fix it, and until then it didn't really matter what others thought. How could I fix a problem if I didn't know there was one? Until that day, nobody told me of my shortcomings. That same day, after work, I visited the community college and signed up for English 101 and Grammar. I didn't expect to take any other classes, after all, I didn't finish high school, but I knew that I had to fix the immediate problem.

How wonderful it felt to be going to school again. I wished that I could continue but I believed that my lack of a high school diploma and financial situation wouldn't allow it. That is where you first came to my rescue. I learned that my employer would pay for any classes that I wanted to take as long as they were job related and nobody cared that I didn't finish high school as long as I passed the entrance exam. I didn't have a clue what that meant but I knew that I would take advantage of anything that could make me a better employee. The thought of a diploma of any kind never entered my mind.

Over the years, at the beginning of each term, you would sit with me to review and select possible classes. You patiently explained how each choice could allow you to give me new job responsibilities that would improve my possibility of advancement. For ten years you watched over me until I had earned first an AA degree, then a BA from the local university. You were so much more than my boss; you were my best friend. With your help over the years, my job title changed from the lowest clerk to a senior cost accountant.

Sadly, you left the company a year before my graduation, and I moved on to a larger company with more opportunities right after graduation. (It took ten years of night school to earn the BA.) The education bug stayed with me and as part of the contract with my new employer was the promise that they would pay for my MBA.

I'm sorry that I lost track of you and that I never had the opportunity to tell you how knowing you changed my life. I am sure that you would be proud of the confident business woman that I became. As a commercial once said, "You've come a long way, Baby," and it would never have happened without you, my best friend and mentor.

FROG LEGS

Joan L. Connor

I called her Pammy. Of course, I didn't spell it that way. I never wrote her name. I was four or five years old, not quite in kindergarten, and loved to play with Pammy.

Today I lay in bed feeling despair covering my memory. Sadness envelops my thoughts. Why would these feelings occur? Surely, I should be dancing like Snoopy on my husband's birthday card at the delight in writing about Pammy. Twitches erupt inside me as thoughts of Pammy drift through. It is foggy, these memories. The writing gurus say to just keep the pen on the paper or in this particular case, my keys tap, tap, tapping on the keyboard. The memories regenerate, come more alive, develop their personas, and all this scares me.

Pammy was my earliest playmate, and she became lost soon after I entered elementary school. Was it because we were not in the same grade level? Was it because her dad remarried, and they moved? Was it because her grandparents died? Where did Pammy go?

Pammy lived across the street and down at the end of our block with her grandparents and her father who came and went, perhaps a truck driver. His name was Arlan—Arlan Lamprecht—and Mr. and Mrs. Lamprecht were the grandparents. Pamela Lamprecht was my first best friend.

I am a bit nervous recalling these names for you readers. They come so vividly to me 75 years later. They say the long-term memory becomes more vivid as the short-term memory diminishes. (What exactly did I fix last night for supper?)

Pammy's big square white house had a large front porch, a front door with see-through glass, and a heavy door probably with beveled glass. They built doors to last back then. There was also a side door, accessed using three or four cement steps like many of our small-town Iowa homes. I would knock on the front door.

"Can Pammy play?"

Most often the answer was, "Yes…PAMELA," Grandma would holler.

And then our collective imagination muse took over. We would go upstairs to her big sister Sally's room and play dress-up. Not with cast-away clothes like Patty Nutt and I played in my basement, but with the current fashions that Sally wore. We were in Sally's closet with her latest teenage styles begging for our attention. Sally was a high school cheerleader in our town of 1,200 solid folks who tended to the surrounding rich farming industry. My daddy ran one of the two hardware stores uptown. Downtown meant it was a city. Daddy's Coast-to-Coast store was uptown.

We never put Sally's cheerleading outfit on. It was blue and gold with a short, pleated skirt and a chenille Trojan on the sweater, surrounded by a very big D for Dysart. We played dress-up in her skirts and blouses, dresses and shoes, perhaps touched a few pieces of jewelry. We walked from bedroom to bedroom just as the ladies of town walked around. I am talking about church women that go shopping. We didn't know about any other kind of woman.

If Sally came home, we would scamper to put everything away just as we found it. Sally never corrected us. She was real pretty, very popular, and liked us. Then off she would go. We scattered outside too, eager to create hollyhock dolls by the back door, perched on those cement steps.

One time I was invited to stay for supper.

"They're having frog legs, Mom. I have never eaten frog legs. Please can I stay?"

I was given permission.

The Lamprecht's home is where I ate frog legs for the first time.

The Lamprecht's home is where I ate frog legs for the only time.

I wonder if Pammy ever came to our home to eat.

Around the 6:00 supper hour, if the phone rang at the Lamprecht's house I was out the door in a flash.

"If that's my mom, tell her I just left," I would blurt over my shoulder.

Home for supper, but no frog legs at my house. We Woodleys didn't eat frog legs. That wasn't something they sold in the butcher shop next door to Daddy's store. I am quite sure Arlan and Grandpa Lamprecht went frog hunting. I never heard of Daddy frog hunting.

The gurus are right-on. The more I write of these long-ago memories, the more I become reacquainted with one small town block in mid-America, during the late 1940s where the corn grew taller than Jack's beanstalk and the girls' basketball forwards didn't cross the middle line.

MUDPIES AND TIME'S GOODBYES

Christine Hassing

I wish I could remember what brought us together, my first best friend, Lori, and I.

I remember what separated us.

Simply adulthood and the passage of time.

As my age increases, so does my curiosity. How has Lori's life progressed after high school? Married? Children? A grandmother? Did she move out of Michigan? What have been some of her greatest joys? Her hardest losses?

Does she remember the summers we camped with my grandparents before the teenage and elderly years introduced the four of us to a universal truth that time does not stay the same forever?

Does she still love to drive with a friend around the countryside without a specific destination in mind, deciding at each stop sign to turn left or turn right, sometimes getting lost, but always regaining a sense of direction to find the way back home?

Our friendship included inseparable moments like when one of us fell ill at school, the other feigned ill. The librarian never judged the validity of both of us little girls sick at the same time as she gently ushered us to the two cots in the elementary library, a resting place until our moms could pick us up.

We were entrepreneurs before the age of ten. We had a store. I still remember our cash register, considered extremely old-fashioned by today's standards. It was red and the cash drawer dinged a bell sound when it opened after summing the total of a customer's purchases. Our store's specialty of homemade pies consistently drew in the same customers, though they never actually ate our desserts.

We had the biggest oven for baking those pies! Larger than the one in my friend's mom's kitchen! The oven was the full length of a wall in our outdoor baking area. I have less recollection of our table where we stirred our special cream fillings, hand dug and blended with water. Also known as mud.

When we weren't running our store or making the ingredients for our one-of-a-kind desserts, we raced cars. My friend's car was painted purple and mine green. Or maybe vice versa. We become pretty dang good at racing them through the sand pile!

We were also architects and builders, when we weren't learning math, science, and reading. Nor jumping rope, swinging with the goal our shoes would touch the tree branch overhead, or spinning on monkey bars during recess.

My ability to keep my belief in Santa Claus a little longer was because of Lori's dad and one of her brothers, though we didn't know it was them at the time. When they made foot and hoof prints in the snow on the roof and in the yard of Lori's home one Christmas Eve night, both of us *knew* Santa existed. She had proof!

Sometimes I wish I understood the significance of grief like I do now. We were seven years old when Lori's other brother died tragically in a construction accident. I didn't have an awareness of how sorrow can live in a house when a bedroom and place setting at a table become empty. I don't recall Lori and I talking about her brother or her sadness. I suppose that is how innocence is designed until life introduces wisdom in naivete's place.

Though I know that time is what evolved us from best friends to good friends to a meaningful chapter of the past, the little girl within me whispers through a childhood memory a quote by Elizabeth Gilbert from her book, *Eat, Pray, Love*. "But I was always coming here. I thought about one of my favorite Sufi poems, which says that God long ago drew a circle in the sand, exactly around the spot where you are standing right now. I was never not coming here. This was never not going to happen."

We were either getting into or out of Lori's mom's car. The rear door closed on Lori's thumb. Initially her mom couldn't get the car door open, kicking at it from inside, pulling at it from outside. The only thing I could do was try to comfort Lori's pain-filled wails with my sense of helplessness and even more than that. A longing that it was me instead of my best friend.

I remember sharing that feeling with Lori after her mom got the car door open, after an emergency room visit and a finger splint, after the tears had dried and the pain had subsided. I remember Lori's response in a tone with words that conveyed I was ridiculous for feeling that way. She couldn't understand someone else wanting to be in another's shoes like that. Not even her best friend.

That moment didn't separate us, so many more years of realized slumber parties, dancing to songs playing from our 45 RPM vinyl record collection, painting an LAV rock and roll radio station logo on the athletic director's wall. Her laughing at how engrossed I got when I was writing. Me laughing at her aspiration to be a band groupie for either The Police, Rick Springfield, or Duran Duran.

I know Lori's father passed away many years ago because I saw his gravestone when we were placing my dad's ashes in a grave in the same cemetery. Lori's mom was a few years older than mine. I wonder if Lori is blessed to still have her mom alive. I hope she has the same fortune I do—my mom still lives.

I don't know all the ways that Lori and I grew into the uniqueness each of us now is, but I know we have a couple of things in common. One. Neither of us returned to class reunions. When I see posts of reunions that have occurred, neither of us are in attendance.

And the second commonality. Before time's goodbye, Lori and I both knew the gift of having a best friend.

COMMON GROUND

Susan Marsh

When I was a child, the harshest scolding my mother could deliver was this: "You look like a Carey kid!" This declaration usually followed one of my forays into the patch of forest behind our house, where I dug for (imaginary) fossils, made mudpies, and climbed trees.

The Carey kids lived below us on the far side of a gravel road, in a small, dilapidated house that my mother called a shack. The condition of their property and the grubbiness of the children reminded her of the families that hers had looked down on as white trash.

Forbidden to approach or play with them, I sneaked behind the laurel hedge and looked down our steep hill for a view of their sagging porch. Four or five dirty-faced Careys stared back as if they'd been expecting me.

As soon as I appeared, a volley of stones came zinging my way. If I took one on the arm or forehead and ran wailing into the house, Mother was not sympathetic. "How many times do I have to tell you to stay away from them?" she demanded.

Her ire failed to stifle my fascination with the Careys. Like me, I could tell they had been instructed not to associate with the neighbors, who they must have seen as interlopers who lived in a newly built subdivision, in clean houses with fireplaces and picture windows. We threw rocks because it was the only form of communication available.

I risked the ever-improving aim of the older Carey boys in hopes of making contact with the girls. Cathy, the oldest, was tall for her age and walked like an adult with a self-possessed swing in her arms. Her blond hair was cropped to just below her ears and I never saw her wearing anything besides denim overalls. I thought of her as interesting and mysterious, elegant and poised. She never acknowledged my existence, not even to hurl a rock my way. For my part, I scarcely noticed her younger sister Rose, a quiet presence with long wavy hair. Unlike her sister, Rose wore dresses. Unlike her brothers, she did not throw rocks.

One day after school I ran along my well-worn footpath into the forest, heading to my "tower"—the broken trunk of a cedar snag at the edge of a log landing from when the original old-growth forest had been cut.

When I reached it, I stopped short. Crouching in a pool of sunlight, not 20 feet away, was Rose Carey.

We eyed each other warily. Her hair, fastened with barrettes, fell to the waistband of her flowered blue dress. With my smudged shorts and dusty tee shirt, I might have agreed with my mother: I looked more like a Carey kid than she did.

Rose regarded me for a moment before turning to a pile of crayons at her feet, spilled from one of those big boxes with 64 colors and a built-in sharpener. She selected the stub of a color I recognized as cornflower. She pressed its blunt end into the weathered cedar wood and when she pulled the crayon away it left a fat waxy dot.

I widened my focus to take in the splatter of colors on the tower—magenta, yellow, orange, pink…and cornflower. The sun must have softened the crayons to make those marks, perhaps because she'd laid them out intentionally for that purpose.

She pushed another dot onto the wood. I fumed in silent confusion, immobilized by this unexpected situation. She had dared to invade *my* forest to deface *my* tower with random and garish blotches.

Rose sat back on her heels to study her work. Then she turned in my direction and offered the crayon.

I can't remember any verbal exchanges between us as we covered the tower with dots of cornflower and aquamarine, raw umber and midnight blue, until she heard her mother calling.

Together we gathered the crayons, and she stuffed them into their box. "Bye," she said with a smile before she ran toward home.

As her cascade of hair disappeared into the shadows, my chest warmed with the guilty thrill of having played with a Carey kid. Beyond that, I realized that I'd enjoyed her company. She was sweet and amiable and had shared her crayons. In less than an hour we had turned from enemies into friends.

Something else stayed with me after she had gone. I realized that the forest served as a haven for someone besides me, someone who may have needed respite from mean-spirited brothers and younger sibs who might have stolen or broken her precious crayons. That ten-acre remnant of forest, which I had thought of as my secret personal friend, welcomed both of us. It didn't matter if one lived in a "shack" and one stood behind a picture window, hoping for another glimpse of Rose. There, beyond the disapproving gazes of adults, we had stood on common ground.

I turned back to the fort and gazed at our handiwork, a galaxy of multicolored dots. It was beautiful.

FRIENDS IN NEED

PUTTING DOWN A HORSE

Marie Unini

Today I will put down my mare, Bahiana. "Put down" has always seemed such an ambiguous term for me. I think, no, there is something better, something more exact. "Put down" is what you do with your knife and fork at the end of a meal. Put down the baby for a nap. Put down a rebellion. Put down someone by way of insult. But putting down as a way of ending life, well, I know what the dictionary says, but it just doesn't resonate with me. But "euthanize." Now there's a word. But it's all the same. I must order her compassionate death by injection.

There are choices, naturally. "Let nature take its course," that's a good one. You can't just allow a dog with cancer, or a cat with kidney failure, or a horse who can't stand, to just languish and fade in nature's own good time. Who could do that? Were this a human proposition, we would call in hospice and get support from social workers, nurses, caregivers. That's what I did for my mother, when it was clear that she did not want to move forward in this life. Told the doctors, "No more treatment." Isn't that somehow equivalent to "put her down"? I don't know where the greater mercy lies. But I must make some phone calls.

"You want to get things ready, Marie," Steve said as he was packing up his shoeing tools two weeks ago. "Here," he said, guiding my hand, "feel her legs." They are hot, not the normal cool they should be. "One day soon, you're going to come out here and find her down, she won't want to get up. It'll be too painful for her to stand. You don't want to be taken by surprise."

He's telling me what I know and don't want to face, that my 29-year-old mare is at the end of her life, that her chronic inflammation is no longer treatable, and I need to make the preparations to end it for her. Put her down. It is not a simple, single act—it's a project requiring several coordinated working parts, anticipation and planning. I need to get started right away, I know. And I don't. You could call this denial. So yes, I will be taken by surprise.

My work life has been busy, and yes, I've been meaning to make those phone calls, get everything lined up, but of course today is the day I walk from the house to the corral, and find her lying down, a Sphinx, half upright, forelegs curved under, her devoted sidekick Calypso hovering, vigilant. I'm not too late, of course, but this event signals urgency that eclipses all other demands.

I make three phone calls: to the vet, the brothers with the backhoe, and my closest friend, Connie. She is the hardest. Connie will want to come immediately, hover over me that way Calypso does Bahiana, waiting for me to show need, to do the thing that rarely happens that aggrieves her so: support me. I closed down my heart years ago, she says, when my brother died. "You've changed. You are not the friend I knew." She's half right perhaps. What shows on the outside changed, anyway. But I do still feel, really, I do. It just can't interfere with what must be done. That's what I did when Eddie died. I did what needed doing and took care of the people who didn't seem like they were going to make it through this intact. My parents. The man who felt responsible for the accident. I grounded them, a lightning rod for their emotions. And I just kept being busy, like an engine that hasn't been turned off. That's what she sees. She remembers the "before" me—the wilder, uncensored one, and she laments its absence. And when she does, she's the last person I want support from, because that noisy longing for me to be different is attached to it. And it drains me, distracts me from the doing.

We are wired differently. Tears erupt for her at the smallest provocation—her estranged siblings, children in cages at the border. I was not crying, as habit, long before my brother died. She requires support, often dramatically, demands it even. Once, she called at 6:00 in the morning and told me she couldn't get out of bed, and would I please come. She lived on a remote alfalfa ranch and didn't do well with the isolation sometimes. I drive 80 miles, climbed into bed with her and we speculated about what could possibly get her up and moving again. Shortly a brightly colored hot air balloon landed in the field closest to us. She declared a miracle, and got out of bed, fully restored.

But right now, what I really want to do, I just want to sit down with Bahiana. I don't want to awaken my husband, Bob. Nothing. No calls, not yet. It's 6:30 a.m., quiet, a light breeze brushing over us from the east, the earth still cool to the touch from the night. I give Calypso his morning feed, and he wanders off, but continues to glance at us between mouthfuls. I sit down and lean against her—something that would have been impossible before. She sighs and stares at me. Take your time, she seems to say. Twenty-nine years of memory wash through me: how tiny she seemed at 6 months, just barely my height, how trusting she was, and patient, how ignorant I was—a first-timer who had no business with a horse. Our great adventures, how she took care of me, rather than the reverse. The time I got us into a tight passage, how she backed us out and side stepped up an almost vertical slope, gently letting me slip out of the saddle, and scrambled back down while I slid behind her. The first time I knew that she read my thoughts, riding bareback and I thought about turning right, and she did. Feeling that connection pass between our skins.

Bahiana was 15 when we brought Calypso to live with us, and they merged in a classic mare/gelding bond: she led, he followed and doted. Some of this is herd habit, but with them it was more their personal chemistry. She was bossy. He was mellow. Grooming, he would doze off, standing. He was trusting and liked people. But his connection to Bahiana was fierce. If I took her out without him, he would pace as we left and whinny until we were out of earshot. He would often stand there, rooted, until we came back in range again and then, when he sensed our proximity, he'd start up again.

I have known her longer than I knew my brother, longer than half my close friends. I don't want to call anyone, I wish we could just do this alone, Bahiana and I. I wish I could just lie here with her and feel her slip away. We sit for an hour like this, and when Bob comes out to feed and discovers us, I have nearly drifted off in daydream. I make the calls.

Dr. Marteney tells me to let him know when I've got the backhoe on site, he promises he won't be more than 30 minutes away. The Clutter brothers arrive and begin digging where I indicate, one of them managing the enormous tractor and scoop with a jeweler's delicacy, the other measuring and directing. Connie arrives, asks what I need, I say I don't know, just be here. I'm glad that you are. She examines me. I have cried, a little, but not so much that you would know. She positions herself at a short distance outside the corral and shifts her weight from one foot to the other, her nervous little dance.

Bob asks what we should do with Calypso, who is now on high alert. "Do you want him to see this?" I hesitate. Without waiting for my response, he halters him and takes him to the far west side of the corral, behind a dense screen of junipers and out of sight of what Marteney and I will do, and the backhoe after us.

Marteney asks me if I'm ready. He is usually so chatty with big energy presence. Making small talk, imagining all the golfing he will do when he retires, someday. Always someday. Today he is soft, slow, calm. I feel his sadness. No, I joke, could we just press rewind and start our relationship all over? He smiles. You're going to have to get her to stand, Marie.

We can't do this when they're lying down, too much danger of them thrashing. On cue, Bahiana stirs and stiffly brings herself up onto all four legs. It leaves her a little breathless, and so we wait. He administers the first injection, a kind of horse valium that he uses when he files their teeth. She sighs and begins to sway ever so gently. The second injection is effective, and in such a surprising, graceful way, this thousand pound animal sinks in soft folds to the ground, like a dropped heavy linen dinner napkin. This all seems so peaceful to me, and now I'm crying, tears of relief, and Marteney places an arm across my shoulders. And then I hear it, from the west. A wail, a howl, a high full-throated bellow, an other-worldly trembling of enormous vocal cords, and it drives right down into me, lightning seeking ground. Bob will later tell me that he knew exactly what we were doing, and when, because Calypso began to pace and circle, pulling toward where we were, and he knew, when he cried out, that it was done.

The Clutters complete their impossibly gentle, delicate job, and Connie joins me to stand by Bahiana's fresh grave. She has brought a bright bouquet of plastic flowers from Vallarta Market, which will survive the elements for two years. She opens her arms to me, and she is crying, of course. My precious loving surrogate. And I step into them, and I feel my own grounding in there, in that embrace.

Previously published in *Tulip Tree Review*, Number 13, Spring/ Summer 2023.

LONELY? YOU'RE NOT ALONE

Barbara Rady Kazdan

I define connection as the energy that exists between people when they feel seen, heard, and valued; can give and receive without judgment; and derive sustenance and strength from the relationship.

—BRENÉ BROWN, PH.D.

One day I received a survey from my temple for "households with only one adult member." They'd found that 25 percent of members fit that description. How, they wanted to know, could they better serve them?

I wondered, who are those single members? Once married; divorced; widowed like me; never married, not yet or not interested—had I forgotten anyone? I completed the survey, but I wondered why it hadn't asked the jackpot questions: Are you lonely? How can we help?

Gerontologist Dr. Bill Thomas calls loneliness, boredom and helplessness the "three plagues." I'd suffered from all three: loneliness often breeds boredom; when I couldn't fill that void I'd feel helpless. In this big wide wonderful world isn't boredom some kind of personal sin? Felt like it.

Several years into widowhood, my circle of friends had grown, so now someone would usually ask, "How about a movie this weekend?" Or "Want to meet at the farmer's market Saturday?" Weekdays would offer up social and substantive fare—planned and impromptu. But sometimes Friday would roll around with nothing but white space on my weekend calendar.

"Get busy," I'd tell myself. "Find something to do." But I couldn't always muster enough energy and ingenuity to carpe the diem. Can you keep a secret? I'd binge-watch TV, milking my streaming subscriptions for all they're worth. Sometimes on the weekend I'd go to the grocery store or to Starbucks just to interact with other human beings. No substitute for engaging with friends or family—but it sure beat sitting home with my dog all weekend.

When I was married, mothering, and immersed in my career, a drive in the country offered soul-reviving solitude. Since I've lived alone, not so much.

During those weekend stints in solitary confinement, when my children would call from their dots on the map and ask how I was doing, I'd never answer, "isolated, longing for company." We'd catch up, schmooze, and plan our next visit.

Meetup CEO Scott Heiferman says America faces a "loneliness epidemic." Research confirms that social isolation is increasing. Why? Because today's way of life reduces the quantity and quality of our relationships. Fewer people live near family. Many delay getting married and having children. More people of all ages are living alone.

Since losing Dan, like the old song says I was "alone again, naturally." I spent years walking into rooms of name-tagged strangers—joining, volunteering, looking for social connections. At the January meeting of a discussion group, when we'd shared New Year's resolutions, I'd said, "To find a new best friend."

I'd left my BFF behind—tearfully—when we'd left Houston. That friendship, steeped in shared confidences from our children's playdates through their wedding days, seemed irreplaceable. Although she's a phone call away, as a widow I'd needed someone nearby who cared about me and to care about, someone to count on for companionship and support.

Turned out that desire was not just wishful thinking, but essential to my health. The trend that prompted my congregation's survey concerns medical professionals as well. Dying of loneliness isn't just an expression. Social psychologist Bert Uchino found that people with little social support have a mortality rate as high as alcoholics; conversely, the impact of making friends has a comparable effect on your health as giving up smoking. A primitive, primal need for connection is hardwired into our brains. No wonder I'd felt an urgency to fill that void.

Harvard's 85-year study on adult happiness concluded: "Good relationships keep us happier and healthier. Period." Having someone to rely on helps your nervous system relax, keeps your brain healthier for longer, and diminishes both emotional and physical pain. Study director Dr. Robert Waldinger noted, "It's the quality of your close relationships that matters." I didn't need a research study to reach the same conclusion.

My congregation reflects a societal trend. Psychologist Susan Pinker's research revealed that people "with frequent face-to-face interactions were not only physically and emotionally healthier, but also lived longer...."

Sadly, Pinker notes, "a quarter of the population says they have no one to talk to."

The most popular category among Meetups' 15 million US members? Socializing. Transient Washington, DC is an especially challenging place even for someone with an outgoing personality like mine to find and develop an emotionally intimate friendship.

Aristotle said, "Friendship is a slow-ripening fruit." Although I'd urgently needed a new best friend, the process required time, first to find a kindred spirit, then to deepen the connection. Time to share our stories, to color and fill in the background so when we ask, "What's new?" the answer would fit into a full, nuanced narrative. It required honesty, the willingness to give and receive confidences in the quest for understanding. Impatience aside, it was worth the wait.

A confidante is a woman "with whom private matters and problems are discussed." When I called a friend recently—someone I've become close to over several years—I explained why I hadn't called recently:

"I've been an emotional wreck, worrying about Stacy's health. I was waiting for an update before I called." She listened. We talked.

As we hung up, she gently chided, "You didn't have to wait. You could've picked up the phone to tell me, 'I'm in a funk.'" Our friendship, she was telling me, could handle the raw, unprocessed stuff of life. Mission accomplished.

THIS IS WHO SHE IS

Kimberly Krantz

I watch.
She is giving and loving, yet demands respect at all times.

I learn.
She manages difficult situations with ease, never turning
    anyone away who needs help.

I listen.
She understands my good days and the bad ones. Always
    speaking with kindness and compassion.

I ask.
She hears about my deep-down thoughts and worries.
    She tells it like it is, assuring me that I will survive.

I admire.
Her zest for life and that she is more beautiful on the
    inside than on the outside.

I love.
The angels brought her into my life at a time when I
    didn't realize I needed her.

Guides me with her light
An unintentional mentor.

Honored she's my friend.

LESSONS FROM FRIENDSHIP

Sue Kusch

There is a black-and-white photo of me as a young child, sitting on a snowbank, looking at a distant group of children playing in the snow. Years ago, while looking at this photo, my gregarious mother remarked that I had difficulty making friends as a child because I was overly shy, which caused her to worry about me. Throughout my childhood and adolescence, I was what most people labeled a loner.

I wasn't entirely friendless during those years: in the fifth grade, Jill, Jane, and I were the popular girls in our class, as well as the tallest ones and the first to wear training bras. We challenged and changed the school dress code forbidding girls from wearing pants by presenting a petition to our school principal. I still remember our group hug in the hallway—jumping with glee and feeling the closeness of camaraderie.

That spring, my newly divorced mother announced we would move as soon as the school year was done. We would move three more times over the next seven years. My family was a mess: divorce, alcoholism, emotional neglect by one parent, and abandonment by the other. There were secrets to maintain and unpredictable behaviors in my home life, so having friends over was never an option. As my family spiraled out of control, I sought safety in books, libraries, and public parks and later escaped via drugs and alcohol in my teens. I wasted a fair amount of time partying with other unhappy teens, names long forgotten, but I never considered them friends.

Over the next three decades, I healed and matured into a responsible college student, wife, parent, and higher education professional. I developed a friendship with a woman named Vicki. We met in a class, eager older students in a sea of young, bored faces. She helped me get a part-time position at the college, an opportunity that turned into a 20-year career. We walked together several mornings each week, sharing our thoughts about what we were reading and discussing our plans for the future. We critiqued each other's academic papers and celebrated our graduation together. One month after we completed graduate school, she was diagnosed with leukemia and died six months later. I was devastated and grieved for a long time. Her death was one of the most painful lessons I learned about love and loss. I dislike the phrase best friend, but at age 36, I lost my first best friend.

As I matured, I recognized that I wasn't overly shy, as my mother had sadly declared, I was highly introverted: quiet, reserved, serious, independent, and a deep thinker. I was curious about the world and had a long list of activities and interests. I had many acquaintances at my workplace and was respected and valued. However, I had difficulty relating to most of them beyond professional conversations. One year, I joined a group of co-workers for a season of dinners and plays, but our conversations consisted mainly of gossip and complaints about our workplace. I didn't join them the following year.

In my forties, I pursued my interests and passions independently. Now and then, I would ask a friend to join me, and I soon realized that I not only liked my solitude but needed it to recharge my energy. I often turned down the occasional invitation to socialize, and eventually, the invitations stopped.

I developed a friendship with a new colleague during this period, initially bonding over our similar childhood experiences. We spent a lot of time together, doing things that she liked to do. She struggled with low self-esteem and negativity and often criticized my lack of professional ambition, my failure to dress for success, and my lack of interest in talking about work. I slowly realized there was a cost attached to our friendship: neglecting my interests and stuffing my emotions. It drained me, and I ended our decade-long friendship. I learned two important lessons about friendship: do not lose sight of yourself in any relationship, and I couldn't help someone who wasn't ready to accept it.

With no close friends, though many acquaintances, I reflected on my friendship skills, thinking I could adjust my personality and be a better friend. What was wrong with me? Why didn't I fit in? It took a while for me to redirect my reflection. Why did I need to change? What did I want from a friendship? Was I willing to compromise parts of myself to maintain a friendship? Do friendships genuinely allow a person to be who she is? Is it okay not to have a close friendship?

Introverts are often misunderstood. While extroverts find energy in groups and parties, I pin myself against the wall and wait for the best opportunity to exit. I am not shy, afraid to talk, or socially anxious. Small talk or chit-chat? I got nothing. But if you want to talk about the best places to camp, favorite hiking trails, the current wildflower bloom, what I'm growing in my garden, or what I am reading, knitting, or thinking about...well, let's sit here and get to know each other. But that doesn't happen. As an older woman, when I meet new people, they often seem less interested in learning about me. Once, a woman told me she didn't need any more friends. I was a bit stunned by that honest statement, but I think I understood that friendships take time and energy.

In my younger years, I experienced bouts of loneliness that I now attribute to cultural pressure to be extroverted and have an abundance of friends. I no longer experience loneliness; I prefer to be alone for much of what I like to do. But I am not isolated or friendless. Sometimes, friendships develop slowly. Thirty-five years ago, I met Ann at a restaurant where we worked. We were young mothers, separated from our husbands, struggling with our lives. We could talk easily and enjoyed each other's humor. A year after meeting her, I reunited with my husband and moved 1500 miles away to start a new chapter in my life. Long-distance friendships can be difficult to maintain: our lives were busy with work, family, and college. Birthday and holiday cards were sent, an occasional phone call, but over the years, we drifted apart.

In November 2011, I called Ann to tell her that my husband had died in a horrific accident. Her compassion during that period of grief was one of the best gifts I have ever received. We began to chat and email regularly, catching up with each other's lives. When I visited my parents, who lived in the same state as her, we tried to spend at least one day together.

In 2016, we had a misunderstanding over the heated politics of that year, and I decided that our differences were more substantial than our similarities and fondness for each other. I missed our friendship terribly and blamed myself for giving up so easily on our relationship. Three years later, she messaged me, and since that simple note, we have fully opened our hearts and embraced our friendship. Our differences are still present, but we focus on our similarities. Now in our mid-60s, we text several times a week, write an occasional letter, and chat on the phone. We share our lives: the good, the bad, and the heartbreaking. And that turned out to be the most important lesson I learned about friendship: it's not about shared activities and interests but about sharing our most genuine version of ourselves.

DEPARTURES AND DOUBTS

Deb Johnson

The night before my crack of dawn flight to move from California to New York City I was in a hotel a half a mile from John Wayne airport with Suzi, my best friend—reflecting back.

Sitting on the well-worn beige couch, I watched some folks playing pool at a neighbor's 40th birthday party. A woman I barely knew with thick, wavy, reddish-blonde hair walked past me and said, "Hey, bitch."

I ignored her. My improvisation skills were not going to help at a big party. And I felt hurt. Why did she dislike me if she'd never even spoken to me?

Although no one had ever called me a bitch to my face, for some unknown reason, I felt we would be good friends. I tried several times to invite Suzi to go for a hike (I guess I should have told her to take a hike after she insulted me.) She kept reiterating, "I'm busy." She finally agreed to go hike with me.

One typical Southern California 70-degree morning we went for a long walk, both of us dressed in our leggings, T-shirts, tennis shoes, and our long hair up in ponytails.

As we ambled out of our gated neighborhood, Suzi's most poignant question was, "What would you do if you knew you wouldn't fail?"

The words slipped right off my tongue. "Go into politics." I continued to speak after pausing a moment. "I've thought about it, but life got busy when I married at 25 and worked full time; I had two kids in two years; then a painful divorce."

"Now what do you think?"

I gazed up and to the left trying to find an honest answer. We walked on one of the two main streets in our 'hood, heading north towards a regional park. "I don't know. How about you?"

"Dude, I'm telling you, I'd start a restaurant downtown," Suzi replied with a big smile.

I took a sip of my bottled water as we started hiking up a steep, rocky hill. "You should." We were both breathing hard, so we slowed down our conversation. I was biting my tongue so as not to query her about the first time we'd met. I was uncomfortable, but climbing another hill gave me some endorphins and increased my confidence enough to bring up the tough question. "Why did you call me a bitch at Rhonda's birthday party?"

She said without hesitation, "I thought you were so cute, and that's how I express it."

I retorted, "Have you ever considered it could hurt someone's feelings to call them that?"

Suzi looked puzzled. "Hm, I hadn't thought of that. I can try it differently, 'Bitch, but I mean it cuz you are so darn cute.' Is that better?"

I smirked.

"Come on, look at your perfect Maria Shriver jaw line and green eyes."

"Ah. Thank you," I said. We both laughed.

I smelled my own stench. At the end of the hike, before she went left and I went right, she gave me a tight warm 30-second hug—and not one of those fake half ones with one arm, or a pat on the back. I felt self-conscious as my shirt was soaking with sweat.

I turned around one last time to engage with her. "I'm so glad I kept bugging you to do something with me."

I ran to Suzi's house many times when I struggled with my kids. On a happy note, we spent many Valentine's nights together when her husband, nine out of ten times, was out of town, and I had no date. We had a unique banter which was lively and upbeat. I'm convinced that God wrote her number on the palm of my hand in a black sharpie pen and my number in ball-point pen on her palm—because she was so tentative about being friends with me and I was certain.

I was a single working mom with two kids in elementary school when we met, and the only single mom in the entire neighborhood. She was a stay-at-home mom with two younger towhead boys. We soon became so close that if she called me a witch, instead of a bitch, I could be Elphaba and she could be Glinda from *Wicked*, best friends forever.

We had a wonderful friendship enjoying many cool activities: Blues Travelers at the House of Blues; California Adventure with the kids; cycling over 30 miles on our heavy mountain bikes to Balboa Island and back; and many hikes.

Over the years at parties, I heard her exclaim to other women over a dozen times, "Bitch, you are so cute—but I mean it in a nice way."

She learned.

...

We've been friends ever since. Together we couldn't commit a crime as our strands of long blonde, fallen hair would leave DNA everywhere. That night in the hotel room near the airport, we sat on ugly brown, fake leather chairs around a kid-sized Formica-top table. My sole belongings for the next three weeks were lined up by the door in two super-sized suitcases. Two weeks earlier, a moving truck took my furniture items across the country. I sold my home a year prior and had been renting nearby. Although there was no kitchen, the room smelled of burnt toast.

I could tell by Suzi's squinted eyes that she knew I wasn't good. I smiled but it was a fake smile.

"Hey, honey. What's going on?" she asked in a warm voice as she touched my forearm.

"Suz, I don't know what I'm doing." Tears started rolling down my cheeks. "I can't do this. I don't know a soul there. All my friends and family are here."

"I know. We talked about this. Seriously girl, you are fierce, you're warm, and you make new friends fast. You have talked about this for years, and the opportunity opened."

"What if I don't find work? What if I don't make friends? I made a mistake; I can't do this. And there's my kids."

"They're grown up," she countered. "Let's go for a walk and get you out of your head. Grab a sweatshirt, it might be a little nippy out."

We walked in the dark to a fast-food place. As we waited to order, I looked on my cell phone to see if by some chance my flight had been canceled tomorrow. That would be a sign. But it was still scheduled for 6:50 a.m. I started tapping my toes, thinking I should hit "cancel flight" on the website and get over this fear of failing.

Back in the hotel room, we sat cross-legged on our beds to eat dinner and talked about the time one of our neighbors pushed me into my pool fully clothed. I laughed.

"Honey, you feel better?" Suzi asked as she wiped salsa off her cheek.

I stood up, threw out my left-over food, and paced the room. "This is too much for my brain. It's been my goal to move to New York and now I'm scared. I don't want to make the worst mistake of my life."

She put her hand on her hip and shook her finger at me. "Since I have known you, you've accomplished everything you've set your mind to. Aren't you the woman who won the City Council seat and got our Citrus Ranch Park built? Aren't you the one who ran a successful consulting business?" I shrugged my shoulders. "Okay, and like traveled to so many countries around the world, I can't keep track. You can do it!"

"You're right—as usual."-

After waiting a minute, she insisted, "Dude, you want to find love, happiness, and have excitement. It's your turn, girl." She was working hard to sell me on taking the leap. "Don't forget you want more culture and theater in your life. NYC has that as well. There are a million reasons to go."

I was escaping. Yes. But I was also going toward something I'd only dreamed of doing for so long.

"But just in case, can I come home if I don't like it?" I probed.

Suzi started crying. We both wiped away our tears and hugged. When she wasn't looking, I pulled out my cell phone and thought about cancelling my flight.

UNEXPECTED FRIENDSHIPS

MY GIRLS GOT ME THROUGH
Jude Walsh

Thorns may hurt you, men desert you, sunlight turns to fog, but you're
never friendless ever if you have a dog.
—DOUGLAS MALLOCK

My son loved all our dogs, but if asked his favorite, he would always say Lucie. Bren named her Lucie because, at the time we got her, he was watching the old black-and-white reruns of I Love Lucy on television. Lucie was black and white, so it seemed appropriate. There are three dogs in our family. In addition to Lucie, we have her littermate Luckie, who is so named because we had thought we would only get one Coton de Tulear and felt very LUCKY to get a second. Our Yorkie, Lottie Ann, is the boss. Although smaller, she was two years older than the Cotons and made it clear she was in charge.

Bren would often carry Lucie around with him, tucked under his arm like you would carry a football on a long play. She tolerated this well and was even content when he squeezed her into a chair next to him while he played Wheel of Fortune on his computer. All three dogs slept in Bren's room: Lottie Ann on the bed with him and Lucie and Luckie in a large crate that comfortably lodged them both. The Cotons often curled around one another as they slept.

When Bren and I were driving home and still about a block away from the house, he would call out in a sing-song voice: Lottie Aaaaaannnn, Luuuuuuuucie, Luckie, Luckie, Luckie, Luckie! We were convinced they heard us and responded by lining up at the top of the stairs to welcome us home, barking and wagging their tails.

Bren assumed responsibility for taking the dogs out at 6 a.m. and giving them their breakfasts. It was one of the great joys in my life to awaken to Bren talking to them, often singing to them, as they passed by my bedroom door on their way out. Bren loved to sing, and the dogs were usually treated to whatever was his current favorite. One that recurred was Katy Perry's "Roar." I asked him why that one kept coming up and he assured me, "It's the girls' favorite. Especially the part about Ro-a-a-a-a-rrr." If not singing, he might be sharing his plans for the day or perhaps telling them details from the basketball game we attended the night before. Bren insisted we leave the radio on at home, and tuned in to the game so they could hear it too. He thought it was a shame that dogs were not allowed in the basketball arena.

Bren had been very sick as a child. He was constantly in and out of the hospital. Eventually, we figured out that he had severe food allergies and a congenital kidney defect. Once we changed his diet and he had surgery to repair his kidney, his health improved. Then, in his thirties, some heart problems surfaced, and he had a pacemaker implanted. Despite all those health challenges and some developmental delays, Bren was one happy guy. He loved swimming, going to basketball games, and trips to Red Robin for fries. He volunteered at the local hospital and participated in several social groups. But what he loved best, by far, were the girls, our dogs, or as he referred to them, his sisters, and his and my best friends.

My concern about Bren's health resurfaced when he kept telling me he felt really tired. He was sleeping more and did not have his usual energy. I took him in for a physical and all checked out, but he continued to be fatigued. I took him to his cardiologist where they did an EKG and followed up with an ultrasound. All clear.

Then one night, Bren again said he was feeling tired. "Would you mind taking out the dogs in the morning?" he asked. He said he wanted to sleep in. This was an unusual request but one I was happy to fulfill. The next morning, I got up early and crept into his room, whispering to the girls to be quiet so Bren could sleep some more. When the girls and I returned about 15 minutes later, Bren had not moved.

He had died during the night.

The shock was indescribable.

I called 911 and the paramedics came. They ordered me out of the room and worked on him for a while, but I knew in my mother's heart he was gone.

After they left and I was waiting for the funeral home staff to come, I sat with Bren's body. The dogs were still locked in another room where I had put them when the squad came. I went to get them to allow them to say goodbye. Lottie Ann and Luckie charged into the room and immediately began to surround and sniff Bren's body. Lucie screeched to a halt at the door to the bedroom and would not come in. I picked her up, held her, and talked to her as I sat next to Bren. Eventually, she reached out with her face and sniffed gently. She collapsed in my arms and let out a pitiful cry. That was exactly how I felt. I just wanted to wail.

Over the next few days, as I made funeral plans and took care of other details, I was wrapped in the love and care of so many of my human friends. I allowed them to shepherd me from task to task and ate whatever they put in front of me. Most of the time I just sat, stunned by grief and bewildered as to what my life would look like going forward. The dogs never left my side, snuggling as close to me as possible. They refused to go into Bren's room and slept in mine. I was glad to have them.

Most remarkable was Lucie. For days, every few breaths, she would exhale a small moan. It was a heartbreaking sound. Sometimes I would sigh or cry with her. Once the services were over and the girls and I were alone again, I spent hours and hours on the couch, surrounded by them, listening to Lucie mourn and mourning alongside her. We faced this immeasurable loss and unimaginable grief together. My three girls helped me make it through those first agonizing days. They helped me figure out a way to live on. Step by step we created new daily rituals, new ways of being without him. I talked with the girls, reminding them of all the things we did with Bren and how much we would miss him.

We still do. I still call out "Lottie Aaaaaannnn, Luuuuuuuucie, Luckie, Luckie, Luckie, Luckie '' when I am turning onto our street. And when I come home, the three of them are lined up at the top of the steps. But they are not alone. I always sense Bren there too, right next to his Lucie, Luckie, and Lottie Ann. It makes coming into a house without his physical presence bearable. Sometimes I even sing, sometimes I even sing "Roar." And I know Bren hears me and is chiming in, still singing to his girls and his mama.

MY OLD FRIEND

Mary Jo West

I didn't choose this old house,
it chose me.
When I stepped into
this craftsman dwelling,
I felt as if
we had met before.

Wood, plaster, glass,
books, and vision
transformed this house
into a treasured bungalow.

It's my family's biography,
our souls are embedded in the walls.

Like an old friend,
it's a place of harmonious rhythms,
that calls me back
again and again,
giving me a sense of well-being.

Hopefully, like a loving companion,
it will be my safe haven
for the rest of my life.

ME, MYSELF AND I

Debra Dolan

I am blessed to have experienced wonderful female friendships throughout the past six+ decades. I have had intense intimate bonds with women who appreciated those significant emotional relationships. As described best in the memoir, *She Matters: A Life in Friendships*, by Susanna Sonnenberg, I relate to the following: "The best friend who broke up with you. The older girl at school you worshipped. The beloved college friend who changed. The friend you slept with. The friend who betrayed you. The friend you betrayed. Companions in travel, in discovery, in marriage and divorce, in grief; the mentor, the role model, the rescuer, the guide, the little sister."

When I was a kid, I could spend hours playing by myself and never be bored, although there were always neighbourhood or schoolyard or Brownie playmates available. As I developed, I was blessed with a vivid and overactive mind talking to myself, out loud, communicating with imaginary *compadres*. I was awkward, bright, social, and shy in grade-school. I started reading and writing whilst young, finding wonderful companionship in books, and a lock-and-key diary gifted at 11 years. As a young girl I loved spending time with my friends on the weekends. We would go downtown and shop with our babysitting money or allowance. As a teenager I was not in a crowd that had boyfriends. I spent Friday nights, usually at the movies, with high-school chums and afterwards long introspective chats at the local downtown Chinese joint where we would have tea and egg rolls thinking we were so sophisticated and forming our own clique.

I have been told I am a good friend, yet I have also received more than one "Dear Debra" letter when someone has distanced, needing to be away from my company. I recognize my intensity and the demands I place on those I reveal myself to. My deepest significant friendships have been with women who are direct, independent, and unconcerned, at least visibly, with outside judgment. They all have rich lives, with their normal human achievements and struggles, and I have leaned on them. I value the trust they have bestowed in me as well as all the many memories we have shared. I have fallen in love platonically with some of these women and I have often wondered if these friendships are there to fill a gap left by my parents or siblings. I was always struck by the saying, "Friends are the family you choose."

Many years ago, I learned that friendships come in and out of your life, like lovers, and to let them. Friendship might spring from shared values or hobbies, workplaces, neighbourhoods, or always bumping into the same someone on a daily commute, or meeting friends-of-friends. The desire for friendship has always been woven into what I feel I need for a healthy support system. They help me not be so alone in the world. During my life I have often painfully been harmed in believing that another is capable, willing or understanding of what I need in friendship. The notion of a deep intimate friendship with another woman as being central and paramount in my life is somewhat foreign to me. Of course, I want connection with others, and I want to engage and do activities with others, yet I don't look upon my friends for something that I can't manage on my own. They are all complements to who I am, at a certain time or phase of living, and this changes as I change. There has always been tremendous diversity in my friendships as I prefer 1:1 rather than groups. Very rarely do I ever bring my friends together. I am selfish that way.

Without question, the best friend I have ever had is me. It feels somewhat silly to put this in writing, however, it is my truth. It wasn't always that way. Once I learned to appreciate myself, flawed and beautiful as I am, I became my dearest friend who I learned to count on as she was always nearby and willing to help, laugh at my jokes, and did exactly as I wish. With the ability to turn to myself for deep, lifelong companionship, I have always found someone who is up for an adventure, or in for a quiet night. I can be my own best friend forever and make my simple & uncomplicated world a better, brighter place simply by loving myself.

Popular ideas about friendship suggest that a true friend is someone who is on your side, no matter what; watches out for you, and will never betray you or make you feel bad. That's me to me. Through thick 'n thin, ups 'n downs, joys 'n sorrows, I rarely abandon or admonish myself. Even after all the disappointments and embarrassments of being my friend I still crave my own company. I am the first person I want to celebrate with, walk with, cry with, share a special moment with, mourn with, shop with, sleep with. When I listen to myself, and write through my body, I understand the richness of what I can offer myself in friendship:

unconditional big-big love, encouragement, and support. I believe this quote from Eleanor Roosevelt, "Friendship with oneself is all important, because without it one cannot be friends with anyone else in the world."

Friendship is not always easy, however, there's a lot that I like about me as bestie to myself. I like being alone with my thoughts, feelings, daydreams, and memories. I like having my own personal space. I like going shopping by myself. I like going to the movies by myself or eating in a restaurant solo. I like being able to change my plans at the last minute and have it affect no one but me. I like that I get to see myself every day in the mirror. I like that I have never forgotten my birthday. I feel fortunate that I am perfectly comfortable doing my own thing. Although I still put myself out there and welcome new people into my life, I have slowly accepted the fact that I don't need to socialize very often. I don't mind being my own best friend. In fact, I love it.

FINDING A DIFFERENT RHYTHM

Beth Mattheus

Friend of mine, you have lived with me a long time.
Every time I changed the way I cope; you met me in a
    different way.
You were a faithful friend. You visited every day. Some
    days insistently.
Other days were just a brief reminder that you were
    always present.
I learned to live my life guardedly, waiting for you to set
    the pace.
I kept my world small so I could bounce and sway to
    your demands
Avoiding anyone's judgment or the "good advice" on how
    to handle you.
The world would say, "oh, you look so good." It was
    difficult for others to believe that discomfort, ache or
    you, friend Pain, were on the inside ever constant.
Ever constant, coloring each interaction. Each decision.
    Each activity.

Initially, Covid's isolation was no friend to me but was a
 friend to you, Pain.
It was harder today to join the world; it was easier to
 disengage from in-person contact.
Yet Covid opened up a different door. As we connect
 through digital space, we increase human contact.
 Different Zoom communities open up choices.
Zoom has allowed me to join the world, to lessen the
 impact and loneliness you fostered as I go through day
 to day.
Through these Zoom groups, I am with people who hear
 and see ME.
You, old friend Pain, are not center stage here in the faces
 that are pictured across my screen. We the people here
 are central. Cyber friends with warm connections who
 help overcome the loneliness of life with you.
Learning lessons of self-care that move us away from you
 at center stage.
Making room for me to be the lead actor in my own
 story.
Perhaps I will lose some battles to you, Pain.
But I will be the one leading and taking you along with
 me to the places I choose to go.
Still with me, but this time as a real companion.
Still living together but now, we sing my song.

MY BEST FRIEND

Mary Jo West

I love cats and have had cats as far back as I can remember, but there's
one I'll never forget. Her name was Spotty, and she will always have a
special place in my heart.

We were visiting my grandfather in Fairmont, West Virginia, when
I first saw her. Only a week old, she was trying to nestle in between
her siblings to nurse from their mother. A pretty little calico kitten with
brown, black, and orange patches on her white, sleek fur. Her forehead
was divided into two strips of color, one black and one orange. It was love

at first sight. As a seven-year-old, I used my sweetest voice to convince my parents to let me take her home. I named her Spotty.

Wrapped in a small towel, she lay nestled in my arms during the six-hour trip over the Blue Ridge Mountains to Washington, DC. Every two hours I fed her with an eyedropper filled with a mixture of Carnation milk and water.

When I was in school, my mother fed her every four hours, but she was my responsibility the rest of the time. I could hardly wait to get home after school, change my clothes and play with Spotty. She fit in my jacket pocket, and I took her with me everywhere. She slept in the crook of my arm every night, and every morning she woke me up with kisses under my chin.

One day, when Spotty was about six weeks old, I came home and couldn't find her.

"Mom, I've looked in all her hiding places, and she isn't here."

"I don't know, Mary Jo, I've been busy. Maybe she got outside. She's got to be around here someplace."

But she wasn't.

Every day after school, for several weeks, some of my friends and I would ride our bikes around the neighborhood looking for Spotty. I never got home before dark.

I felt so sad and had no interest in school or playing with my friends. I moped around the house, hoping she'd turn up.

I finally gave up on that notion, and figured she was gone for good.

One afternoon, I answered a knock at our front door. My best friend, Jane, was standing on the porch with her hands behind her back.

"Hi Mary Jo, I have a surprise for you." She swept her hands in front of her holding a small, furry ball. "I found her!"

"Oh my gosh, it's Spotty." She handed her to me and I kissed and nuzzled her face next to mine. "Where did you find her?"

Beaming, Jane leaned toward me and said that when she was walking by a neighbor's house about a block away, she saw Spotty in their yard. "I knocked on their door and told them this kitten belonged to my friend! She's been looking all over for her." They believed her and let her retrieve my kitten.

"Thank you, Jane, I can't believe it." We jumped up and down with joy.

When Spotty was older, she had several litters. She always chose to have her babies in the coal bin in our back yard. We'd clean the coal dust off of their fur and put them in a box in my bedroom, where I looked after them until they were old enough to be given away.

At home, Spotty was my constant companion. She followed me everywhere. Whenever I sat on my bed to read or study, she slept on my lap like a living shawl.

In 1956, when I was seventeen, and looking forward to my senior year at Wheaton High in Maryland, Dad announced we were moving to Newhall, a small rural town in California. I naturally assumed Spotty would go with us, but Dad explained that since we were driving across country, she would have to take the trip later. Mom had already arranged for our neighbors to look after her for a few days, and then they would put her on a train to California.

I hesitated for a moment, then blurted out, "Dad, how long will that take?"

"Ten days to two weeks. A conductor will feed her and give her water. She'll be fine."

Cuddling Spotty in my arms, and looking into his eyes, I pleaded, "Please Dad, she won't be any trouble. I'll take care of her."

"No, this is the best way, and that's final."

Two and a half weeks later, we picked Spotty up at the Saugus train station. She looked so thin, and her eyes were glazed over. When we got home, she ran under my bed and wouldn't come out. I stayed in my room for the rest of the day, talking to her in a soft, hushed voice. Finally, two days later she appeared, but she could hardly walk.

Had she stopped eating because she was pining away for me? Had anyone really taken care of her on the train? It didn't matter now, she was home with me, and I was sure I could nourish her back to health.

I decided to have a local vet check her out. He wanted to run some tests, so I left her there overnight. The next morning, he called to tell me she had cancer, and there was nothing he could do.

Wanting to see her again for the last time, I went to the vet hospital. On the way to her cage, I called to her. When she heard my voice, she lifted her head and looked at me. She tried to stand, but she was too weak. I gently picked her up, and she let out a long, almost human moan. Cradling her, I stroked her head until her body went limp in my arms.

I lost my best and only friend in an unfamiliar place where strangers surrounded me.

GAZEBOS

Lisa Nackan

gazebos go back for centuries in classical
    civilizations, and i didn't know that.
i failed my architecture exam because i didn't
    know the meaning
of the word gazebo

i had to design one and i couldn't so i wrote my
    name and the date 1985
nothing else would come out
my children love this story of me not knowing the
    things they do

they point out gazebos whenever they can
today i sit under one
not like the red-walled gardens of classical
    literature

but amidst flowers in raised boxes in the rain
there is something about gazebos
and spending time with the elderly that is regal

rain bursts through the first layer of sky
tries to reach us sitting side by side at the slatted
    table
with the wooden canopy over our heads

you colour the canvas and move paint around
    with your fingers
we compare the shapes of leaves
i listen to your stories "ek is lief vir jou," you tell
    me in afrikaans

a tree holds an open nest and we speak of the way
    of flowers
you tell me you want to paint them next
a swallow shuffles its feathers and you pick me
    out for my pronunciation

rain covers the ground leaving a dry circle where
    we sit
the world shifts around us
the word gazebo comes from the word to gaze

i see it all now
thirty years have passed since i left that room
with a blank page and no structure to call my
    own

under this gazebo on a rainy afternoon
i realize how little that matters now
the things we lose can become the things we win

when i left that page open devoid of anything
not aware that there was a word for a structure
    open on all sides
with a view

i opened up a path that took half a lifetime to
    find
i failed my architecture exam.
yet construction doesn't feel as significant

as sitting with someone observing their stories
    emerge on a blank page
in colour with texture
the certainty of blank spaces.

i walked my path for the most part alone.
only when i abandoned my belief that being
    solitary was strong,
did i realize that two pairs of eyes seeing really see

in this moment we are both so alive
there is nothing empty under this gazebo
everything is bursting with meaning

FREE AT LAST

Stacy Ann Parish

I didn't grow up with a whole lot of agency as a kid, but there was one thing that I was always allowed to do. Every summer, I was free to go outside, and ride! And although my very first bike was a hand-me-down, she was all mine. And that bike—she was my best friend.

She had a bright metallic blue body with coaster brakes—long mustache handlebars, a white basket and this badass white banana seat—covered with purple, red and yellow flowers. On the ends of the handlebars were these streamers that went "rat tat tat tat tat" in the breeze as I cruised around town.

My favorite place to ride in the summer was up to the elementary school for our rec department's summer playground. My legs—always considered too big, and too chunky—would pump away up this HUUUUGE hill on the way there. At the beginning of the summer, I'd have to stop and walk my bike to make it to the top, but by the end of the summer, I could make it all the way without getting off my bike. Yesssss....

I made this ride every day for the summer playground, but also because...there was no feeling in the world like screaming down that hill on the way home. The wind in my face, my hair flying all over the place—I felt so alive, so free, like this is where I BELONGED, and...I felt like I could fly.

When I graduated 8th grade, I got my own bike—a fancy red, lady's Schwinn ten-speed bike with curled handlebars and skinny tires. I rode that bike all over town, and late in the summer, I rode it to and from tennis practice. One day after practice I was carrying a teammate's gear on my handlebars along with my own.

While riding my usual path, the bridge was full of people and there was no room for me to cross, so—I attempted to bypass the bridge by riding on the grass alongside it. I suddenly realized the grass was going to run out and I'd go over a cliff if I didn't get back on the bridge. I tried to reach for my brakes but got nothing but a handful of sweatshirts and tennis rackets. I couldn't stop.

My bike and I sailed over the cliff, into a culvert, tossing me face first into a stone wall. Everything went in slow motion—just like you hear in the movies.

I don't remember feeling any pain when my mouth hit the wall—just a cold, hard, impact.

The next thing I remember, I was sitting in shock on the ledge of the fieldstone wall, while a half dozen people looked for my teeth in the bottom of the culvert—at that point we didn't realize they were embedded in the roof of my mouth.

I tried to ride a bike again, on occasion—maybe half a dozen times in almost 40 years, but I'd inevitably have this moment of panic rush over me at some point, and I'd have to stop.

The story I told myself was that I'd had this terrible accident when I was 14, and it was only natural that I couldn't ride. Some people can—I just wasn't one of them.

But in 2018 I started dating Jeff. He's a psychotherapist by trade, and he spent many years working with adolescents doing wilderness therapy. Outdoors. In the dead of winter. In Wisconsin. The guy knows how to survive—and being with him made me feel safe.

In the first few weeks of our dating, he completed a 50-mile race in our town called "Bike to the Beat" which combines music and biking… and I was so envious. I genuinely missed biking for the first time since giving it up, and something in me wanted to try again.

The following spring Jeff took me to a local bike shop where you can ride the bikes right out the door of their shop, and onto a safe trail to try them out. I was veeeery shaky at first. And yes, I had a few moments of panic—but I was resolute, and Jeff was right there encouraging me. I tried out three or four different bikes and found one that felt just right! (And for any bike geeks, she's a black LIV Rove 3 with teal details) I also made the decision that day to start to train for my very own 50 mile "Bike to the Beat" ride!

One Sunday while training, I went out for a really early ride while the rest of the town was still asleep. Listening to and singing along to "Señorita" by Shawn Mendes and Camilla Cabella. "I love it when you call me Señorita…." I was blissed out—God, I LOVED my bike! I really had recaptured the feeling I had as a kid. I was BACK!

Then I noticed a sketchy van coming to a stop on a road perpendicular to me. It was the kind of van whose photo would be in the dictionary next to the words "sketchy van". Like a really long body, no windows, double doors in the back. It was 6 a.m. on a Sunday and I hadn't seen another vehicle all morning, so it just struck me as odd. The driver started to pull through the intersection and did a double take when they saw me. They stopped in the middle of the intersection, did a Y turn and started driving in the same direction I was traveling in…and they were driving SLLLLLOOOOOOW. Slow enough that I could easily catch up to them.

GODAMMIT. I was just blissed out!! Now I've got this sketchy van in front of me, and I don't feel safe riding my route anymore.

I turned my bike around and started riding in the other direction—slowly at first, and then as fast as I could. *That's when it happened.* That old familiar panic. Instead of steering my bike to safety I lost control of it and went straight into a curb—where my bike stopped, and my body kept going. I flew over my bike and landed hard on the ground banging into the frame as I landed. The wind knocked out of me, I lay there stunned, unsure about whether I could get up.

As I picked up my bike, I sobbed and sobbed, feeling that my carefree bliss, my friend, had been taken away again. I began to think that bikes just weren't for me after all, and this was the proof.

With tears running down my face and adrenaline coursing through my veins, I got back on my bike and started riding. The old expression about "getting back on the horse" kept running through my head.

As I continued to ride home, my tears of sadness turned to tears of rage.

I began to feel like "Nobody, and I mean NOBODY is going to take my best friend or my freedom away from me now that I just rediscovered it."

I spent about two weeks off my bike, letting some bruised ribs and a very sore knee heal. But after that? I continued to ride. I kept training for that 50, because I'm stubborn like that. And I found a hill to train on.

At first I had to get off my bike and walk it—but soon, I could ride all the way to the top. Happy for these big ol' muscular legs.

And as I was screaming down the hill—with the wind in my face, and the scenery flying by, I felt a NEW kind of freedom. Because I knew that biking was forever MINE, and I'd be safe at the bottom of that hill. And in the end, my injury did in fact keep me from completing a 50-mile ride—BUT Jeff and I *did* complete a 30 "Bike to the Beat" together—and as I crossed that finish line—for the first time since that little blue bike with the streamers, I wasn't alone and KNEW I could FLY!

A Sonnet to a Purring Friend

Ariela L. Zucker

I run my fingers through her soft, silky hair
She looks at me with those baby blues
Her eyes clouded with love so rare
Make me melt all the way to my shoes.

On my old creaking rocking chair
The flames dancing in the wood stove
Sitting with no worries or care
I suck the warmth in like a sponge.

She curls next to me, her head on my knee
I rest my hand on her head
Only the both of us, you see
Like a picture in a book I once read.
I brush my fingers through her soft white hair
And lose myself in the melodious purr.

FAMILY FRIENDS

LOVE, FRIENDSHIP, AND NEW YEAR'S EVE KISSES

B. Lynn Goodwin

I've been thinking a lot about Art and Deloris, who were the closest people I had to living grandparents. It seemed like they'd been married forever. They slept in twin beds, since it was the '50s, and when I was a teenager, I thought of them as best buds more than a romantic couple. The romance was a memory, but the partnership and support for one another was a daily practice. Older couples need more than romance to survive. They need friendship.

Deloris had severe arthritis. She could still move around her kitchen and make a Thanksgiving dinner from scratch, but standing up from the dinner table or going down the front steps of their apartment building was painful. I remember the anguish I saw on her face and these days I channel it when I get up from a chair or go down my own front steps. Even though we're not biologically related, I feel like I inherited her arthritis. Art would do the yard work and carry her purse when they went places. He was in the driver's seat.

Then he had a stroke. A bad one. It shut down the part of his brain where the ability to read resides.

They used to go grocery shopping together. Art would seat Deloris in the front of the store, in the days before the disabled carts that you could ride in. He knew what they needed, but he couldn't read the labels, so he'd take the cans or meat packages to her so she could check the labels. They were a team. They were partners. They were best friends, I am sure, and all these years later, I know they were role models for me.

You see, my husband and I have been going through medical trials that come with life as a septuagenarian—two heart attacks and diabetes for him; arthritis, a hiatal hernia, broken ribs, and a concussion for me. The last two came from a futile attempt to keep our RV from going over onto the passenger side. I *never* blamed him for the accident.

Unlike Art and Deloris, we married late in life. Like them, though, we trust, love, and care about each other. Despite the fact that we're both stubborn and independent, we're good friends. We love each other in the same mature way that Art and Deloris did.

They visited my family of origin on New Year's Eve during my senior year in high school. I didn't have a date—or a boyfriend—so I was in the living room with my family at midnight.

I will never forget Deloris hoisting herself off the sofa, walking over to Art, and kissing him on his lips at midnight. I saw love in a new way that night. There was something about the way Deloris walked, despite her arthritic pain, that mixed love, selflessness, and partnership. It always stayed with me.

I desperately wanted that for myself someday. Finally, in my 60s, I was lucky enough to get it: a marriage with love and friendship and New Year's Eve kisses year after year.

MY SISTER'S HAND ON MY SHOULDER

Laura Santos-Farry

Looking over old black and white candid photos of my childhood, one of the earliest photos of me is on a clunky wooden highchair. I was ten months old, my infant head still not more than a veil of thin dark baby hair. On the edge of the table to my right sits my five-year-old sister, Rose, dressed in fashionable pedal pushers that were the rage in the 1950s. A white cotton top is tied neatly in the front, and she sports a short dark bob with bangs. I can see my sister's laughing face, that perpetual contagious giggle that always seemed to be splayed across her face and would later cause us both to be sent away from the dinner table. Her skinny tanned legs dangling off the tabletop but posed so close to me as if she had been instructed to stay close to tend to her baby sister. She always assumed the role of watching over me and she took her responsibility very seriously.

A second photo is of Rose and me under a large beach umbrella, with the ocean in the background. Both of us in our bathing suits. I look to be about three years old, making Rose eight years old. Rose, in tight pigtails and short straight bangs, looks intently into the camera, her right hand on my left shoulder. I am looking away from the camera, but I look content, relaxed, and at peace; mainly because my big sister is right behind me. Again, I sense that Rose is taking on her role as big sister very dutifully.

The third photo finds Rose and I standing in front of a tall shrub in the front yard. I am about five years old, Rose by now is ten years old. Both of us dressed in cap-sleeved summer frocks, I sport a pageboy while Rose has evolved to wearing a high, wavy ponytail but still with short straight bangs. Rose is standing behind me. She is posed with her hands firmly on both of my shoulders almost like she is holding me in place, as if I may suddenly dash off.

Most of my childhood photos are of Rose and me in various times of our lives but I note how in each picture, Rose either has her hand on my shoulder, or she is poised very close to me. In each photo, I look calm, at ease, and content.

When I started school, Rose was entering junior high. When I entered junior high, Rose was already in high school. When I was in high school, Rose was away at college. When I started college, Rose had graduated and was married. When I married, Rose was having children. When I got pregnant, Rose was getting a divorce and was then a single mom. It seemed for a while that we were never in sync with each other's lives but despite this, Rose was always there for me.

In high school, trauma hit me. I was sexually assaulted and then to compound the issue, I found myself pregnant. Still, I was so full of shame and guilt that I could not speak my truth. It was only Rose that I could confide in, and she got me through that rough year by standing by me, a gentle hand on my shoulder, steadying me in the maelstrom I found myself in.

For years, we were inseparable. We were in constant communication with each other, calling each other several times a week even though we lived 175 miles away from each other. Rose became a high school counselor, and I became a school district safety director. She was handling the emotional and mental needs of students, and I was in turn handling the physical and environmental necessities to make all students safe. Between school shootings, teen suicides, teen pregnancies, and other school violence threats, we had plenty to share of what was going on at our respective jobs.

We never lacked anything to share. When most of our phone calls and visits would end, one of us would inevitably chime in, "Oh, I forgot to tell you..." and we'd chat for at least another hour.

Through new relationships, marriages, births, illnesses, traumas, parenting challenges, deaths, and personal growth we shared our most private thoughts, our greatest vulnerabilities, our deepest regrets, and our innermost secrets. There wasn't anything I couldn't tell Rose, she was my rock, that hand on me to let me know she was there for me through thick and thin.

Then one late evening, Rose called me to let me know that the breast cancer she had long since recovered from, had returned and returned with a vengeance. It was then that the tables got turned, I found I had to step up to be there for her now. It was my turn to become the big sister, the protector, and the caregiver.

The next couple of years were the worst, Rose first went through several rounds of radiation and then chemo. Nothing seemed to be helping, and she slowly got weaker and frailer. One day Rose called me and told me she was done. She had made peace with her higher power and was ready to go. None of us—her family, our family, and especially me—were ready to let her go. But it was my turn to place my hand on her shoulder, to assure her that she wasn't alone and assure her that I would stand by her regardless of her decision.

Rose had made up her mind, and her doctor, knowing there wasn't much else that could be done for her, put her on hospice. She insisted on staying at her home and for her last remaining months, I dutifully drove up the 175 miles every weekend to spend with her. I would sit with her, read to her, write for her, and just listened to her. She had long ago taught me what it was to be a good listener, I had learned from the best.

One cool March morning while I was visiting, I helped Rose walk out to her front porch that overlooked her medicine wheel garden she had once taken such pride in creating. Medicine wheel gardens are considered sacred places for the healing and tranquility of the people who created them. Rose had painstakingly planted herbs, flowers, and shrubs in this garden the year before her returning cancer, but the garden now sat neglected and in decay.

"Isn't it miraculous how nature works?" Rose continued. "With the seasons, all the trees and foliage die but in just a few months, the greenery and the flowers will once again come alive." Then she paused and said almost to herself, "I wonder where I will spring up?"

We both fell silent. I glanced back over to Rose and saw she was in deep thought as she pondered this deep philosophical query. I had to look away, I didn't want her to see my tears. I had vowed to stay strong for her, but I wasn't sure how I would be able to fulfill this one task for her. I couldn't let her go, she was my muse, she was my best friend.

A month later, she was gone.

It's been ten years now since Rose has been gone. And although I now find myself surrounded by many wonderful friends, none are the same as my sister, Rose. None were there when I was born; none put up with me as I grew up; none ever rested their hand on my shoulder to assure me, comfort me, keep me in line, or let me know I was safe.

Rose was my best friend; she was by my side my entire life, until she wasn't. She was always there to celebrate the good times, and to help me work my way through the bad times.

Now on full moon evenings, I sit out back alone in the dark and talk to her. I feel her hand on me still and sometimes I can even hear her giggle. She lets me know that I'm still not alone.

HEARTBEATS

Eileen Harrison Sanchez

"I had my hand on her chest. I could feel her heartbeat. Thump, thump, thump, thump. Then it stopped." My cousin Diane said these words to me at her daughter Bridget's wake.

My own heart sank. How should I respond? How can I comfort a woman in such pain? I reached out to hold her hand and said, "You were there. Bridget knew it."

Diane explained that she had been at the hospital for days that seemed to never end. Bridget's years of alcohol and drug abuse did their damage. There was no hope of recovery. Diane and her husband had to make the unthinkable decision to turn off the machines that were keeping Bridget breathing. The doctor explained that it was possible she could stay alive after life support stopped, it had happened. The expectation was that she would live for a few hours, a few days at the most. Bridget was gone in minutes.

As this grieving mother spoke to me of these last memories of her beloved daughter, her haggard face became energized, and light shone from her eyes. The corners of her mouth turned up slightly, which at another time would have been the beginning of Diane's lovely smile but her words betrayed her. "I felt her first heartbeats and her last."

The emotion I had held back spilled from my eyes.

Diane and Jack had three daughters. All three died before their time and for three different reasons within 20 years. Bridget was the middle daughter, she was 38. I couldn't help but wonder why some families have such traumatic events? Is this random? Or is this some test?

The next day, a terse email announced the funeral and the hours of Shiva for Rebecca, the daughter of my colleague, Miriam. The second sudden death of a young woman before her time, Rebecca was also 38. That old wives' tale of bad things coming in threes worried me.

How could I help Diane and Miriam? All I could think to do was to go to the wake and Shiva. Two distraught mothers; two daughters taken from them. A token card or flowers wouldn't be enough to express my sympathy.

I was compelled to be present.

I have three adult daughters. The echo of "three" haunts me. I can't contemplate the possible tragedies that could take one of them from me. The loss of a daughter, or a son, and all the hopes and possibilities that their life can offer is incomprehensible.

Do I prepare myself for pain by witnessing theirs? If I share their pain will I be spared?

I hear Diane's words over and over. "I felt her first heartbeats and her last."

My own heart quickened at the news that life was growing inside me. Being present for first heartbeats is a joy I experienced three times.

Being present for my mother's last breath is also a memory I hold precious. The hospice nurse looked at me with knowing eyes and I nodded my head. I said, "It's 1:26 pm."

Thinking back on that moment I realized that my mother witnessed my first breaths, and I witnessed her last. This thought brings me comfort now. It's an intimacy I can never experience with another person. Mother and daughter love is unique.

First heartbeats and first breaths represent hopes and dreams.

Last breaths and final heartbeats are a testimony to a life that deserves to be remembered.

Grief is love with no place to go. Being present for a friend is an act of love.

MUSINGS ON FRIENDSHIP

Sara Etgen-Baker

I have always struggled to make and keep friends. Don't get me wrong. I have friends, but most don't know me beyond the surface. And I don't know them beyond the surface either. We smile and talk about our day-to-day lives; but in truth, those smiles hide a lot of unexpressed feelings, emotions, fears, etc.

My struggle became more pronounced since Covid with more and more people working from home and intentionally isolating themselves from the chaotic and politically divisive world in which we currently live. Plus, everyone around me, including myself, wrestles with balancing the demands of family, work, and other responsibilities. When Mom was alive, I didn't feel this pronounced absence of friends, for Mother was my best friend. She was the one with whom I felt safe, with whom I vented, and with whom I could be emotionally vulnerable. Since her passing, I've often wondered how this strong, invisible bond came about.

Seems as if cooking together was the way we formed our bond of friendship. My first attempts at cooking were simplistic—peanut butter and jelly sandwiches, grilled cheese, cooked spaghetti with a jar of sauce poured on top. Fortunately, my skills improved over the years thanks to Mother's help. Every night I watched her cook a fabulous meal for the family, and I was her sous chef, watching her meticulously follow a recipe but leaving out the onions because she knew of my distaste for them. When times were tough, I watched her magically create a recipe out of whatever was available in the kitchen. As time went on, the kitchen became a safe place where we talked about anything. She opened up about her fears and concerns and let me know it was okay to do the same. Our bond as mother and daughter only grew stronger as we shared our deepest thoughts while chopping vegetables and preparing the family meal.

As a result, I told my mom everything. As soon as something significant or meaningful happened in my life, I couldn't wait to share the news with my best friend. I knew Mom would be happy for me when I told her my good news. Likewise, she was kind and empathetic when I told her about my bad choices, my bad news, and my disappointments. She was the one I looked to for counsel when something was bothering me. She was the first one to give me a shoulder to cry on when I was emotionally wounded, afraid, or filled with doubt.

In her early 60s, Mother developed dementia and was slowly and silently robbed of most of her memories. Naturally, the conversations between us dwindled. I often sat beside her holding her hand noticing that, although she was physically present, she wasn't really there at all. Our scattered conversations revolved around the little she did remember and the jumbled pieces from her past. The almost daily phone calls I came to expect from Mother stopped, because she was unable to pick up the phone and remember who she was calling.

During the last three years of her life, I thought I had accepted the fact that the mom I had known, my best friend, had quietly disappeared. So, when Mother suddenly died from a heart attack, I thought the grief would not be difficult to traverse because she was already absent from my life. I was wrong. Her physical and emotional absence only amplified the lack of friendship in my life and the presence I shared with others.

Mom knew me completely and made me feel whole and stable. Without her friendship, I was adrift. Some days, I felt like a phantom— someone without substance floating through life and going through all the motions. I could no longer deny my loneliness and had to confront the lack of friends in my life.

Although no one could ever replace Mother and our bond of friendship, I made a conscious effort to make deeper connections with the people who were currently in my life. I intentionally enrolled in classes hoping to find someone my age who shared some of my interests and passions. My husband and I joined a senior center and have found another couple our age with whom we bonded and can get together with regularly.

Over time, I discovered some truths about friendship that I'd like to share with you. Friendship is a treasure trove of emotions, experiences, and memories that shape our lives in profound ways. From the laughter shared during late-night conversations to the unwavering support during tough times, true friendships enrich our life journey. Through friendship, we self-select into some of the most affirming, safe, and sacred relationships of our lives. Having close friends at any stage of life makes us feel whole, increases our ability to be empathic, and helps us figure out who we are. Likewise, friendships are an integral part of healthy aging.

A humbling truth also became apparent to me: Each of us has the power to strengthen friendships, if only we put aside our fears and invest in them. And it's worth it, because when we value our friendships, we can transform our lives for the better. In the big picture, friendships benefit society as a whole, for they increase trust, and cross-group friendships can decrease prejudice.

As I reflect upon my friendship journey, I humbly offer this advice to you: "Don't wait for a calamity to rock you into realizing friendship is priceless. Engrave friendship on your heart. Make being a good friend a part of who you are, because a deep and true core that needs to belong lies within us all."

MY HUSBAND, MY FRIEND

Linda Healy

Today would have been our tenth wedding anniversary. Sadly, we didn't even make it to our first one. I married my best friend after three years of friendship, including a year of engagement.

I met Chuck six weeks after my dad had died. He was a minister to the dying at the hospice where we worked, and so I leaned on him for his counsel as I grieved for my dad. We became friends quickly.

I felt a special spark when I met Chuck and always knew we were meant to be together. I never brought the subject up. As the loss of my dad became less intense, I sought his support less often. Still, we often worked closely together with hospice patients, and had lunch together occasionally, continuing to develop our friendship.

One and a half years after I came to work with him, we accidentally met at a facility where we were both visiting patients. As we sat on a bench together, he asked me to lunch. I felt stronger than ever that we were meant to be together. He told me much later that he had felt it, too, some weeks earlier at a work lunch. This lunch was different than our previous friendly lunches. It was more like a job interview or a first date. He was asking me about my previous relationships and if I would ever be able to love again. At that point, I told him my palms were starting to sweat! We fell in love that day over a three-hour lunch, but we did not talk about how we felt that day.

The next week was Valentine's Day. Chuck and I were sitting at a table together at work. In the middle of the table was a bowl of Valentine candies that had little sayings on them. Chuck dramatically lifted the bowl and started digging through it until he found the one he wanted.

Then he handed the little candy to me. The one he picked for me read, "Be Mine", and so I was.

Since we were in the sixth decade of our lives, and were already dear friends, we became engaged six weeks later. During a visit to a jewelry store, he dropped to one knee and proposed. Then we did a year of pre-marital counseling to get off to a good start. We learned much about ourselves and each other and became even closer friends.

Chuck wanted to marry in a log cabin in the Colorado Rockies. I thought to myself, "Well, that's not going to happen!" And yet we did just that. We eloped to a log cabin in the mountains that my love had always yearned to see. How grateful I am that we had that trip, as it was his last.

Six weeks later Chuck was diagnosed with a brain tumor. Our lives turned from building our friendship and marriage to ICU, brain surgery, chemo, radiation and the dying process. He lived six months after the wedding. That was a hard year, as I said goodbye to my 11-year-old Labrador on December 23 and my husband on December 29, my two dear friends.

In Chuck's last weeks I kept him at home and hired a young woman to help me with my 6-foot, 2-inch husband. She said she learned a lot in those weeks about love and friendship from us as she watched us support each other.

As Chuck died, I sat holding his hand and talking to him. I watched as his breath became air and I was left with cards, pictures, letters, a journal he wrote for me in his last weeks and memories of the best friend I ever had. His picture still hangs in my bedroom and ten years later I still think of him every day, my chosen friend for life, my husband.

SAFE PASSAGE

Teresa H. Janssen

We walk single file toward the ramp of the ferry boat. Four middle-aged sisters, like stairsteps, the nuns used to say, descending every two years until I appeared—the bottom tread. Tighter than family, we are fast friends.

One of us, the oldest, carries an oak box. Inside lie the ashes of Aunt Rita, our father's never-married sister, who died peacefully after slowly drifting away from us, a victim of Alzheimer's. The funeral mass took place several weeks ago. Our final act of caregiving is to inter her remains near her parents' graves in a cemetery across Puget Sound in Seattle.

Boarding the ferry, we step past a security officer with a leashed German Shepherd sniffing for bombs. It is post-911, the nation still on edge. We walk inside and head down the aisle. Like a single-cell amoeba, we slide into bench-seats next to a window. The oldest sister places the box on the table.

We sisters lead diverse, independent lives when apart. But when together, we slip into birth order roles: Big Sis, Second Sis, Third Sis, and myself—Little Sis. Though in my forties, I am called the "baby" of the family, a title that still exasperates me and tickles my sisters. Like best friends, we schedule getaways at a hotel or cabin, lunches together, and sometimes vacations.

As little girls, we played together, our favorite game called "Teenager." Each sister dressed the role and enthusiastically acted out one of two personas: 'razzmatazz' or 'polite,' as though there were no other kind of teen to be. I always wanted to be 'cowgirl' instead, but it was not an option, according to an unspoken rule of consensus that remained a mystery to me.

We look out at Puget Sound. Gray gulls plane in the breeze. A flash of white sail a quarter mile away. We turn our heads to watch a police boat zip by, its machine gun poised to take out any terrorist boat gunning for the ferry. The loudspeaker crackles. "Welcome aboard the Washington State Ferries. Please do not leave backpacks, packages, or luggage unattended." Passengers are reminded to immediately report any suspicious item to the purser's office.

Few words pass between the four of us, who have shared so much over the years. Crowding into one double bed during the lean years when our father went 'missing'. Basking in the attention of his sister, Rita, who visited every week, safeguarding us with her love, promising to never abandon us. Confusion during the difficult years after our father returned home (as if he had been out for a ten-year stroll), surprised that none of his daughters knew him. Collusion as we planned our departures from home when we each turned 18. Grief, acceptance, and forgiveness after our father's untimely death.

Third Sis caresses the box. "Aunt Rita was so patient. I loved her red polish so much, she let me lick her fingernails when she visited."

I nod. "I adored the feel of her nylons. She let me run my hands over her calves while she talked."

Big Sis chuckles. "Remember the year we made her a birthday cake? We couldn't agree on which color for the frosting, so we dyed it green, blue, yellow, and red."

"It was fine until we decided to swirl," says Second Sis. "The colors ran together, and the frosting turned an ugly gray."

"And she didn't complain, though it looked awful."

"And tasted bad. Didn't we accidentally triple the salt?"

We laugh so hard we begin to cry. Big Sis squeals that she's going to wet her pants.

Second Sis wipes her eyes. "Ooh, I need a coffee."

Third Sis decides to go with her.

The two head to the galley, while Big Sis and I remain with the box. We discuss what we'll do at the graveyard. Recite a poem, a prayer, a eulogy. But no singing.

We'd sustained eight years of Catholic school and the organ dirges of daily Mass, the singing gone out of us. We often tried to fathom our missing father's religion, (our Christian Science mother little help), by playing 'church' in our basement, kneeling to receive communion—hosts of Necco candy placed on our tongues by Big Sis, always the priest because she was the oldest, assisted by Third Sis, who wanted to be a nun. Despite years of practice and enough candy to rot four sets of teeth, the religion didn't stick.

Big Sis and I catch sight of our middle sisters with their coffees, heading our way. We leave for the restroom. When we return ten minutes later, their seats are empty. The box is gone.

We inquire of a man sitting across the aisle. Were two women just sitting here? The man, who admittedly looks a bit out-of-it, shakes his head.

We panic. Someone must have taken the unattended box to the purser. I can imagine the 'suspicious package' on his desk, the security officer summoned, the German Shepherd drooling over it. The bomb squad, already notified, prepares to clear the ferry on arrival, ready to detonate the explosive within. Aunt Rita's ashes blast into the sky.

Big Sis hurries toward the purser's office. I run to find our middle sisters. They've disappeared. I climb to the upper level, race around the deck, and finally check out the restroom. On the counter, unattended, sits the oak box. Second Sis comes out of a stall. Third Sis steps out of another. They are surprised we left the ashes alone. Anyone could have walked off with them.

We make it to the cemetery and find our aunt's plot near those of our grandparents. We have accompanied her to her final resting place, as we will do for each other when the day comes.

As we sprinkle dirt over the box of ashes, disoriented pilgrims wander through, seeking directions to the grave and memorial for martial-arts hero, Bruce Lee. We point them to the nearby site. A robin alights on a branch of fir nearby. It cocks it head, wondering what the fuss is about.

Second Sis, forever razzmatazz, tosses confetti into Aunt Rita's grave. Third Sis, still polite, recites a poem. Big Sis, our guide through life's serpentine path, offers a prayer. And I, at last a cowgirl, lasso the memories with a short eulogy. For extra assurance, we implore the spirit of neighbor, Bruce Lee, to guard our aunt's remains, as fiercely as she once protected us. We depart to finally leave her at peace.

A LASTING LEGACY

Cindy Jones

A print of a Fred Maroon photograph of Wisconsin Avenue in Georgetown just after a snowstorm hangs in my front hall. A daily reminder of my brother and the extraordinary friendship we shared. I met him for the first time when I was ten years old. A brother I never knew I had. Both of my parents had been married before and, while I'd grown up with my older sister from my mother's first marriage, my father never spoke about his son. Therefore, it surprised me when, at 18 after graduating from high school, Douglas came to spend the summer with us. I'd always felt like an outsider in my family. An awkward, shy girl who preferred books to people and whose primary goal in any social situation was to be invisible. I couldn't have anticipated how his time, attention, and acceptance would be a defining influence in my life. From that first visit, the bond that we built changed the narrative that I told myself about what I could accomplish and what my future self could be.

After that year, he visited us every summer while he was in college. We lived in Catonsville, a suburb of Baltimore, about an hour north of Washington, DC, and, at least once during his visit, we would spend a day in Georgetown. We window shopped lingering at Brentano's bookstore because we both loved books and reading so much. He introduced me to literature and authors who were his favorites. Most times, we ate lunch at one of the local restaurants and he encouraged me to try new flavors and dishes I'd never had before.

The summer of 1967 was extra special. I turned 13 years old and, in the fall, would start high school. Instead of our regular route into the city, we headed towards Bethesda. Unbeknownst to me, our destination was Saks Fifth Avenue. Specifically, the store's beauty department. Douglas had it all planned out. Standing at the counter, he explained to the saleswoman, "I'm buying a first lipstick for my sister." She smiled and said, "I think I have something that will be just perfect." She showed us a rosy-pink glossy gel in a pale aqua tube. It was from Estée Lauder, a grownup brand that exuded all that I hoped my life would be. I felt I could glimpse my future, and it would also be light, airy, and full of wonderful smells.

It was the first of many surprises he had planned for me that summer. Jim Rouse's vision for Columbia, Maryland, was just beginning to become a reality, and one of its central features would be the Merriweather Post Pavilion. Douglas bought tickets for its July 1967 opening night. The program featured Van Cliburn as a guest soloist playing Rachmaninoff's Second Piano Concerto accompanying the National Symphony Orchestra. The concert debuted a piece commissioned from composer Morton Gould that celebrated the new town of Columbia. Douglas's enthusiasm was contagious; however, at the time, I didn't grasp the significance of the event. Whenever I listened to music, it was on my little round Panasonic AM radio to Johnny Dark and the Top Forty for the week. My only exposure to classical music had been the red 45s of the Nutcracker Suite that we had, and I was never sure exactly why we even owned those.

Summer rains in Maryland seldom create significant problems; however, that summer, the rain overwhelmed the newly constructed pavilion. Although the open-air amphitheater itself was mostly finished, it became an island surrounded by swamp-like ground when the recently laid sod couldn't absorb the water. We tromped through muddy puddles and tried not to slip and fall on the hastily laid wooden walkways to make our way to our seats. Still, it was a memorable night. So many firsts for me: seeing Van Cliburn play, hearing Gould's unusual new orchestral piece and watching the audience filled with elegantly dressed women and men. Of course, everyone's muddy shoes somewhat overshadowed their elegant appearance.

As the years passed, Douglas often planned other experiences to show me a life far different from my small, circumscribed life in the suburbs. After he graduated from college and moved to Boston, I visited him in his small, exquisitely decorated apartment on Beacon Hill in Boston. We ate an amazing Easter dinner at the Ritz-Carlton, visited his friends at their elegant Marblehead home, attended a screening of Anna Karenina, to name just a few. However, my memory of the concert in Columbia shined like a lighthouse, highlighting all the possibilities that my life might include.

Later, when he moved to Chicago, we only saw each other every few years when I attended conferences that were held there. I didn't know when I saw him in January 1991 it would be the last time I'd talk to him. Awkwardly, he confided he was HIV positive and would be moving to a small town in Maine, near Portland, where he'd grown up. He needed to have heart surgery; however, since he was HIV positive, they wouldn't operate on him. I told him that after he had settled in his new home, I would come to visit. Later, I realized he'd been saying goodbye.

Fourteen months later, his friend called and told me Douglas was dying. Raymond convinced me not to come to see Douglas because he was in a coma. He wouldn't know that I was there. Days later, he was dead. I was devastated that I was never able to speak with him again. I'll always regret that I didn't follow my heart and go. When I saw him laid out in his coffin at his funeral, I was stunned. Instead of my brother, I saw an emaciated old man. He was only 46.

I miss him and sometimes still, all these years later, I think about calling him to tell him about something that reminded me of him. I hope he knew how his acceptance, friendship, and encouragement changed my life from the day we met.

MIMI AND TOTTIE

Merimee Moffitt

My two grandmothers, friends to each other and to me
rarely met, their visits contingent with space in-between,
one then the other, both widows with husbands dead at 63
cirrhosis, whiskey—their medicine and poison
their houses were sold, down-scaled to solitude, small pensions
both had soft hands and fancy dresses put away
one with mink and diamonds drove a big Buick fast
the other speeded in her Studebaker from a son-in-law's lot
both made special food upon arrival: Boston baked beans
all day in mother's slow-cooking oven, the other,
applesauce cooled in freezer trays until we got home from school
seeing either car gave me joy enough to run fast for hugs
their decades and single womanhood
each a strong peg staked into the unknown
one to mass daily, early and almost alone
I'd go along to fourth floor chapel with the nuns, my teachers!
for hot chocolate and warm Lenten donuts in the basement cafeteria
the other attended mass at whim (she a heathen convert)
an occasion to bring out the mink and diamonds
her ample warm side a pleasure to lean into
both wore corsets with laces and bones, pink powdery
things over chemises, under slips, with ties and hooks
complicated things; both wore shoes with a heel
as if their feet needed slope
the non-mink sang at the piano, had a teaching degree
wrote her own music and what Mother called silly little poems
the mink always quiet in self-manicured nails, perfect face and hair
the Studebaker bought her own brand of cookies, less eager to please

the Buick liked afternoon tea in a china cup and saucer in her tiny
  kitchen
bought a whole case of strawberries once, so I could eat my fill
the Studebaker told me to make something of my life
ferociously holding my collar close to pale blue eyes under white halo
the other gave me pre-war paper dolls I played with for years
both were 87 at the end, first one, and then the other and I was too
broke in New Mexico to make it to their waning health and funerals—
their joy already planted in the pearly evening bag of my heart

SERENDIPITOUS FRIENDSHIPS

RAVEN

Lin Marshall Brummels

Big Jeff got married in Vegas,
new wife, Raven, from Georgia,
is a trucker by trade.
She drives her trailer-less electric blue

semi-tractor to our house,
sounds the truck's horn
like a shepherd calling sheep
from the hills with a trumpet,

invites me to climb aboard.
She grins broadly when I open the door,
offers me a hand up into the cab,
Honey, let's go, in her southern drawl.

Blue-black hair sweeps from her brow
in an Elvis pompadour,
falls in waves across her shoulders
and over the collar

of her snap-front black western shirt,
tucked into old Levi's
shielding the lion's share
of her dusty slate engineer boots.

Raven jams the truck into gear,
tears down these dusty roads
north, then west, south,
and finally,

a half mile east to Big Jeff's place,
shows off newly acquired
mink, ferret, and a rattle snake
to celebrate her Celtic roots.

It is not clear how exotic critters
celebrate anyone's background
but her enthusiasm is contagious.
I smile, admire her treasures.

MEETING ANDREA,
"SOMEONE WHO LIGHTS UP A ROOM"

Jeanne Zeeb-Schecter

My relationship with Andrea began in August 2014, the day I wandered into the nearby Studio City Library to return and get more books for one of my great-grandsons. Before checking out, I always take a walk around the information desk looking for announcements about what's going on in the library and community. I immediately came across a flyer for a six-week writing class on Thursday evenings, starting the next week, no charge, at the library. I think the picture of the teacher, Andrea Beard drew me in, her vibrant, palpable energy that seemed to pop off the page. I signed up on the spot.

I went home and said, "What the heck did I do? Why did I do that? Creative Life Writing? What is that? Memoir writing? OMG! Reading about my personal life in front of other people? Writing? I journal but I'm not a writer. What was I thinking? What possessed me to do that?" It felt like someone else had made that decision for me and only because I'm a spiritual Jew, I looked up at the sky and said "Okay, I don't understand. I don't think I like it, but okay." and then I cautiously showed up the next week.

I spent the next five weeks mesmerized by Andrea, this small ball of creative energy which seemed to emanate from her core and oozed from her pores. She was Tinker Bell and Cinderella's fairy godmother all rolled into one. She brought out the best in every one of the 21 participants. We had assignments we wrote at home and brought in to read to the group. We had prompts during class that brought out the most surprising creative expressions in our writing. It felt like she sprinkled each of us with fairy dust as we entered the large room, sitting in a horseshoe formation at our tables around her.

At home I floated about on her inspiration, grabbing spare moments and hours to write every chance I could. She had awakened something in me that I didn't even know was there. I often whispered short prayers of thanks into the heavens.

However, I wasn't reading aloud in class. I would pass each time she came around to me. She didn't push me, but I felt a pressure from within myself that I was only half participating. I needed to push myself out of my comfort zone. Arriving early before our last class, I went up to her. "Andrea, I've been so afraid to read. I have to read tonight, please don't let me off the hook. I have to do this. Please." There was so much urgency in my voice. I thought she must think I'm someone who forgot to take their medications that morning, I sounded nutty.

She had an amused look on her face and simply said, "Okay."

Well, with a flushed face, a shaky voice, a trembling body and the sweet woman next to me with her hand on my leg, anchoring me to my chair, I read. I even remember the piece from 10 years ago. It was titled, "The Clan of the Women." It was an excerpt from my childhood memories of holidays at my paternal grandparent's home. I wrote about the year I was inducted into the kitchen clean-up, the family gossip, the womanly things after our holiday dinner with my grandmother, my aunt and my mother. It was in some small sense, a coming-of-age story. I became part of the family's inner women's group.

Everyone seemed to like it. Several of the women came up to tell me how much they enjoyed it after class. But Andrea just smiled and said it was an excellent piece of writing and she hoped to hear more from me over the next class sessions.

I felt like Sally Fields when she tearfully accepted her Academy Award, saying, "You like me, you really like me!"

And, did she say the next session? My prayers had been answered. I went on to do her next two six-week classes. I learned so much about her over those next three months. I watched her bring a homeless vet into class, an almost toothless old guy who hung out around the library because it was safer than a lot of places. Bob was big, respectful and always spiffy clean. I loved his New England accent. He said he had PTSD from the Vietnam War. Another, a homeless woman who lived in her car was so talented. She wore expensive clothing that reeked of old cigarette smoke. A couple of us brought in spiral notebooks and pens for them. Andrea brought the homeless writers back into the world that they had dropped out of years ago, managing to sidestep their registration. Her heart was enormous.

By the time the classes stopped, Andrea and I had become friendly. She invited me to join a small group of women in a private class she offered. I showed up. Then a year or so later I added her second class to the mix. I felt like I had been invited into the inner sanctuary since most of the members had been writing together for twelve years. The talent in that room was stunning. It was the beginning of my learning so much more, climbing to a higher level of writing and making several dear friends that are with me today.

As the first group got smaller, I realized that each of the four women left, including myself had a book they wanted to write. I begged Andrea to take us on with this change in venue. I begged without mercy. It took her a month to decide but finally she gave us a yes. Later she thanked me because she said she grew, it stretched her, tackling something new with each of us as the next couple of years passed. She was incredibly adaptive and talented. We wrote, we critiqued, we rewrote, we got closer and closer to developing our dreams. Andrea created that sacred writing circle that she learned about from her mentor, Christina Baldwin years earlier. She began talking about writing a book herself that would train others to teach Creative Life Writing.

At some point Andrea and I became friends. We spent many an hour on the phone and set up writing dates in restaurants during their off hours. Then we laughed when no writing got done because we each had just "one more thing" to tell the other. Talking to a couple of her other friends I realized she had the gift of making you feel like you had been friends for a lifetime. A few of them had been dear loyal friends since they were teens. It was truly a magical time in my life. Who would have believed that I could develop and grow as a writer as I went into my seventh decade of life? Andrea spouted a fountain of youthful energy that made you know there was still plenty of life left.

Then her mother became ill and started to fail. Her younger sister, Lisa, had been diagnosed with early onset Alzheimer's like her father and needed to go into a facility. She took me with her on a few of the visits to spend time with Lisa. It was amazing to watch as she showered her with so much love. Lisa miraculously responded to her energy, the songs Andrea sang to her and her antics.

Sadly, her mother passed away and then Lisa. Andrea had a mild heart attack and began to deteriorate in the midst of all this chaos. She stayed home most of the time. Then Covid hit with its enforced isolation.

Andrea now lives in a Memory Care Facility and battles the same disease that took her father and sister.

It felt like I had lost her. But that core part of the wonder of Andrea lives on in my heart. I can hear her sometimes, that raucous laughter, her shimmying to music as only Andrea could shimmy. I can see and feel her close by sometimes. I feel the encouragement she so freely dispersed. Her voice is recorded in my mind. When I sometimes feel unsure of my writing, I just hit the Andrea play button and the ink flows. She is my muse. She is my friend, and she lives in my heart.

ANCHORS IN FOREIGN PORTS

Terry A. Repak

I would not have survived our lengthy sojourns in foreign countries—nine years in Africa and five in Europe—without the women who became lifelong friends; women who happened to land on the same distant shores I did. They became mentors and companions in my efforts to adapt to other countries and cultures.

My husband's public health work took us to west Africa when the AIDS pandemic was at its height, decimating families and villages in the 1990s. I agreed to move to Ivory Coast because his work would help save lives while mine (freelance writing) could be done anywhere.

It was a lonely venture, moving with two small children to a place with an inhospitable climate where we didn't speak the language. What saved me were the women I met who welcomed me at book group and women's network meetings. Most of the women had landed in Ivory Coast before me and were happy to be living there. I wanted to embrace the local cultures as they had and help my children feel at home in Abidjan.

The first woman to become a close friend was an American who was married to an Ivorian. She knew the country well after living and working there for a decade. Carol hosted a monthly book group meeting, and she invited my family to spend Thanksgiving and Christmas with her friends and family. Through her I met other women who got me out of the Embassy bubble and became close friends.

Friendships develop fast in foreign settings since friends are lifelines when your extended family is far away. With friends I did volunteer work and ventured into parts of the city I would never have visited on my own. After two years in Abidjan, it felt like home.

It was a blow when Carol told me later that year that she'd accepted a job in Pakistan and would leave Ivory Coast. It was one of the hardest things for me to get used to while living overseas—that friends would come and go in our lives sooner than we liked.

I learned other hard lessons through the friendships I made in foreign countries. One was that you can't control where a relationship will go or how long it will last. I wish, for example, that things had gone differently with my friend Mona, a brilliant woman who worked for the African Development Bank in Abidjan. Our friendship fed my desire to get to know women from African countries and not just spend time with other expats like me.

I was a little in awe of Mona. She was an insightful thinker who offered alternative perspectives at book group and professional women's meetings. She became my closest companion and confidante after Carol left the country. We walked together in the evenings and attended theatre and music events in the city. We could talk about everything from our personal lives to life in general and what we believed in.

Yet Mona wasn't an easy friend for me. When she was in a good mood, she radiated warmth and drew people to her. But she could also be abrasive and scornful, and she had little patience with people who bored her—like another close friend of mine who attended our book group meetings. Ula was a timid expat who for some reason Mona didn't like.

One spring, Mona and I decided to take a trip to Paris to escape the rainy season. Ula happened to be recovering from a nasty bout of malaria, and when she heard about my trip to Paris, she asked if she could go along. I didn't have the nerve to say no even though I knew Mona wouldn't like it. Ula ended up going, and Mona rarely spoke to her that week. It was more of a hardship for me than it was for either of them since Mona frequently went off with another friend she knew in Paris, and Ula was happy to be with me.

A few months after we returned to Abidjan, Ula and her family decided to move back to Germany. I was sad to see her go as she was a kindred spirit who truly cared for me. Mona and I continued to walk together in Abidjan and see each other regularly. Then she met a French woman who was training for the New York marathon, and she decided to train with her and try to run the marathon too. I had developed hip bursitis by then and could hardly walk, much less run.

I felt the loss deeply when Mona stopped calling me. She didn't answer my phone calls or emails, and when I finally reached her one day, she attributed her silence to a misunderstanding we'd had several months prior. I had hoped we would work things out, but she found it easier to stop talking to me.

At the end of that year, my husband and I decided it was time to move back to the US. I didn't get to say goodbye to Mona, and I grieved the loss of our friendship for months.

One year later, I returned to Abidjan to visit the places and friends I'd been missing already. I called Mona to arrange a lunch date, and we talked as if nothing had come between us. At the end of the meal, I worked up the nerve to ask her why she thought our friendship fell apart. "I'm really sorry about what happened between us," she said somberly. "I suppose I should have talked things over with you, which is how friends are supposed to work things out. But I didn't know how to do that." It was a relief to clear the air with her, and both of us cried when we hugged goodbye.

It occurred to me later that cultural and situational differences had complicated our friendship. Mona was a single mother with a full-time job and heavy responsibilities that she bore alone, whereas I had a trusted partner and was able to write and be at home when my children returned from school. She didn't have as much free time as I did, nor did she need or prioritize my friendship as I had hers. Perhaps my "need" had been part of the problem. I had overvalued Mona's friendship and chose to spend more time with her than I did with Ula, who was a more devoted friend in the end.

What also complicates friendships is the expectations we bring to them and the emotional investment each one puts in. It's one of the most important investments we make in life, particularly if we want to take a friendship to a deeper level. We make an unwritten contract to be there for each other, especially when one needs something that the other can give. Yet we have to allow for hurts and disappointments since all of us make mistakes and let each other down. Honest discussions about needs and hurts are critical to maintain trust and intimacy, even though it may take extra effort to get past cultural differences.

Over the years, Ula and I kept in touch and visited each other when I was in Europe or when she came to the United States. I regularly see my South African friend and another German woman with whom I studied in London forty-plus years ago. I've stayed in Oslo numerous times with a Norwegian friend, and I get to see a handful of American women who became close friends in foreign cities. Foremost among them is Carol, who landed in the Seattle area not far from me.

Most of my friendships stood the test of time because we loved and trusted each other at pivotal points in our lives. These friends sustained me when I lived in foreign countries, far from home and from my extended family. In fact, I was willing to move abroad again and again because I knew that old and new friends would be there for me.

I'D LOVE THE COMPANY

Lucy Painter

I was living alone for the first time in my 24 years in a strange city where I knew no one. My husband Charlie was far away in Washington state and then in Louisiana undergoing US Army training. I had landed a teaching job at Liberty Middle School in a town 45 minutes away, again where I knew no one. The faculty in that small school had been together for years and were not welcoming to a newcomer, never inviting me to join them at the coffee shop after school. I taught my classes and drove back to the empty apartment Charlie and I had shared for only three weeks before he had to report for duty.

To describe our apartment as modest is to be kind. Apartment #6 lay in a row of ten identical boxes lined up side by side on a dead-end street. Cox Avenue Apartments looked as if a builder had simply stopped construction at ten units, deciding that the whole project was just too ugly to continue. There was no driveway, no porch except three crooked brick steps supporting a concrete stoop, very little yard and no shrubbery. Asphalt and scrubby dirt surrounded me. A heavy metal door atop the stoop was the only entrance into and the only exit from a three-room box, a home invader's dream.

Dark stone, the color of wet mud, covered the floors, always cold even in summer. We were too poor to buy our own furniture, so we used what the landlord had available. The vomit-green couch was synthetic, vinyl or Naugahyde that adhered to any exposed skin so that rising from it had to be done slowly and with forethought. Our other furniture consisted of one battered fake-wood table, two mismatched chairs, a double bed, and a mattress that even today I shudder to think of sleeping on. There was no TV, no radio.

I had not lived in Asheboro long enough to know anyone. I watched neighbors, mostly single men and women, come and go at various hours, never lifting their eyes to see me or their hands to wave hello. They seemed a sad lot, hurried and worried and as alone as I was, but not interested in friendship.

I came to know a loneliness that pulled the breath from my lungs. It took all the energy I had to drive to and from school, to come home to sit on the couch and read, forgetting to eat. Awaking at night to silence, I was afraid to turn on a lamp for fear that its light would fail to penetrate the darkness. I often left the bed to lie on the cold floor so that the iciness let me know I was alive, that I actually did exist outside of Liberty School.

When a knock sounded on my door one Saturday afternoon, I almost ignored it, thinking it must be a salesperson. I didn't know anyone else. An older woman stood on the little stoop, the one exactly like hers next door, with a Coke in one hand and a cigarette in the other. She was the neighbor I seldom saw outside but sometimes glimpsed as she sat in her front window, staring at the scrubby field. Her hair was silver, not gray. A radiant silver. She carried an air of elegance about her that I had never noticed. Now she stood tall and willowy in my cramped doorway, the fall sunshine sparkling off her silver earrings and on her warm face when she smiled at me.

"Hi, I'm Frances. I hope you don't think I am being pushy, but I noticed that you're alone and thought you might want to watch TV with me tonight. It's the Miss America pageant. I know it's corny, but just too much fun to watch by myself. Will you come over and let's be catty about all those beautiful girls? I'd love the company."

Of course I went. Frances and I shared a bottle of wine and laughed at the inane questions the gowned and coiffed young contestants had to answer. Over the hours of that September evening, Frances and I discovered we had much in common—the books we read, the songs we loved, our fondness for old cats. Her fat gray tabby cuddled in my lap as if he had been waiting for me.

Two women, one young and unsophisticated, the other older and polished, bonded in our shared loneliness. We began to talk every day, to keep an eye out for each other. If I had a late parent conference at school, I let her know. She did the same for me when she was to be away or late from her work as paralegal downtown. We met in her apartment or mine on weekends to watch TV or a movie. We took in each other's mail and often shared a simple meal or a glass of wine.

Most importantly, I was not invisible any more. And neither was she.

FLEETING FOREVER FRIENDS

Ellen Notbohm

"How long do you have to know someone before they're your friend?" my young son wondered, struggling to understand the devilishly nuanced concept of friendship. How would he know if they're a real friend? We had long talks about friendship, how they come in all degrees. They can last for years, or they can be brief and situational, but unquestionably genuine. This I learned as a child myself.

Even eight-year-olds dressed up for airplane trips in the 1960s. Hence my flying from Oregon to Chicago in a bright white pique dress with a black-and-white checked hem and sash. From my aisle seat at the back of the plane, I could see my parents and little brother several rows ahead. I didn't mind sitting alone. I felt worldly. The stewardess brought breakfast: eggs over easy, toast triangles soaked in margarine, a tiny cup of canned fruit cocktail. My mother despised margarine and fruit cocktail, so I felt even more worldly gobbling them, quite literally, behind her back. The greasy damp bread and slippery grapes would never have been a first choice for breakfast, but opportunities for small acts of defiance rarely came my way. That made them delicious.

However, the egg was trickier. Hard-boiled or scrambled, those were acceptable ways to eat a yolk, but this one ran all over the plate like yellow blood from a paper cut. Revolted, I tried to cut around it delicately, to pop small bites of the whites into my mouth. Even on an airplane, it felt rude to reject the meal, even if politely.

Then, calamity. A splotch of egg yolk, blinding as the sun, landed on my white collar, spreading through the mesh fabric like an inkblot.

I must have gasped in horror, because the man seated next to me glanced over. As I scraped at the stain with my napkin, he said gently, "That will only make it worse."

Indeed, little balls of napkin stuck to the stain, unchanged for my efforts. When my tears welled, the man spoke again. "It's just a small stain. I'm sure it will come out. That's such a pretty dress. It doesn't ruin it at all."

"My mother will be angry," I told the nice man, which wasn't true. My mother never angered over small mishaps. I was angry with myself, dribbling food like a two-year-old. I added, "We're going to see my grandparents," doubting whether he could understand how rare and important this was.

"I'm sure they'll be so happy to see you that they won't even notice a tiny spot on your dress."

I finally looked up at this kind man, who had magically said exactly the right thing. Sandy-colored brows topped his light blue eyes, and he wore a black uniform with brass buttons and white braid trim. He said he was Captain Smith, and that he had a daughter about my age.

"She calls me Cap'n Crunch," he told me, making me giggle in spite of myself. "But we still won't buy the cereal." I nodded, no, my mom wouldn't buy it either. She bought things like Cornflakes and Puffed Rice and suddenly I was telling him why I thought Puffed Rice was ridiculous. It just sits there on the milk, bobbing like balloons in a bathtub, until it soaks up enough milk to sink and turn to mush. Captain Smith laughed and said I'd described Puffed Rice perfectly, yes, it was like eating Styrofoam, and thank you, because now he would remember me and never eat it again.

At O'Hare, I introduced Captain Smith to my parents. He told them what a charming daughter they had and wished them a pleasant time in Chicago.

Hurtling down the expressway in our rental car, my mother remarked, neither kindly or unkindly, that Captain Smith wasn't a real captain, not in the U. S. military, nor an airline pilot. He was a captain in the Salvation Army.

The Christmastime bell-ringers with the coin buckets? How did she know this? Something about his uniform? I wondered what I was supposed to do with this information. It made no difference to me. Captain Smith knew just what I needed to hear at the moment I most needed it. He was indeed my salvation. He was my friend. Even if ever so briefly, real enough for me.

...

A few years into a new millennium, *Fly the friendly skies* is now a laughably antique ad slogan. I'm standing in a long line waiting to go through customs, to be questioned by unsmiling fellow American citizens so I can end my research trip and get back to my own country. The line snakes between coils of nylon ropes back and forth, back and forth, ensuring that I'll end my exhilarating adventure in this most boring manner possible.

To pass time, I mentally catalog the crowd ahead of me. One thing's for sure: no one dresses up to fly anymore. They barely dress at all. Women in sandals comprised of cardboard-thin soles with pipe-cleaner strips of grimy plastic for straps. Women wearing tops that expose their brassieres. Men displaying several inches of underwear above low-slung pants. Wait, are those pants—or pajama bottoms? Two charmers have skipped the underwear and treat us to an inch of butt crack.

My eyelids grow heavy with tedium.

"Ma'am? Step up, please." A man behind a counter beckons to me, his shirt as white as my long-ago dress. Navy blue and gold epaulettes gleam from the shirt's shoulders; detailed cloth badges garnish the chest and sleeves. He takes my passport and says, "I have to ask you to step out of line and follow me."

His ID tag smacks away any trace of indifference I have been nursing. *It can't be.* But it is.

Cap Smith

Cap Smith might be all of 38 years old, a study in deadpan coolness. He leads me to a female agent. I don't allow myself to wonder anything. My backpack contains nothing remarkable. Laptop, trail mix, book of crossword puzzles. The female agent asks me to step through a metal detector. Nothing unusual there. But then I'm taken to a private side station where she says, "I'm sorry about this. I have to pat you down. Please put your arms over your head." I feel the reluctance in her hands as they move down my body, under my breasts and between my legs. With another "I'm sorry about this," the agent pulls the waistband of my pants out a few inches and peeks down.

Now I balk. "What is going on here?" I ask, in a pointedly reasonable tone. But the agent simply repeats, "I'm sorry about this," and tells me to turn my palms up. "I have to swab you," she explains-apologizes.

"For what?"

"Traces of explosives."

Now I find my full voice. "What reason do you have to think—"

The agent quickly runs a fabric-covered wand over my hands and inserts it into the detection instrument. No lights blink. No alarms sound. She turns and looks me in the eye, a look of empathy and compassion. "None, ma'am. We're randomly testing every 20th person today. It's September 11."

"So someone with explosives on their hands has a 95% change of not getting caught."

What can she say? She has no more voice in these procedures than me.

"I know you're just doing your job," I say, shouldering my backpack. There's a weariness in her smile as she directs me back into the mainstream of the customs area, where the po-faced Cap Smith flicks his eyes from my passport picture to my real mug, then hands my passport back and wordlessly gestures me to a line funneling the random 5% through a door and back into the main concourse. Just another heifer in his cattle drive.

A suppressed snort collides with my sealed lips and shoots up my nose as I hear my son's voice in my head. *Tell it, Mom!* Oh, yes, I'll tell it. How a long ago one-hour friendship has stayed with me a lifetime. I wait until I'm three steps from the door, bolting distance, before I turn back to the implacable Cap and call to him, "I knew Captain Smith. I flew with Captain Smith. Captain Smith was a friend of mine. You, sir, are no Captain Smith."

Fat Friends Forever

Lorinda Boyer

Chunky cheeks, chubby thighs
Swimsuit fabric stretched thin
Blonde hair, bright blue eyes
Shoulders rolled back, not in

Standing in the pool
Legs submerged to her knees
Next to a boy who's cool
Both notice when I sneeze

Snot bubbles from my nose
My face flushes red hot
Gazing quickly at my toes
Did they notice or not?

Bracing for their teasing
I cautiously lift my head
Feel my body seizing
My heart filling with dread

But upon inspection
The boy's no longer there
She's headed my direction
Bringing her towel to share

"Don't worry, it's okay."
She whispers, I wipe my face
"Nobody looked your way."
She assures kindly with grace

"Let's get ice cream cones."
She clasps hold of my hand
We follow square steppingstones
To the concession stand

We amble and we chatter
I suck my stomach in
Trying hard to make it flatter
I notice her grin

She pushes her belly out
Pats it with her hand
Erasing any doubt
She may not understand

Our friendship's made that day
The summer of fifth grade
Bonding over the way
We're both pudgily made

And forty years since then
Through thick, thin or whatever
Devoted we have been
We're best Fat Friends Forever

FRIENDS WITH WORDS

Donna Cameron

Making friends was easier when I was a child. "You wanna come over to my house after school and play pirates?" was all it took to set up an afternoon of imaginary swashbuckling. These days, my imagination conjures all the reasons why someone would say no: *She has better things to do than spend time with me ... I'm just not that interesting ... She probably has all the friends she wants....*

Playdates today are much harder to come by. So are friends.

That's why I was so grateful when Ellen emailed me to ask if I had any interest in being her critique partner. She, a successful author of many nonfiction books and a shimmering novel—all award-winners—wanted to venture into short prose and hoped I might be interested in similar exploration and experimentation. I was. My own book had done well and kept me busy with follow-up articles and speaking engagements, but I was ready to get serious about personal essays, while also getting more playful with my short-form writing.

Ellen and I had met only once when I gave a reading at her neighborhood bookstore. She bought my nonfiction book, and I bought her novel. We both liked what we read, which led to email exchanges and a growing mutual admiration. We planned to meet up again at a writers' conference in the spring of 2020 where our books were both in the running for awards. These best-laid plans were soon curtailed by a worldwide pandemic.

Ellen's suggestion a few months later led to a long-distance playdate and a friendship I've come to treasure.

We started cautiously. While we both claimed to have thick skin and to want critiques that were direct and hard-hitting, *did we really?* Turns out we did. While of course we welcomed praise for our writing, we genuinely wanted to hear about what hadn't worked, what hadn't landed with freshness and precision, what would have been better left unsaid, what we'd missed, and how we could have said it better.

We shared works in progress, both works we were proud of and cringeworthy efforts we'd never shared with anyone. And we took seriously the task of critiquing—always appraising the writing and its effectiveness, never the writer or her choices.

Over the course of sharing our stories, essays, and creative nonfiction back and forth, we inevitably discovered many things we had in common and many we didn't. Our opinions dovetailed and differed in refreshing and interesting ways. We debated, deferred, nudged, and sympathized. We found that great minds can cheerfully agree to disagree. We learned from each other.

Quite naturally, our emails strayed into histories and recollections, plans and adventures, and the everyday challenges of life, family, health, and ice cream. Though we live 200 miles apart, our email interactions often left me feeling that I'd just taken a chatty walk with my friend Ellen.

As our critiques progressed and our friendship grew, we both found the courage to explore things we never thought we could or would write about. The safe and nurturing environment we had created proved to be fertile—and even healing—ground.

Before long, something else began happening. The essays and stories we'd worked on started getting accepted by literary journals. Not just a few. *A lot.* When I received an acceptance, Ellen was the first person I'd tell, and she cheered my success as if it had been her own. I celebrated her many acceptances with the same gusto.

We knew it was more than luck. We had taken our writing seriously. We had taken our critiquing seriously. At the same time, we took ourselves less seriously. We'd also done our research—checking out journals, sharing ones we found attractive and that were publishing work complementary to our own. Of course there were rejections—plenty of those. Although we both reject that word, deeming it self-sabotage. Instead, Ellen calls them "no thank-yous," while I refer to them as "declines." Together, we relished the kind ones: the personalized messages that praised our prose, invited more submissions, and wished us well. And we hooted over the tone-deaf declines that mangled our names, sported glaring grammatical errors, or hit us up to donate money in the same sentence they spurned our words. Bullets dodged, we agreed.

As we head into our fourth year of collaboration and friendship, we look both back and ahead at a partnership that works because of some core tenets:

We don't keep score. We trust the process as well as each other. There are times when one of us has a surge of work ready for critique, while the other is going through a spell of blank-page-itis. It all balances out. We learn as much from critiquing each other's writing as we do from the appraisals of our own work. And, more often than not, critiquing primes our pumps.

We judge not. Once it became apparent that neither of us would make judgments about our partner's thoughts and ideas, we felt freer to express honest and sometimes painful feelings we had heretofore resisted writing about. Writing through our vulnerability produced some of our most powerful stories and essays, ones that were snatched up quickly upon submission.

No comparisons. No envy. We've both reached a time in our lives where we feel no need to prove ourselves, outshine, or one-up anyone. We're now more focused on having fun and continuing to learn. People may eye us skeptically when we say we celebrate each other's successes as heartily as we celebrate our own. But it's a splendid truth.

What happens in Vegas.... An effective critique partnership/friendship becomes personal and intimate. Sharing our deepest thoughts requires equally deep trust. We both knew instinctively that honoring the sanctity of our two-way "confessional" was essential. As trust grew, so did our writerly courage and proficiency.

The precepts above might be more than guidelines for partnering with a writing buddy; they could apply to most any friendship. And maybe, just maybe, they're not bad instructions for life.

At a time in life when losing dear ones is unavoidable, a new friend is a jewel of great value. What started as a writing collaboration has ripened into a deep and lasting friendship. Should she need me, I wouldn't hesitate to jump in my car and drive a few hours to offer Ellen my assistance and support. And I know that if I asked her, Ellen would say, "Arrrrr, I'll play pirates with you," and show up at my door in a tricorn, boots, and sash.

ACCOUNTABILITY FRIENDS
Patricia Daly

We met online, not through a dating app, but in a writers coaching program we both subscribed to. We saw each other in the same room every Tuesday on Zoom from opposite sides of the country; I'm in Florida, Andrea lives in California.

At some point in the coaching program, Andrea and I connected outside the Zoom group when she asked me through chat if she could learn more about my indie-published book. She was interested in my spirituality. I made an appointment with her through Calendly to meet up on her Zoom account. Our friendship was born.

Neither of us belong to the online coaching program anymore. But we have maintained contact by becoming weekly accountability partners to each other. Every Monday (sometimes Tuesday if one of us forgets!), we send a bulleted list of actions taken, things written, videos watched, webinars attended, books and articles read, and just about anything having to do with writing and publishing. The list of accomplishments during the prior week is followed by our goals and scheduled events for the week to come.

At first, I wasn't too keen on the idea of being (or having) an accountability partner. It sounded like I was adding yet another task to my already-full plate of writing responsibilities. Neither of us was sure about the value of the practice, but we decided to try. We've been communicating weekly for almost three years now.

I knew that being accountable to another writer would improve my consciousness of the use of time, but I did not expect it to be as enriching as it has been. I think I speak for both of us. There have been slow periods when we questioned the benefit of continuing to report weekly. Whenever we ask each other, "Is this worth it?" the answer always is "Yes." We recognize a deeper benefit to our communication. We enjoy sharing with and learning from each other. We understand each other's challenges of time, energy, and need for friendship.

I am accountable to Andrea, but it means being accountable to my writing goals first. It also means I must remain focused on my work. If it weren't for Andrea's mutual commitment to our practice, I would be less aware of the cumulative effect of what I'm doing day by day. The week would fly by on autopilot with little sense of accomplishment if I were not documenting tasks and sharing my list with Andrea. Although it requires keeping track, documenting, and giving time to report writing, it's never a time hog because of the benefits I receive in return.

Andrea and I schedule things the old-fashioned way, on a paper calendar that shows every day in the month. Over time we've gotten creative at documenting even the smallest writing-related tasks. I am frequently surprised how to-do list items add up, and how baby steps toward a goal begin to show results.

We don't pressure ourselves or each other to perform or produce. We simply report by sharing a list. We learn from each other. We inspire one another. Sometimes we send a message in response to the other's report asking for clarification or expansion.

In spite of the fact that Andrea and I have much in common as authors, we follow divergent writing paths that don't conflict, nor are they competitive. Andrea is focused on creating a business for income that includes course creation, book coaching, website subscription programming, ghostwriting, and editing. My focus is on writing creative nonfiction in the genres of spirituality and self-improvement, indie publishing, copywriting, Amazon Ads, and a growing interest in building a business on my website selling books and digital products.

Andrea and I are in our 70s. We're single. Through this accountability relationship, we have a common meeting ground where we are familiar and comfortable with each other. We encourage one another and offer ideas.

We catch up on Zoom every two months, on average. There are no dead spots in our conversation! Sometimes we share disappointments, other times there may be a small success we celebrate. We ask each other for advice and opinion. We give feedback and suggestions. We are held together by our love of writing and by our mutual efforts to learn, grow, and be there for each other.

Our relationship has become a wonderful, unexpected gift to my writing journey. I feel Andrea's respect, her sincerity. I have the best of both worlds: the love of a friend and the support of a fellow writer. We'll probably never meet in person. That certainly isn't necessary to keep our friendship alive and well. It's not as easy to make new friends later in life that result in feeling you've known each other for decades. Yet, Andrea and I have hit upon a fine balance of mutual admiration and a commitment to personal and professional growth that has enriched us both.

THE EMPOWERMENT OF FRIENDSHIP

Denise Larson

When I moved to San Francisco in my early twenties I had one goal in mind: to become an actress. I enrolled as a drama major student at San Francisco State College (now San Francisco State University) and plunged into learning the craft. It was my vision of heaven. I loved discovering all aspects of theater and digging deep into the nuance of developing characters for the stage. But there were other lessons to learn as well. Number one: the business is competitive. Competing against other young women for coveted roles at auditions was daunting. Later I learned that the same competitive spirit was needed to get an agent, attract publicity, and get a seat at the table in the theatrical community to attract the attention of producers and directors. You had to use your elbows to push through the crowds of other female hopefuls, and your fingernails to claw your way up the ladder. It's also worth mentioning that at the time (the early '70s) men exclusively made casting decisions and helmed theater companies, movie studios, and television stations. Once you got cast in a play or movie you could become friendly and develop acquaintances with other actresses, but it never ran too deep because the next job, the next audition, would pit you, once again, against each other. I didn't excel at this viciously competitive process.

But then, almost accidently, certainly serendipitously, I created my own female collective theater troupe: Les Nickelettes. We came together initially to do outrageous skits at an afterhours film program at a porn theater (we weren't a pornographic act—but that's another story). And then an unexpected thing emerged, we discovered that when we came together, we shared the same sense of humor—not the mainstream (patriarchal) humor but a hidden, suppressed female sense of humor. Since none of us had banded together like this before, it was a revelation. As a group we laughed hysterically at the oft quoted cultural lie that, "women aren't funny."

We had fun together. We didn't compete with each other; we cooperated and formed a special sisterhood. Our confidence grew as we thumbed our noses at cultural norms. On my own, I would never have been brave enough to challenge the status quo. But within this unique group I audaciously proclaimed that we *were* funny! Our brazen humor trailblazed a different take on second-wave feminism. What do you think of when you think of feminism? Women carrying signs and marching in the streets? Political activists leading the effort to pass the ERA? Gloria Steinem and *Ms. Magazine?* The #metoo movement? Do you ever consider comedy or satire? Les Nickelettes addressed serious feminist issues through a female satirical lens.

In a *Village Voice* article "Rhinestone Politics: Bay Area Experimental Theater," Ellin Stein observed, "The serious themes of their [Les Nickelettes] thickly plotted musicals are buried beneath a barrage of puns, visual jokes, cheap laughs, plot complications, and every melodramatic cliché in the book. They circle around the message, approaching it in an oblique 'feminine' way in contrast to the more overtly feminist companies who dramatize similar issues in a 'masculine,' i.e., direct, way."

By using satire and silliness the group addressed myriad women's issues: Demeaning and competitive beauty contests (Ms. Hysterical), women's reproductive rights (Birth Control Blues), patriarchal supremacy (Peter Pan: A New Wave Fairytale), aging women being devalued and sexual harassment (The Didi Glitz Story), patriarchal religion (Oh Goddess!), etc. This approach was unheard of in the '70s and '80s. And yet, women using humor to highlight feminist issues made it more palatable and accessible. Comedy and satire have long been subversive tools of activism and significant elements of the history of political theater and film. We set out to upend female stereotypes and unsettle the patriarchy.

The troupe continued for 13 years and during that time deep friendships developed. It was empowering to be with a group of friends that I trusted implicitly. Trust, that was the key. My generation was socialized to be suspicious of others of our gender. Part of the competition revolved around the threat that other women would steal your boyfriend, betray you, or use gossip and lies to undermine you to others you were close to. It worked as a disinformation signal from the patriarchy to keep us separated from each other and reject our inherent connection. And yes, there were some women that came into the circle who never really fit in. But a core group of friends emerged and persevered. A group of women that I could be myself with, reveal secrets, share a laugh, and do the most stupid things imaginable and yet never feel judged. We laughed *with* each other not *at* each other. What I treasured above everything else was the amazing friendships with these wonderful and audacious women—a shameless blast of zany, escapades sheltered in an affinity of family. They were the best friends I have ever had. And, forty years later, some of these women remain my very best friends. We still get together and laugh ourselves silly whenever we can.

In my retirement I have been blessed to forge new friendships with my peers—not an easy task. I'm now working with a group called The Cosmic Elders Theater Ensemble. Coming together with like-minded elder women to create theater again blows my mind—in the best sense of the metaphor. I'm also part of an older women writing group that freely shares stories of aging, youthful adventures, and deep feelings held in for far too long. It reminds me of the old saying: Make new friends, but keep the old, one is silver, and the other gold.

TWO PEAS: EACH TO HER OWN POD

Shawn LaTorre

We couldn't have been born into more disparate cultures: she, of deep, warm Southern stock and a drawl to match and me, of cold, industrial North sensibilities and no patience for lollygagging. Not long after she walked into the English office of the central Texas high school where I'd already been working for a year, I scratched my head wondering how someone like that could've been selected to work with students from the East Side, an area of town with gangs, little concern for the integration they were a part of, and graffiti bigger and more colorful than anything this school's art department could ever pump out. When I heard her growling about students speaking "Mexican" in her classroom, I worried that this hire was just plain wrong somehow. I had to work with HER? But she was a native Texan and as a bilingual import from Michigan, who was I to judge?

Instead, I endeavored to befriend her. Maybe my hopes were a bit high-minded, but in an odd sort of way, I felt like those students from the East Side were my own brothers and sisters. I understood them. I'd worked alongside Mexican field workers many summers growing up in an area of the North where freshly grown apples, pears, peaches, blueberries, watermelons, asparagus, and cherries reined king during short, but beautiful, sunny growing seasons. These crops brought in many families from the South as migrant workers. I thought if the two of us teachers could plan together, maybe some of my insight would rub off on her and the students would surely benefit.

Within a couple of months, I noticed her appearance wasn't as professional as it had been earlier. Her hair appeared greasy, clothing wrinkled and unclean. When I asked her if everything was alright one morning, she broke down crying and admitted that she was living with her soon-to-be ex-in-laws, and they were making life miserable for her. They complained about the amount of water being used for showers and washing clothes. They complained about her two little girls making messes in the house. Soon, she would find a place she could afford and get out of there, she told me. And somehow that's just what she did. It wasn't easy living on her own, raising two daughters, and teaching high school. But I saw a true pioneering spirit emerge that I greatly admired. It was a side of her that I'd not seen, and it added a new facet to our emerging friendship.

We're both retired now, and she is one of my very best friends. She has a way of laughing at life and letting things go—including three husbands. I don't know what I add to her life, but I've stood by her over the years and made keeping in touch a priority. She's kept me afloat through some very tough times. To this day, I still prefer texts and she, phone calls. She still speaks with that Texas drawl and clings to her religion faithfully. I've drifted away from organized religion, and still say "fie-er" for fire and she says "far." She's a Republican to the core while I'm a conservative Democrat. We disagree on many fronts, but we do so respectfully. I have a sneaky suspicion we'll be voting for the same person in November though. This is the power of our togetherness. This is the transcendent power of friendship.

THE NEIGHBORHOOD LADIES

Julie Ryan McGue

When the save-the-date card arrived for the wedding of my friend Sara's son, I didn't simply affix it under a magnet on the fridge door. Nor did I think, "How nice. I wonder if I should go." Rather, I plucked up my phone, entered the date into my calendar app, and RSVP'd via the online link.

In the comment section, I wrote, "Can't wait to celebrate such a happy occasion." I signed my name next to three heart emojis and hit send. Attending Bryan's wedding meant celebrating with my friend and her family, but it was also about reconnecting with dear friends whom I hadn't seen in a long while.

In August 1993, my family relocated to Chicago's western suburbs after a year-long expatriate assignment in Mexico City. One week after closing on a charming clapboard Victorian near a bustling neighborhood park, my two daughters started at the local grammar school. Because the preschool in which we'd enrolled our four-year-old son, Danny, didn't begin until after Labor Day, he was home with me while I continued unpacking.

I'd sliced open a moving carton, pulled out some Legos and Matchbox cars, and left him to play quietly in his new bedroom. A little while later, I called out to him from the kitchen. When he didn't answer, I scrambled up the back staircase, glancing into a vacant space.

"Danny, where are you?" I yelled.

Nothing. Not a far-off, "Mommy, I'm in here," or the familiar *vroom-vroom* sound he often made with his cars. As I screeched his name, I charged through the unfamiliar house, the bitter taste of morning coffee souring my mouth. Whipping the back door open, I shouted into the fenced-in yard, glaring at our old collie, as if he might indicate where his little buddy had disappeared.

Hands shaking, I combed through my purse for the names and numbers of two neighbor ladies, Sara and Patty. The week before, the pair had appeared with a plate of brownies the moment our moving truck arrived. Both women promised to comb their yards and quiz their kids.

Before alerting the police about my missing child, I took another pass through the house. A bright blue cloth in the upstairs bath caught my eye. Danny's T-shirt. A trail of clothes—khaki shorts, white socks, and black Velcro sneakers—led to the door of his room. Inside, I spied a lock of mousy brown hair peeking out from the comforter on his bed. He'd tucked himself in for a nap. Gulping back tears, I phoned Sara and Patty to share the news and thank them for their willingness to help at a moment's notice.

Within days of the "misplaced child" episode, Sara and Patty introduced me to another neighborhood mom, Cathy, who had two preschool-aged boys. I felt lucky to have landed in the neighborhood, and I also felt as if I'd joined a sisterhood. Between our four families, the kids numbered 14. Clustered in similar age groups, our children began to spend a lot of time together. If the girls hung out at my house after school, the boys played in Sara's basement, or in the yards of the other two moms.

When Sara's son, Bryan, dubbed our tight little band, "the neighborhood ladies," the nickname stuck.

As we got to know one another, we swapped babysitter phone numbers, restaurant tips for *date night,* and information about kids' camps, community activities, and music lessons. We car-pooled, hosted potluck dinners, and trick-or-treated together. And when we met up at the park or lingered on the street corner, we commiserated about the daily joys and challenges of motherhood and marriage. There was always a shoulder to cry on, and usually it was Sara who chased away our tears with her infectious laugh and humorous spin on the predicament.

Time and shared experiences crafted the four of us into soul sisters, fellow warriors entrenched in the ongoing, often uphill battle of parenting. Our mindsets were aligned: to nurture our kids' diverse interests, to provide safe opportunities for them, and to ensure they stayed clear of trouble. We also wanted to achieve those expectations while maintaining our sanity. Humor, humility, honesty, and camaraderie made it possible.

As our clans splintered off and attended various local high schools, "the neighborhood ladies" cultivated our connection. At monthly lunches—which often stretched two hours or more—we shared and listened. Nothing was left unsaid. We chatted about our personal goals and interests, husbands' careers, and what the kids were up to, including their latest screw-ups. Each of us had more than a few colorful and tender stories to relate.

Yet, we didn't judge or pity. We consoled, empathized, and boosted. And we hoped. Hoped that the children we knew since pre-school and had grown to know and love like our own would succeed, thrive, and find happiness. Some of our collective children, young men like Sara's son, Bryan, faced bigger obstacles than most, and carried those heavy challenges far longer than any of us imagined. Yet, they made it. He made it.

As I took my seat at the wedding reception with "the neighborhood ladies" and their spouses, I glimpsed Sara's face at the adjacent table. She watched her son on the dance floor twirling his new bride. She glowed. Her full dimpled cheeks held pride, joy, and contentment. Relief, too. Sara's son had championed all the many forks in the multiple roads he'd encountered. Happiness had been won at last.

Sara caught my eye, and I winked. A year ago, she might have thought all the same things of me as my son Danny walked to the altar and married the girl he loved. When Sara and her husband came around to our table, "the neighborhood ladies" and I giggled like we had when we were those young moms decades ago. As Sara slid into the fancy skirted chair next to me, she said, "Thanks for being here," and then she pressed a tissue to the corner of her soulful brown eyes. "There were times when I didn't think ...."

My friend didn't need to complete the sentence. I hugged her hard and said, "You had your doubts, but..." I waved at our friends. "We knew you'd mother him through all the detours. Besides, we all had a kid we worried about more than the others."

I giggled conspiratorially, "Remember ...?" I reminded Sara about "the misplaced child" episode and the time my husband heard a noise in the middle of the night. The house alarm had been set, but he got up to check it out anyway. About 15 minutes later, he slid back in bed, chuckling.

"I caught him," he said. "Your son was using the only unarmed window in the house—the one above your desk—as a route to visit a girl or some other kind of trouble."

"I'll call the alarm company in the morning," I'd said

"Good idea. I bet he's not the only one who's been climbing in and out of that window."

My friend, Sara, tossed her head back, laughing at the reminiscences. "I remember those." Then she pulled me in close. "Do you remember when one of my kids shot the dart gun and it landed," she pointed to her tall handsome son Bryan, "in his calf?"

When Sara finished the story—one which culminated in an ER visit and a painful tetanus shot—another one of "the neighborhood ladies" launched into an equally outrageous tale involving recompense for the bully on our block.

I grinned at the familiar faces around the table. "It's truly a miracle that our kids survived their childhood. And that we did, too."

Soon, the groom motioned to Sara to join him on the dance floor, and she stood, her dark eyes filling. "I'm glad all of you were able to come tonight. It means so much."

Around the table, "the neighborhood ladies" and I shared knowing glances. Our presence had many layers. Of course, we had come to witness and celebrate the marriage of a young couple. But mostly we had been eager to support our friend Sara, to relish in her son achieving happiness, and to catch up with one another.

Weddings are not just celebrations for the bride and groom. They commemorate shared history and reaffirm our belonging to the people we cherish.

FRIENDS — GONE BUT NOT FORGOTTEN

A CONVERSATION

Eileen Harrison Sanchez

Carol left with a big hug and a calm "Goodbye, I left something for you, you'll know what to do with it."

A big black phone from the 1950s was on the dining room table. How did Carol put it there without me seeing her do that? It was next to the file box of paperwork with the death certificates for Jack's pension and life insurance and on top of the form I needed to complete. The phone shocked me into the past. I was whisked back to the time it took a special reason and Mother's permission to use the phone.

I rushed to the door, but Carol was gone. I couldn't do what she wanted me to do. It was weird. Yesterday she gave me an article about a phone in the forest. Someone hung a disconnected rotary wall phone on a tree. It was for people who need to talk to someone who is no longer here from the solitude of the wooded surroundings. The article had a photo. Tacked above the phone was a message:

"This phone is for everyone who lost a loved one. The phone is an outlet for those who have messages to share with their lost friends and family. It is a phone for memories and saying the goodbyes you never got to say."

I didn't have time for this. I needed to finish the form and send it off by certified mail. The insurance company wouldn't send the benefit check without the form. The phone stopped me. Panic set in. I was so angry. It was as if the d#?% phone called out "use me, use me." I rushed to move it out of my sight. The handset fell off and dangled by the cord. I grabbed it. It felt comfortable in my hand as I placed it back in the cradle. I held onto it.

This wasn't what I wanted to do. What was I supposed to say? We had our goodbye's. Was I supposed to dial 1-800-HEAVEN? My heart pounded. My hand sweated. My finger fit into the rotary dial, and I made the call.

"Is this Heaven?"

Pause.

"Is Jack there?"

Pause.

"Hi, I miss you."

Pause.

"I'm doing the paperwork for the life insurance."

Pause.

"You told me it would be sent immediately."

Pause.

"No, it didn't come because you didn't put me as your beneficiary."

Pause.

"No, you didn't!"

Pause.

"It's going to the estate!"

Pause.

"I know! But I have to probate the will to get the estate!"

Pause.

"I'm sorry, I know you did everything to leave me comfortable."

Pause.

"Yes, I'm crying! I'm upset."

This is stupid. I slammed the handset into the cradle and sobbed. I looked at the big black phone and felt like a fool. I was mad. How many times had Jack told me not to worry, all the papers were in order. He must have told me a hundred times that the life insurance would come automatically. When I got the letter with the insurance company's return address, I was sure it was the check. But it was a letter explaining that the funds would be sent to the estate since the beneficiary box was blank. Now I had yelled at Jack, we never yell like that. I had to call him back. I held the handset up to my ear. It felt good, it was a level of connection to Jack that was familiar, tangible. Like the days that Mother would hand me the phone and announce, "It's Jack—for you." I spun the dial to call the number.

"Heaven?"

Pause.

"I need to talk to Jack again."

Pause.

"Oh honey, I'm so sorry I yelled."

Pause.

"I miss you too."

Pause.

"Yes, the kids check in with me every morning."

Pause.

"And Carol has been a great friend, this phone call was her idea."

Pause.

"It's the nights that are the hardest."

Pause.
"I love you too."
Pause.
"That's a good idea."
Pause.
"Yes, I'll call you tonight before I go to sleep."

I put the handset down and moved the phone over so that I could finish the form. It felt good to talk to Jack. I got to tell him about the problem with the life insurance. And I can call him anytime.

MY FRIEND'S MOTHER

Terry A. Repak

Why does it make such a difference to me
that my friend's mother has passed away?
A diminutive woman deep in her nineties,
in palliative care for a few short days,
she died sooner than anyone expected.
She made a difference to me decades ago when—
as a young foreign student trying to find my way—
my friend sent me to stay at her mother's house
as a landing pad till I found my own place.
Even back then her mother impressed me
with her acerbic wit and grace; so much so that
my sojourn with her stretched from days
to weeks and into a month.
She worried about me when I gave up
and returned to my country without the degree,
yet every few years when I visited the UK
she welcomed me back wholeheartedly.
I can honestly say that I loved and admired her
as much as I did my own mother
(if one can measure such things),
a wise woman who meant so much
to her family members and many friends,
and who showed such delight in seeing me.
In our last few visits every year or so,

she would grip my hand and beam at me
as if surprised that I still kept turning up—
her exuberant younger American friend—
which is why, after hearing of her passing,
I'm trying to convey what a difference it makes
that my friend's mother is gone from this world,
and how much I appreciate the gift my friend gave
of sharing her singular mother with me.

MY MARILYN

Stacy Ann Parish

I rang the doorbell, and her daughter Marla welcomed me in. "Mom's in here," she said. And there she was. My Marilyn.

Sitting at the kitchen table in a wheelchair, wearing cotton jammies, covered in bright red cardinals. A once stout woman, the pajamas now hung on her like a blanket fort made with kitchen chairs.

Even though she was now in full hospice, I was heartened to see she was wearing a neon pink zip hoodie; the kind she used to wear to chair yoga. Her eyes were puffy, and she looked weary, but that smile of hers still lit up her face, and her eyes still twinkled.

We met at the Menasha Senior Center, where I worked over a decade ago. I came to love so many of the people there, but Marilyn— she became like a surrogate mother to me.

The women were gathering as they did every Tuesday. Marilyn adding powdered creamer to her coffee and Shirley waiting impatiently behind her. "Oh, for God's sake, Marilyn" Shirley scoffed. "Do you have ANY idea how many chemicals are in that garbage?" Marilyn glanced over at me with a sheepish grin. She winked, stirring her coffee, and licked the straw.

Shirley frowned in disgust, "Ugh, for God's sake!'

And thus began another gathering of "Breakfast for Your Brain"—a program I created for the Center a decade ago.

This morning, I began our session with great enthusiasm (if I had a tail, it would've been wagging), "Today, we are going to blow bubbles!" I told them, "It's a great way to lower cortisol levels in the brain."

The ladies all unscrewed the lids on their bottles and began pulling out the dainty yellow plastic wands. "For God's sake! What're we supposed to do with this!?" Shirley asked.

"Just pucker up and blow, Shirley," Marilyn instructed. Then Marilyn demonstrated for us all; blowing softly, she achieved the perfect little string of bubbles from her wand. She watched in wonder as the bubbles sailed up and out of sight. Meanwhile, Shirley was puffing in hard short bursts and wasn't getting any bubbles. The madder she got, the harder she blew and the harder she blew, the higher her cortisol levels.

Once back inside, Marilyn retrieved a huge shopping bag bursting with Tupperware, plates, spoons and paper napkins. She dug inside and pulled out a still warm loaf of homemade blueberry bread.

Next, she pulled out a tub of Cool Whip, waving around a well-worn wooden spoon from her kitchen like she was conducting a symphony. "Help yourself!" she proclaimed!

She didn't have to ask me twice.

I piled a bunch on my piece and Marilyn approved. "Atta girl!" she said.

"Oh, for God's sake!" Shirley said. "Isn't this fattening cake enough for you two without smothering it in chemicals?" Almost in unison we both said "Nope."

Shirley continued her rant, "I don't ever eat that stuff—NO FAST FOOD for me either! And don't even get me started on the Colonel's eleven herbs and spices."

"Speaking of herbs," Marilyn interjected, "Here's a fun fact. Do you know the difference between an herb and a spice?" Her sheepish grin returned because she knew she had stumped us again. "Herbs are the leaves of a plant, and spices are the seeds." When she dispensed that kind of loving wisdom, it stuck with me.

Now in her kitchen, I wished she could lift a wooden spoon and wave it around with the same energy she had back then, but she looked so frail, as if she could hardly lift a finger. I sat down placing a box I had brought with me under my seat.

Once we'd both settled, Marilyn's eyes lit up. "I thought we could have some of the blueberry bread I had in the freezer." Gesturing to her wheelchair she added, "I made it last fall before all of this happened." Marla gently squeezed her mom's shoulder as she passed to serve our bread.

"And Marla, bring that tub of Cool Whip with you!" Then, her face clouded over a little and she said, "They say I can eat anything I want now."

I knew what she meant by "now."

While working at the senior center, my mom died but my family didn't tell me. I'm assuming they did it because having been estranged from her, they believed I wouldn't be interested.

But I would have loved the chance to say goodbye.

One morning when I arrived at the center, Marilyn knew immediately something was wrong. I told her the news about my mom, and she held me while I wept. She whispered, "Stacy, it's never too late to say goodbye. You'll know when it's time to say it."

A week or so later Marilyn stayed after class. "Here," she said, handing me an old American Girl box. Inside were three things: a folded piece of paper and two palm-sized items wrapped carefully with scotch tape and paper napkins. One was labeled "To Break." The other, "To Keep."

"What are these, Marilyn?" I asked her. With a soft smile she said, "Read the poem."

On the paper was the *Legend of the Sand Dollar*. She recited the end of the poem: "Now break the center open, and you will release the five doves awaiting to spread Goodwill and Peace."

"Marilyn," I said, "I know this legend—it's one of the few positive memories I have from when I was little. My mom loved them and hung the poem on the wall of our bathroom."

Now, I swallowed the last of my blueberry treat, reached down and took out the small American Girl box I had placed under my seat earlier. I pulled out a wrapped sand dollar labeled "To Break".

"I've never had the heart to break it on my own, Marilyn," I told her, "I brought them along today so we can break it together."

With her frail hands she showed me how to hold it to release the doves. We cracked it open and out they came. "One, two, three, four…" A little shake released the last one. "Five!"

She then began to talk about what was going on inside of her. "Oh, how I miss the senior center. I miss yoga and you girls so much! They keep telling me I'm grieving and that I have to learn to accept."

Eyes cast down, she swallowed hard.

I suddenly heard what was not explicitly being said.

Marilyn was not only saying goodbye to a life with her friends at the Senior Center, or to a life that includes daily yoga. What she was actually saying goodbye to was life itself—and I could see how unspeakably hard it was. Suddenly I understood that sitting there holding her hands was the deepest privilege.

When she was finished speaking, we embraced in silence. I stood up and she looked deep into my eyes and said: "Stacy, You're always in my heart. You always have been." I tell her "I feel the same—you're precious to me, Marilyn," because indeed she always has been.

The spell is broken when the doorbell rings. The hospice nurse had arrived, and it was time for me to go.

I began to cry and said: "I don't want to leave, Marilyn." She nodded, because she understood why. The nurse was waiting, and I needed to let her take care of my friend. I told her I loved her and backed out of the kitchen as the nurse walked in.

Not two weeks later, she was gone.

I went back to Marilyn's house to see Marla, and she handed me a small white box. She said, "The day before her wake, all of the kids and grandkids came over and we sifted through mom's jewelry. I'm certain that Mom would've wanted you to have this."

Inside the box was a tiny, delicate silver sand dollar charm no bigger than my fingernail. The tears spilled from my eyes as I looked at the delicate pendant.

The moment was pure magic because for the first time I really knew what it felt like to be a beloved daughter and how beautiful it can be to say goodbye.

LOSING A FRIEND:
THE PASSING OF LINDA DEER HEART

Cynthia F. Davidson

Stepping out the door, into the predawn darkness on that November day, my four-legged companion took off, ripping the leash from my hand. The force of her sudden departure cost me my balance. My feet came out from under me, and my chin hit the frost slicked leaves. A searing pain registered in my right wrist.

My dog, Smudge, was already a distant blur, in pursuit of the white-tailed doe, escaping through the forest thickets beyond our property line.

Belly down on the cold ground, I caught my breath. A quick inventory of additional parts included a throbbing in my right shoulder and teeth aching in my jawbone. At least I'd grabbed my jacket going out the door, so I wasn't as soaked as I would've been without it.

At 70, we don't have much choice, except to adjust to reality, as it alters us.

Until the text arrived an hour later, I did not realize my painstaking inventory needed a monumental addition. At the precise moment that deer was bounding by, my dear friend Linda Deer Heart's spirit was passing, from her mortal coil.

Although my panting dog soon returned from giving chase that morning, my relationship with Linda Deer Heart has moved on, into the realm of spiritual pursuits. Like breathing concertedly upon the contents of a smudge bowl, I keep the slow glow going, like sweet, spiraling smoke continuing its rise.

Linda remains dear in our hearts.

In the six months since shedding her physicality, her emotional loss tests my balance the most. Although the energetic cord still thrums between us, especially during Lodge ceremonies, adjustments must be made, in the here and now domain. My husband and I have driven up to New Hampshire, a couple of times already, to help Linda's brother empty her home in the woods, before he puts it on the market. While sifting through her belongings—her artwork, medicine bundles and books— the inventory of our friendship expands and overlaps.

"What's this?" her brother asks, holding up the long stick of a peeled chokecherry branch. A red cotton bundle is tied with red yarn on one end.

"That's one of the 202 sticks we put around the inside of the Arbor each year at the Sundance," I explain.

My husband adds, "I used to put those in the ground." He was the chief FireKeeper at the Mi'kmaq White Eagle Sundance for ten years, in Elsipogtok, New Brunswick, where Linda was a faithful supporter, and I danced as a participant.

But all of this draws a blank with Deer Heart's brother, wife, son, and daughter. They were never drawn to the ceremonies though we extend them an open invitation now, "Anytime."

Her official obituary does not include her spirit name, Deer Heart.

Linda became our Lodge sister in 2006. We met at one of our monthly purification (sweat lodge) ceremonies. Not long after that, following a breakup with a boyfriend, she'd asked me "to put her out," on her first four day fast. That was in the autumn of 2007. Her prayers were answered. She received reassurance about her path on the Red Road, and her purpose.

Deer Heart became the first Lodge sister I passed the pouring rites to…

The next year she found a lump in her breast.

"Throw away that plastic tea kettle," she cautioned. "They found dioxin from those heated plastics in my tumors.…"

Enduring a double mastectomy, radiation and chemo, she was one of only two women who survived in her initial chemo group. From her I learned many intimacies concerning cancer, treatments and suffering. These included what chemo brain does to the faculties of memory.

As a Sundancer, I'd prayed and pierced for her. And gifted her a sacred pipe…she had ceased smoking cigarettes.

After this, Deer Heart had a good decade. Offering ceremonies to others, she continued to share her musical and artistic gifts with her students at the two high schools where she taught music for 20 years, until her retirement in 2015. She was also active in the women's prison, running AA meetings, and working as a sponsor, ever grateful for her own sobriety. She became the musical director at the Unitarian church. For her fellow cancer patients, she volunteered Reiki treatments, and provided singing bowl sessions, even over Zoom.

But the cancer returned, with renewed vengeance. It invaded her spine, skull, and pelvis.

For the last five years, she battled to keep the tumors at bay, outliving her oncologists' predictions. "Dragon feeding day" she called her chemo infusions. From her I heard about genome sequencing, and the range of treatments and experimental trials. They kept her going. "Tamoxifen and Everolimus chemo pills" among them. "I had my last Enhertu chemo. It's not working any more.…"

She documented what it looks and feels like to fight the progress of this disease. In addition to the bone pain, the blisters erupting on her skin from treatments, were excruciating. Her pain meds had to be increased.

Then came the pandemic. When in-person visits were prohibited, the instantaneous magic of social media kept us connected. Her Facebook updates cheered our spirits as we cheered her on. Along with what she was undergoing medically, she posted her "doodlings," beautiful water colorings, jewelry, and paintings. At Sundance, I used the turkey tail fan she made and beaded for me. As I write this, on my wrist is one of her lovely bracelets, black and white, with tiny iridescent purple beads.

She made it to New Zealand on a plein air painting trip. There she visited Bradrona, "where the New Zealand Cancer Society offers emotional support to breast cancer patients." Happy to stop there she made the "deposit of a hat," adding, "There was a super long fence hung with thousands of bras. Made an impression. Love to all"

Thirteen of twenty-six participants came down with Covid and were still isolating there when she flew back to the USA.

"I had the trip of a life time," she wrote on Facebook, generously sharing her photos. "Thank you for journeying with me. Love to all."

May we all be fortunate to journey with such a friend.

DEATH OF A GOOD FRIEND

Sarah Fine

"To everything, there is a season" and one of the seasons of life is dying. There's a timelessness to it, a focus that is beyond weather, daily news, personal concerns.

"How did I get here?" my friend asks from her bed in Palliative Care. I have no answer for her. "Did I give up too soon?" I have a motto of 'never giving up' but I don't tell her that. I reassure her she did everything she could.

Now I regret not visiting more often as I always assumed we would have more time.

I wasn't there for the diagnosis—a return of the cancer she had five years ago. I didn't hear the prognosis—stage 4 with weeks or months to live. When I came to visit in the hospital she told me she would be dead in a few days. She talked about funerals, obituaries, shiva—she wanted none of these. She talked about bequests to the daughters of friends - beautiful scarves she bought several years ago that were somewhere in her house.

Susan lived for almost six weeks after that first visit. While she was in a general ward at a hospital close to her home, we talked about our days as social workers and people we knew. She was much better at remembering their names than I was. She loved telling stories.

We talked about our families and how we spent a Passover Seder together. Her son and my daughter are the same age, and I remembered a fourth birthday party at her house. I now think about the numerous times she came to our house for family celebrations.

Susan was our most loyal fan when it came to musical concerts by my children, my husband, and even myself, when I joined a community choir. She loved all music and would always praise our efforts. She also took me to symphony concerts where we sat in her mother's seats and she explained classical music, introducing me to the orchestra and solo performers.

We talked about how difficult it is to sleep in a hospital, and after she was transferred to a second smaller hospital and a Palliative Care Unit (still surprisingly noisy), I asked her how she liked the new place. "The food is great," she said. I could see for myself when they delivered her lunch on a tray.

That was our last visit. I helped her by unwrapping a salmon and potato lunch with broccoli soup and ice cream in one of those old-fashioned Dixie Cups that have been around since 1908. I suggested she 'eat dessert first' and she did. At the first mouthful of ice cream, she said, "This is delicious." The soup, the salmon and the potatoes got the same rave review. She was even grateful for the instant coffee with milk and sugar.

That was the last time I saw and talked with my friend. She was happy because her "beautiful daughter" was coming to spend Rosh Hashana with her. I put Mozart on the CD player her daughter had organized for her and left her singing along to a piece she definitely recognized. I really believed we would have more time.

For Susan Who Died in September
Backward
Circling of thoughts
I can make
No sense of
These tangled
Knotty
Twists of life

Why some trees
Grow old in the sunshine
While their neighbours
Companions, friends
Die suddenly of disease
Is there a plan
In the forest?
Is there a reason?
Or is it a natural
Whirling along
Where some
Unlucky ones get
Caught in an eddy?

REMEMBRANCE OF FRIENDS PAST

Carolyn Foland

I became 80 years old this year. In addition to losing my ability to dash rapidly from place to place, easily remember common nouns and names, and stand up without being reminded of certain joints, I am also losing friends. After parents, then teachers, friends help us explore the world and discover who we are.

I cope with less resentment with the physical and mental constraints than I can with the death of friends, some of whom I have known since grade school, some of whom I worked with and some that are recent additions to a post-retirement life.

I met Jack when I went to a mental health education seminar in New York for my first job after university in the late 1960s. He graciously gave my friend and me a tour of Greenwich Village, where he lived at the time. Born in New York, he had been to Europe before he crossed the Hudson River. When his work sent him to Cleveland, he was rejoicing in his visit to the West when a woman from Denver exclaimed how excited she was to have come to the East.

Later when I worked with him in the early 1970s, we traveled in our work and on personal excursions. He was a great traveling companion— so enthusiastic about the discoveries. His courtly manners under any crisis were so much a part of him that I could imagine him saying to surrounding companions struggling in the water around a sinking ship, "I am not sure I will be coming up after this next wave, so I just wanted to let you know how much I enjoyed meeting you. Except for this last bit of unpleasantness, this has been a most enjoyable voyage." My friend was a classic; I miss him.

Amelia came bursting into our county workplace late in the 1970s dressed in electric colored jump suits, rainbow colors in her blond short curly hair and a car that declared "Damsel" on its vanity plate. She bubbled with enthusiasm and openly touted her health regime that included high colonics, supplements, and workouts at Jack LaLanne's. Amelia's more outrageous practices mellowed with age, but her zest for living did not fade. I worked with her on and off for decades, but it was hard keeping up after we both retired. Sporadic lunches made up most of our contact, but it was a pleasure to be with her. After a period of no contact, a mutual friend told me of her onset of dementia and the move to her sister's home out of state. Word of her death reached me recently and it was as though the world got a little darker.

My friendship with John arrived when I was working at a state hospital in Kansas in the late '60s and he arrived in the clinical pastoral education program for the summer. A group of us were in the hospital employee dorm—his roommate, the summer intern in the Office of Public Information which I headed, and a host of other employees— made the most of the summer. John later left the priesthood and married the woman who had been my summer intern. Our friendship lasted throughout the decades even though I no longer lived in Kansas but would visit them whenever I could. John died during the Covid period of a lung ailment caused by years of smoking. I was only able to watch the mass for him via a recording that the church made. John had been an imposing figure, tall and burly, but with a wry sense of humor that made him alternatingly lovable and annoying. I still cannot erase the last funny voice mail I had from him.

I knew Judy from grade school. She was always the friend that got to do things that my parents would tell me that since I was their daughter, not her parent's daughter, I could not do. I heard the familiar lecture of "if she jumped off a bridge would you do it too?" Our childhoods were spent studying, writing letters during summer vacations, at slumber parties, and in good conversation—later after sometimes being apart for years. Judy is still alive but descending into the dementia that was her sister's and her mother's fate. It seems tragic that someone who could finish my sentences could not remember my name.

Lisa came into my life when she joined our church. An attorney with a law firm, Lisa was super intelligent, funny, eternally curious and, within a short time, had what she called a mid-life crisis. Ever the idealist, she joined the Peace Corps and was shipped off to Romania. She wrote funny letters about her adjustments to "mystery meats," hanging her laundry outside her window in the winter to have it freeze, the high alcohol content of local "moonshine," and her embrace of the Orthodox church. She returned, maintaining close ties to the people she met there and went to work as counsel for a nonprofit international charity. She traveled almost 100 percent of her time, including returning to the US regularly to infuse us with the variety of her experiences, including her plan to retire near her friends in Romania. We planned to visit her and share her delight in the people and culture.

Her newly constructed retirement home was nearly completed when she wrote us that she had an incurable cancer. She was direct in her plan to receive quality palliative care, remain in her adopted country and die among those friends with her acceptance of what was ahead of her. But she left friends all over the world, including those of us who read her letters from Romania, sent her care packages for her first years in the Peace Corps (a massive amount of peanut butter was air freighted) and always made room for her when she came to town. My instinctive response to that email sent to a group of us was to reply to my fellow recipients with a sole four-letter word beginning with F. As most of them were clergy, it was reassuring that they thought it an acceptable response to an unacceptable situation. She was too young.

At John's service the priest said that the people in our lives have sacred spaces within us, a space that remains empty when they are gone. No one is "replaced"—each space is filled with uniqueness of personhood. My life, my interests, my knowledge, has been enriched by the kaleidoscope of sacred spaces. As these friends leave me, I can only reflect on what they contributed to my life. I would not be who I am without the people that made up—and make up—those sacred places in my heart and mind and soul, who open it to a freshness and growth I could not experience without them.

I instinctively smile when I think of each of those I have lost. I often think of something I want to tell Lisa or John or someone else. There is a sharp pain when I realize I cannot. It feels new, raw. I will always feel deprived.

I have current friends holding sacred spaces and the gifts that they fill my life with— hope, wider horizons, support, and wit. These are folks who have traveled with me, sat with me after surgery, driven me to appointments, listened when I whined, taught me how to laugh at myself. These are the people who choose to be with me, without the obligation of blood. Who tolerated my moods, my political preferences, my introverted ways. Some live near, some far. Thank heaven for social media and email. But distance has always made the connections with friends fragile. A missed Christmas exchange, a change of address—we are a mobile society, and it is too easy to lose touch.

We are obviously supposed to find our own unique self. But these are people who helped me get there—keep challenging me to think, to reach for more understanding, to curb my intolerance without losing my values.

Miguel de Cervantes has Sancho quoting an old saying he believes is true: "Tell me who your friends are, and I'll tell you who you are." Given the quality of the people who have contributed to who I am, I would like to believe that it is true, too.

So Long, My Friend

Kimberly Krantz

As we became friends, we started new ventures.
I did my homework, studied your work.
Gave it my all;
Proud of you—and me.

When you pulled the plug,
You assured me that we're just on hold.
My radar tells me different.
Did you mean to take advantage of me?

Lunch is postponed so many times,
It finally fades away for good.
Christmas arrives, cards are sent.
I ask for a call when you have time, then wait.

Now it's summer and the days are long.

I wish you well.
A note from you would have been nice.
I'll accept the silence, believing I filled a need
In your life.

So long, my friend.

LETTER TO A LONG-DEAD FRIEND

Helen (Len) Leatherwood

I was thinking about your death the other day. About how you had been reluctant to let me know you had lung cancer and then pretended you were getting better just before you died. I was disappointed that you didn't trust me enough to tell me the truth, or was it that you couldn't tell yourself the truth? I guess I'll never know. It seemed more than coincidental that you died on the day that your propane tank ran out. But then again, you always were a practical sort.

We arrived two days later in the dead of winter in northeastern Missouri and met your sons at your home. They had missed your death by a few hours because they had gotten stoned on the way to the Houston airport and missed their flight. Your daughter-in-law, who stayed at home, swore she saw you walking in her backyard at the exact time that you passed away. I wondered about that since you had made it clear to me that she wasn't high on your list of favorite people, and as a new ghost, couldn't you have chosen instead that old Chevy van your boys were driving ever so slowly? They would have been happy to see you.

I think you would have been pleased with the turnout of the Amish who came to pay their respects. They clearly appreciated the time you spent driving them to and fro to town or to weddings or funerals in your van. They came that cold night in dark blues and blacks, the women in their bonnets and shawls, the men in their waistcoats and dress pants, the children little miniatures of their parents. They stood in a circle around your dining room table where you lay in state in one of their homemade pine coffins. They remained there in silence for several minutes before the women turned and started serving the pies and cakes they had brought and filling big mugs with steaming coffee that we had brewed for the occasion. The Amish were in no hurry to leave. They stood in small groups and chatted among themselves, leaving us "English" to do the same. After an hour or so, they headed out into the cold to their horses and buggies and quietly climbed inside. The sky was cold and clear with no city lights obscuring the view of the Milky Way or Orion. The air was clean as it had followed the same path you had when you'd tried to outrun your past, first in Canada and then in the United States.

Back inside, I sat with your family and friends around the kitchen table, and we told stories of you and your exploits. How you'd pulled drowned rats out of the cistern of that very house when you'd moved in and only boiled the water for a day or two before deciding that was good enough. How your dog had kept you warm when you'd fallen two nights prior, before a friend had discovered you prone on your kitchen floor, in the coma from which you would not emerge. How when my husband and your younger son were moving your body from the undertaker's van into the house, your son broke down in tears and left my husband holding all 5' 8" and 150 pounds of you in his arms, dead-weight. "She had the last laugh, for sure," he said, knowing too well what a love/hate relationship you two had had.

I couldn't believe you were dead so soon, only 64, when you had survived so much: World War II in Germany, the dual suicides of your parents when the Russians invaded, the "scales falling from your eyes" when the camps were liberated, and a Jewish woman knocked on your door to ask if you had a comb, the years post-War as a German woman in England with a sadistic new husband who hated your German sons. How could something as small as the endless cigarettes you smoked finally succeed in bringing you down?

You knew I was angry that you had harshly disciplined my oldest daughter when she had "misbehaved." You narrowed your eyes when I said, "If you ever touch her or any of my children again in anger, I will throw you out of my house without a word." Perhaps that's why you didn't want to tell me about your illness. Maybe you thought my reaction was overly dramatic. After all, your second husband had thrust your oldest son into a water barrel and held him there by his heels. You said you picked up a brick to hit him, but he brought the child up out of the water just in time. Perhaps you thought that spanking with a board or a light slap to the face was nothing in comparison. You surely could tell that I didn't give a good goddamn what you thought when it came to the welfare of my children.

The day of your funeral was cold and gray and filled with the sound of horses and buggies as the Amish formed a procession to their cemetery. They had already dug your grave in that cold ground before we came and then used ropes to lower your casket into the earth while we watched. Each person walked by and tossed a handful of dirt on top of your casket, and then all the men grabbed shovels and quickly filled in the hole. I knew you'd be pleased that you were on top of a hill looking out on pasture land, that the Amish made an exception and allowed you, an English driver, to be buried among them, that your closest family and friends were there to see you properly planted.

I do miss you. I miss your passion and vigor, your gypsy nature and sense of adventure, your big laugh, gold-sprinkled front teeth, and deep-blue eyes. You were the first woman I'd ever met who lived life like a man, never limiting your vision or considering a task too big. I loved that you traveled cross-country without a thought and kept a German shepherd as a guard dog so you could walk at night whenever and wherever you pleased. I admired how free you were of all the fears that women share. Of strangers, dark alleys, and breakdowns on a lonely road.

Not you.

It's too bad your temper got the best of you when it came to my kids. That breach was not an easy one to mend, no matter how deep our affection. After all, it required looking a situation straight in the face and naming what was going on.

Trusting in the truth.

I hope you wander across that pasture land and enjoy the open country and the bright, shimmering stars. You deserve some freedom and peace after that life of yours. You deserve some peace, indeed.

I KNOW YOU WILL SEE IT

Lucy Painter

The large photograph of a quiet Venetian scene hangs on my office wall. Its soft blues and grays depict a narrow canal between two tall buildings, four stories of ancient stone. Deep shadows cover one side and strong sunlight the other. Three small boats rest against the sunlit side, each covered with a blue tarp, seeming at rest for the day.

This photograph has hung on a prominent wall in different homes I have lived in over the past 20 years because of who it reminds me of. Her name is Sally Moran Kugelmeyer, Kugie to her friends.

I met Sally on my first day as an English teacher at Warren Hills High School in New Jersey where I had lived for only one month. I knew no one except my husband, whose work had brought us there, and the principal who had hired me. I was nervous walking through strange school corridors to find my classroom when I passed an art room. From inside came a loud voice:

"Yoohoo, you out there. Need some help in here, whoever you are."

I followed the voice into a large room cluttered with paint jars and brushes in tin cans and on the shelves, not one inch of space free. From a wire strung across the ceiling hung dozens of paintings. Student work, I assumed. Still, I saw no one but followed the voice coming from under a paint-stained table.

"I seem to have gotten stuck, damn it. Help me up, will you?"

On the floor sat a large round woman with gray hair pulled back into a bun held together with a paintbrush. She looked up at me with a mischievous grin and grabbed my hand to pull her up. She dusted herself off, secured the paintbrush holding her hair and held out her hand.

"You're a skinny thing, but I think you'll do. Hello, there. I'm Sally, Kugie to my friends, now that you're one of them."

So began a seven-year friendship with a woman who changed the way I see the world. A gifted teacher and artist, Sally taught me to observe everything around me, not just to look at it in passing, but to see it with the artist's eye, the poet's eye. Don't just pass the maple tree outside the school's front door but notice how sunlight dances on her leaves, how her colors change with the day, with the seasons. At home, I stop to feel the silky fur of our cat Betty as she twines herself around my legs. I taste the crisp bite of a cold Chablis on a warm summer evening. With my eyes, with my heart, I practice seeing, and I miss nothing.

Because we lived not far from each other, Sally and I were able to spend hours together. In summer, we walked in her riotous garden where three or four cats roamed and in winter sat in the cozy diner in town sharing cups of Earl Grey tea. During those times, conversations flew, talking about anything and everything from the best shade of red to why men feel it unmanly to cry. I soaked up her enthusiasm for life until it became my own.

A painter of acrylics, of watercolors, and a lithographer and printmaker, Sally fell in love with photography while in the Italian village of Lucca where she traveled to paint one summer. Upon her return in the fall, she came to my door with a large package wrapped in brown paper. It was the Venetian photograph that now hangs on my wall. Handing it over to me, she said, "For you, because I know you will see it."

Sally died seven years after I met her of cancer once thought defeated. What I have of her now is Venice. In it I see her invitation to stop, to rest, to wait and observe. Her love of life and her friendship are ever-present in Venice's shifting shadows and light.

MY CIRCLE TIGHTENS, DOES NOT COLLAPSE

Jo-Ann Vega

On my first vacation since Covid-19 cut a lethal swath across the planet, I made sure to pack a new notebook. One day, instead of recording observations, I found myself penning a letter to a long-lost friend and collaborator.

My dear friend and colleague, now at rest for eight years,

You are remembered and sorely missed. I smile as I consider your greeting and recall the lilt in your voice as you approached me, pleased I can still hear your voice.

Echoes of the Past

I remember my first meeting with Carol more than 30 years ago, at a networking event for women. I had been recovering from a serious car accident the previous summer and was taking steps to get back into my life trajectory. At the time I was the president of the group. My introductory remarks always included an appeal to move the group forward by working together and actively finding others who could take your place.

During the networking session Carol approached me. We clicked as we started talking. Talking led to charged discussions about Carol's idea to form a networking group for women entrepreneurs. Her energy and enthusiasm were infectious. Wow! Someone I could talk *with* who wanted to talk *with* me about ideas and how to make them work. It was intoxicating!

Ever carefully put together, Carol was disciplined and dedicated to living a healthy lifestyle. We were a good team. Together we blended our differences and built a fabulous organization. After I left the organization and then relocated, what I really appreciated were the dinners we shared and the continuing dialogue about so many things.

When Carol called and asked me if I was alone, my internal warning system was activated. When she said, *"I have something to say that is difficult to say and difficult to hear,"* I suppressed a scream.

Intimations of Mortality

It all happened too quickly. It wasn't supposed to be this way or happen to her. I loved and respected Carol. Didn't she tell me she was going to live to be 100 years old? Didn't I always retort by saying there was no possible way I was going to make it to 100. She'd surely be coming to my funeral! They were words, not intimations of mortality.

I'm not as extroverted as I seem; never had a wide circle of friends. Sometimes excessively loyal, I've maintained most of my relationships for decades. I've found, to my disappointment, since I retired and relocated, that making new friends at this stage in life is more a matter of skimming-the-surface than plumbing-the-depths, which I prefer.

In the weeks following the phone call, I did what I always do to cope, gathered pen and paper, went to my room, put on classical music, and started writing.

Intimations

Not ready for you to leave, I prayed for your comfort
Screamed in pain at the cruelty of this illness
that brings the constant companionship
of unspeakable & unbearable suffering

Sure you were as much yourself as you could be
Going beyond your limits to help others
Slipping away feeling loved
Your life force was strong, unwilling to let go,
surrender to the limitations of human biology

Relieved I told you I loved you,
you are a highlight of my life
With regret, I let my insecurities
prevent us from growing closer
Losing you means I lose a piece of myself

The losses of adulthood—*f r i g h t e n i n g*
Yet somehow reassuring
Intimations of mortality remind us to
Pay attention to those who
Love us—despite ourselves

My circle tightens, does not collapse

Bearing Witness

I huddled with dozens, in subfreezing weather, to bear witness
to Carol's interment. When it was my turn, I managed, despite the
numbness in my hands and the frozen dirt, to pick up and heave a
good amount of earth onto the midsection of the tiny, elaborately
carved pine casket. Then I silently said, "Hi, it's Jo." I would not hear
Carol's lilting greeting again. I'd like to believe the dirt, my offering,
landed close to her heart, as I was. I believe Carol's spirit hovered
over the funeral proceedings and felt satisfied at the outpouring of
admiration and affection.

I rail against the creeping invisibility of aging, seek engagement
with others, continue to learn, remain curious. I will always cherish my
friendship and collaborations with Carol, highlights of my life. When
Carol left this earthly plane, I lost a piece of myself; my circle tightened.

*Almost a decade on, I faithfully mark the anniversary of your passing,
pay tribute to the life you lived, the deep impression you left on me. I
miss the easy banter and intellectualism we shared in the service of helping
women achieve life goals.*

I don't know if you would have prevailed during Covid-19. I am sure you would have despaired at the wreckage it brought to the US and the world.

I am now at the age you were when you left, having survived the 60s twice and faced medical crises. I would have enjoyed sharing my personal published writings with you, evidence of the emotional depth I've reached, the integration of head with heart.

What comfort we could have given each other! What enriching talks we could have had in our 'golden years'! Our bonds of respect and affection meant we could agree to disagree and remain connected, qualities in dire need today.

You remain, as always, dear to me, remembered, and never abandoned. Your precious gift of friendship still nourishes me.

Rest in peace, brave heart.

Postscript

Those we love mark and influence us long after their earthly journey concludes. Funeral rites and mourning while grieving, give us, for whom the rites and rituals are designed, a time-out, a way to get through the first difficult days as we move into a new normal—life without the lost family member, spouse, or friend. The strength of my beloved friend and collaborator's memory is a continuing gift and an ache that periodically asserts itself.

The slow time goes by fast.

Intimations of mortality remind us to
Pay attention to those who
Love us—despite ourselves.

TRIBUTE TO A FRIEND

Marion Hunt

I walked into Kim's classroom, my fourth in two years of volunteering with other teachers. I had long since retired from the profession—25 years working with children in grades one to three.

The second I entered, I felt the peaceful environment. The air was fresh and sweet-smelling. Miss Kim, her hair cropped short and spiky, her clothing professionally appropriate—chic in a grungy way and shoes meant for walking—had her first graders seated on the rug and she nestled into a worn but comfy-looking chair.

Her audience sat quiet and looked at their teacher as she welcomed them with her soft voice.

The walls were already filled with graphics related to curriculum, and words of encouragement. One that stood out for me read

TURN AND TALK,
KNEE TO KNEE,
EYE TO EYE,
HEART TO HEART.

I knew instantly I had found my place. I joined the class on the rug. When Kim saw me, she smiled and immediately introduced me to everyone as Miss Marion, who would be helping her. I loved the sound of my name.

I worked with Kim for two years. The classes of multiple personalities were happy and well-mannered. Kim never raised her voice and, always positive and respectful of her students' needs, created a team of children who worked cooperatively together and tried their best.

Kim greeted each child with an elbow bump or kind word EVERY time they entered and reentered her room and said a personal goodbye to each as they left for home or childcare.

She never wavered. Miss Kim's actions and words, like her creative outfits, were a well-worn part of her. She loved her classes, understood each child, nurtured and supported their learning styles, and endeavored to create thinkers and problem-solvers.

One day when I noticed Kim looking on the down side, I told her that she was a perfect teacher. She shook her head and denied my observation, but I insisted. She was my idea of not just a perfect teacher, but an extraordinary person.

After those two years, I decided to move to a class with a teacher I believed could use my help. I wanted to be challenged and more useful.

During that next school year, Kim and I passed in the yard and smiled and waved, but she was always ON and I found no opportunity to connect with her during my time with my very energetic and challenging second grade class.

Then, two months after winter break, Covid opened its mouth wide and roared with ferocity, schools shut down, and, sadly, I was separated from everyone in my classroom life.

Kim was diagnosed with cancer not long after, but I did not learn of it until I got a school message that we were all encouraged to walk a mile for Kim.

My husband Jeff and I went for a mile-long walk in the neighborhood while I thought of my friend with every step.

One day I awoke with a realization. I wanted Kim back in my life for whatever time she had left. Some people suffering with a cancer cocoon and don't want anyone around. But Kim was not one to suffer. I took a chance and called her. She answered the phone with a bright, "Hi Marion," and we talked. Kim was happy to hear from me.

I knew I needed to strengthen our relationship and connection. Kim, always the giver, drew me in, and we began a steady schedule of getting together for a couple of hours, each one fun and cancer-ignored. On Kim's good days (and there were many) she enjoyed life to its fullest, always allowing friends to join her. She was still giving. Loving. Caring.

My love for Kim intensified. I learned to cherish each date with her, knowing her time on earth was so limited. Then, on a day that Kim and I had planned for a walk, I got a message from her daughter saying that my friend would not be able to meet me.

I inquired later and found that Kim had gotten worse, and after a visit to the hospital, it was decided that she would return home to hospice care.

If and when she felt up to it, she might allow visits.

I never got that chance. Several days later, Kim had decided that it was about time to stop her life supporting machines and allow herself to rest and move on.

My organized and generous friend had an important request. On the eve of March 23, 2023, Kim asked that her friends and family come to her backyard with voices and songs to say their goodbyes.

More than 50 people showed. We sang songs and shouted words of love.

"We love you Kim," her friends chanted. They sang songs she loved.

The window soon opened, and Kim's head appeared. She was smiling and presenting the Kim we all knew and loved. Kim thanked us for being there, and told stories that made us smile and laugh. She was taking care of us. We also cried as we didn't want to lose her.

The sun began to set. Kim waved a goodbye, the window slowly closed, and the curtain came down. In minutes, Kim would deny her life support and lay herself down to wait for her exit from this life. She was ready. Strong and accepting. She would rest peacefully, allowing the inevitable to take her from this life.

Though she would never think it of herself, we all knew that Kim—our angel in life—would find a place to spread her wings in another world that would be happier upon her entrance.

In the darkness, we all stayed. We cried. We hugged. We talked softly. We didn't want to leave, but respectful of Kim's desire, we left for home.

Three days later, I received word that Kim had taken her last breath.

I hugged myself and cried. I cried for many days.

At the age of seventy-five, I have learned that death is inevitable and a part of life. I have been sad when I've lost family and friends. But the strength of my emotions with the loss of my friend Kim has been almost unbearable and long-lasting.

I keep wanting Kim to return to me. I feel her inside of me. I try to emulate her goodness. I sometimes use her words.

I am and have always been a good and loving person, caring and respectful.

I will never stop wanting to help others. But Kim inspired an even better me.

Kim lives on in all who knew her. She brightened the world she left behind.

THANK YOU, MY DEAR FRIEND.

ENDURING FRIENDSHIP

FRIENDSHIP FROM ZERO TO INFINITY

Jo Virgil

True friendship can take on so many different forms. How could a dictionary come up with an absolute definition of "friendship"? When we look back on our lives, we can remember all sorts of connections that helped us become who we are, and that remind us of the connection we all share.

A stranger can share the power of friendship. I often think of one time when I was walking downtown from my workplace to pick up lunch. At a stoplight, a stranger smiled at me, and I smiled back. We chatted a bit while we waited for the light to change, and then we walked across the street together, sharing some laughter. And then when the stranger had to go down a different street, she reached out and gently touched my arm and wished me a happy day. My morning had been a tough one, and I guess maybe she picked up on that. She did make my day happy! I'll never forget her tenderness and her smile. I hope she remembers me.

We all have memories from true friends way back in our lifetime— when we were in elementary school, high school, college, early jobs. We all weaved through a lot of connections and friends, but there are always some that remain in our heart forever, just because of the connection we felt, and still feel, even if we haven't communicated with that friend in years. My best friend in high school was a true friend, for sure. We were comfortable sharing our stories, good and bad, and feeling empathy for each other's laughter and tears. We've not seen each other in many years, but our friendship lives on.

In the present, we all tend to have casual friends that matter— neighbors, work companions, members in our discussion groups, even nurses or retail staff or librarians whom we become familiar with and love to share brief chats. A casual friend can matter in so many ways, including what they do for us and what we do for them. Often, I will purchase a bunch of scratch-off lottery tickets and share one each time with the check-out cashier at the grocery store. They always look surprised, smile and thank me; their smile makes me feel happy inside, and I smile back. That's a connection, for sure.

Then, of course, we often have good, close friends. We all can feel that deep connection with some people we meet and share stories, hugs, and compassion. Being able to feel a close friend's emotions, thoughts, opinions, beliefs, etc., can weave us together in ways that help us both feel loved and treasured. Good friends are there for each other during fun times, sad times, confusing times, and even just ordinary times when sharing stories and memories matter. I often think of all my good friends, some of whom have disappeared. One of my best friends from many years ago wound up moving far away from our hometown. Of course we stayed in touch for a while, but as the years went by and as each of our lives changed a lot—having children, then grandchildren, various moves to other towns, busier jobs, etc.—we mostly lost touch. We still connect from time to time, but it's been several years since we saw each other in person. Still, I consider her a good friend, and she says the same about me. A good friend may not last forever, either because of moving away, a disruption of the friendship, or even a death. But a close friend lives always in one's heart, and that's where friendship matters.

And then there is the deepest form of friendship, which some people call "soul mates." A soul mate is one even beyond a close friendship—a true connection that means we can deeply feel each other connected as one being, something beyond just our material selves. Soul mates can be there for each other always, even if they live far away from each other or have very different lifestyles. A soul mate may not always agree with everything the other one thinks, but that has no impact on the friendship. I've had a few soul mates in my life, and I know what that perfect friendship is like, although it is hard to put into words. One of my soul mates was a woman I just barely knew in a book group, and when my marriage fell apart, she was there for me in a way I could never have imagined. She wasn't the "boss of me," but she gently guided me through my own path to find comfort and meaning in my life. Another soul mate started as a friend because our daughters were in an elementary school class together. Throughout the years, we became more and more connected, and even though we both moved far away from each other, we still stay connected and visit often. We've helped each other through tough times and laughed with each other through fun times. Soul mates are a reminder of how true friendship is a connection even beyond love.

Friendship, in many forms, is what gently guides us through life. Without friends, we would just be lost. With friends, we get to explore infinity.

A CROOKED SMILE

Barbara Wolf Terao

The greatest gift you ever give is your honest self.
—FRED ROGERS

Alice was in the lead, brown hair streaming behind her, when—flump!—down I went, pitching sideways into the snow. "Hey, Allie!" Pausing her glide, she turned, saw me waving my ski pole in the air, and erupted into her signature rolling laugh. There was nothing to do but lie there in the snow and laugh with her.

Born a month apart, Alice and I were miles apart in temperament. I rotated through the social circles of our small town, while she generally preferred to stay close to home. Her parents were musicians, so there would sometimes be a string quartet playing in her living room as we passed through. Though I mostly listened to the Beatles, James Taylor, and Carole King, I liked the lilt of classical music as the soundtrack to my friend's house.

We bonded over outdoor activities—climbing trees and swimming in the summer and skating and skiing in the winter. Alice was so strong and coordinated, any team would have welcomed her, but she rarely revealed her skills beyond her backyard (or cross-country skiing in the arboretum with me).

Having Alice in my life grounded me in a way that I needed. Other friends would come and go, while she was a constant. In our daily lives, we were constrained by Minnesota Nice, which often meant concealing our struggles and feelings. Daily weather in the Midwest was a popular topic, but reporting inner weather was not. Because of our long friendship, Alice and I spoke our truths to one another, which meant we could be real. She heard my heart.

When we confided our angst, Alice always came back to one thing. Her face. The use of forceps during delivery caused the left side of her face to be partially paralyzed from birth. When I had sleepovers at her house, I noticed Alice applying something she called "goop" and taping her left eye closed at bedtime but paid little attention to it.

Walking together one evening, she explained the effects of her injury. "You can smile and make friends. My face is lopsided, so I'm super self-conscious meeting new people," she said. "I can't close my left eye all the way or blink symmetrically."

I paused under a streetlight. "Allie, I can't ever really know what that's like, but it must be grueling. You're right, I rely on communicating with my smile, and you're deprived of that common human thing." I got tears in my eyes. Her face was so familiar and dear to me, it was hard to grasp how she saw herself. When I thought of Alice suffering from this, I felt angry. "Did your parents sue the doctor?"

Alice shook her head. "No, they just tried to make the best of it. I don't talk about it much, because it makes them feel bad."

Years later, I mailed Alice a copy of *Autobiography of a Face* by Lucy Grealy, a writer whose appearance changed after cancer and surgery. Alice could relate to her struggles with self-esteem. Then I recommended *Smile: A Memoir* by Sarah Ruhl, who had facial paralysis due to Bell's palsy. As it turned out, Alice's brother-in-law had already sent her the book. Again, she could relate, though having company in her distress was of limited comfort.

A nurturing caretaker of both people and pets, Alice became a physical therapist. I relocated to Illinois and became a psychologist and a writer. For birthdays, Alice sent me gifts of footwear, including slippers, sandals, and a pair of white boots with owls on them, all of which I took as physical support along with her emotional support. She knew me so well, the shoes always fit. Eventually I moved, alone, to an island in the Salish Sea. Four months after my move, I was diagnosed with breast cancer.

That's when Alice showed up. She flew to Seattle, enduring the gaze of strangers so she could be with me. I warned her I'd be weak, wobbly, and weepy, and she understood. But on one of my good days between chemo infusions, I laced up my owl boots and we went hiking through a state park. With Alice's hand nearby to steady me, we walked the whole trail.

THE GOLD OF CHILDHOOD FRIENDSHIP

Lee Ann Stevens

"Make new friends but keep the old. One is silver and the other's gold." A line from a song I learned in Girl Scouts and sang to my children when their IBM-employed father received another transfer offer, and we were uprooting them once again from all that was familiar.

It's true that old friends can be gold, especially in our golden years. Many studies demonstrate the value of a social network to our physical and mental health, but a friendship that has endured for 66 years is something else entirely. I'm lucky to have one such friend.

We met in 1958 when I was five and she was six and my parents bought a house close to hers. Our birthdays are a few days apart, and soon after moving in, my brother, in first grade with Vicky, was invited to her birthday party. My busy mother took one of the presents I had just received for my birthday, a puzzle, and rewrapped it. I stood in the room unnoticed as she did this, with shoulders slumped and a lump in my throat. She rushed past me, since the party had already started, to deliver Scott to Vicky's house with the gift of my puzzle. It's not like the puzzle was my favorite gift, in fact it was probably my least favorite. It's that my mother's action told me I didn't matter enough to keep my own presents. And I didn't even know the recipient of the gift.

That changed when a week or so later, Vicky and two of her sisters came over to my house for a playdate. They brought with them life-sized dolls I'd never seen before, and they were generous in sharing them with me. The oldest of the sisters, Vicky, was a tall and skinny kid, infinitely kind, and bookish like me. From that day forward, we were friends, spending the majority of our free time together. In the summer, freckled and barefoot, we climbed trees, swam in the river, slept in tents in our backyard, and rowed across the river to get books from the library and ice cream sundaes at the Newport Creamery. We also played in the woods, rode bikes, and dared each other to walk across the railroad trestle that spanned the river before the occasional train came rumbling along.

In addition, we regularly spent the night at each other's houses. I was an anxious, sensitive, bed-wetting child, and Vicky's mother scared me. I now can understand that she was anxious herself, and depressed. If I sneezed in her presence, she would yell at me to go home rather than spread germs in their house. While she played creative games with her children and exposed them to cultural activities like the ballet and music festivals, she was often in her room when we went to Vicky's house, with the shades drawn. I was terrified of wetting the bed when I slept over, but when I did, Vicky always told her mother that she had done it, not me. I doubt her mother believed her, but she didn't say anything about it, and I appreciated Vicky's loyalty and protection.

As we morphed into teens, we stayed close, looking like sisters with our long brown hair, embroidered shirts, and hippie skirts. Together we learned about the adulthood that lay ahead of us, sharing knowledge, secrets, and even the first boyfriend each of us had. When I was home from college for Christmas my freshman year, Vicky's mother invited us to join her in drinking some Vermeer Dutch chocolate cream liqueur. She was friendly, asking me about my first semester in college, and teasing Vicky about the frivolous courses she was taking at the alternative college she had chosen in Vermont. I noticed, though, that her mouth was twitching in an odd way. Turns out, she was going through a tough time, with her husband cheating on her, and coping with what was likely the beginning of the brain tumor that would kill her a couple of years later. When she died, I was 21, going to journalism school in Oregon. Vicky was home in Rhode Island trying to keep her family together. On the night Vicky's mother died, it was I who dreamed of her, with a glowing light around her and loving smile on her face. Though Vicky wished she had had that dream, I felt it was meant for me as a way to ask forgiveness. My own mother, who as a nurse had helped care for Vicky's mother at the end of her life, stepped up her role in Vicky's life in the aftermath, staying in touch and visiting her over the years.

While we didn't remain close in geography, and there were years we forgot to be in touch, the bond between Vicky and me remained. We chose different paths in life, and didn't always understand each other's choices. A few years after her mother died, her father died as well, making orphans of her and her siblings. She used her inheritance to buy land in Vermont, where she and her freelance writer husband built their own home over the course of many years. She became a truck farmer, growing and selling vegetables at farmer's markets. When I married my first husband, he was newly employed by IBM, and Vicky didn't hesitate to let him know how she felt about IBM's presence in South Africa, where apartheid still existed. While she remained on her land in Vermont with her husband and two children, I moved around the country with my husband and our two children, living a suburban corporate existence. His preference for stopping at bars after work eventually led to our divorce in 1992.

While I went through a reactionary period to my husband's alcoholism, Vicky continued her hand-to-mouth but happy existence in Vermont. Having lost my grounding, and my sense of self, I rushed into a second marriage out of fear, in 1995. All during this time, we wrote letters, exchanged books, and occasionally saw each other. She was never judgmental about what I was going through, but instead just happy to remain connected.

When my second husband committed suicide in 2010, Vicky showed up to see me through. Two of her sisters had died of ALS, the disease that had also killed her father, so she was no stranger to grief. A year later, I repaid the favor by visiting her in Vermont. At some point we realized that the things we used to take so seriously in our youth, our stand on issues, our differences in lifestyle, made no difference in the reality of our enduring bond, and the arc of our lives toward elderhood.

More recently, during the long first year of the pandemic, when we'd all had time to mull over what matters most in life, Vicky and I started a habit of monthly FaceTime sessions, and we've continued that habit into the present. These days, we are two old childhood friends on the screen laughing about our aging selves, and talking, for hours, about books, about the men we love, our grown children, and our grandchildren. When I look at her, wrinkled and gray haired now like me, I see the child she once was in the aging face of my first true friend.

Gold indeed.

I'LL BE THERE FOR YOU: DRESSING FOR MIDDLE AGE

Irena Smith

My friend Tracy and I are searching for overalls. Not just any overalls, the ones we both owned in the late '90s when the world was full of promise and possibility. The overalls were faded but not too faded, wide-legged, wide-cuffed, cropped to hit right at the ankle. I'm convinced mine came from Old Navy; Tracy thinks hers came from the Gap. Regardless, we both know exactly what we mean when we say *those overalls:* slouchy but not sloppy, light but not flimsy, tomboyish but low-key sexy. The ones that looked like the overalls Jennifer Aniston wore on *Friends* over a white tank top. We were no Jen Aniston, but we were reasonably attractive and *young*—so impossibly young—and why, *why* did we give them away? We shake our heads. Could we have *been* any more stupid?

…

Tracy and I met when our children were in elementary school. She saw me jogging in the neighborhood, pushing my toddler daughter in a jog stroller, and asked me if I ran. We were standing around near the school playground, waiting for our older kids to finish playing on the play structure, and I nodded and made air quotes around the word "run" because I had taken up running only a year earlier, mostly to get rid of the baby weight I couldn't seem to shed after three pregnancies in seven years.

Although Tracy was a more experienced runner, she was injury-prone, so our pace was the same: slow. Slow enough to talk while we ran to trade tips on sports bras that didn't chafe, to debate the least objectionable flavors of Gu, a thick, revolting nutrition supplement that could be sucked down during long runs. Slow enough to discuss the chasm separating before children from after children, when our lives were no longer entirely ours.

We stopped running after Tracy's injuries got worse and I hurt my calf as a result of wearing Vibram FiveFingers, a minimalist shoe designed to approximate barefoot running. My skeptical husband dubbed them "gorilla shoes" because they were contoured to the foot and had visible individual sections for each toe and I hated that he was right and that the Vibrams had not, as I believed they would, turned me into a fleet-footed gazelle.

By then, Tracy's and my friendship was sealed. We started walking instead of running, meeting on Saturday mornings and making sure to include a place to stop for coffee. We walked past luxurious mansions in north Palo Alto and lamented that we were born beautiful instead of rich and dissected our childhoods and aired petty grudges and nodded at the truth of the saying "little kids, little problems, big kids, big problems." Because walking, unlike running, did not precipitate heavy sweating, we dressed in everyday clothes and discovered that our styles were complementary, so much so that we occasionally copied each other. During the pandemic, when both of us worked from home, we walked together during every lunch break, keeping the prescribed six feet apart, the same three-mile loop—Louis to Charleston to Middlefield to Mayview to Ross to Colorado. Tracy was the first person outside my immediate family who knew that my daughter almost died after taking a fentanyl-laced pill two weeks into quarantine. The terror and grief of it made me numb, and when I told Tracy what happened she stopped and put her hands over her mouth and her eyes filled with tears and the knot in my chest loosened a little. Every day at noon, we met on Louis Road and walked and anguished about how awful everything was and when we weren't anguishing, we discussed recipes we saw on Pinterest and houses we coveted on Zillow and Claire's terrible haircut on *Fleabag* and Alexis' outfits on *Schitt's Creek*. We spent a lot of time on Poshmark, and that's how the subject of overalls came up.

. . .

Suddenly, urgently, we *need* those overalls. We scour Target, the Gap, Old Navy, the entire internet. I find a pair at Target, but the stiff denim bib sticks out awkwardly, and they make me look short and squat and have a slight *Whatever Happened to Baby Jane* vibe. Mutton dressed as lamb. Women aging ungracefully. We don't want to be those women.

Then again, it's possible that I'm no longer the woman I was when I had those overalls. Many years ago, I wore them to the beach with my husband and our oldest son, then a toddler, and we tried to get him interested in the fuchsia plastic bucket and yellow shovel we brought, but he was profoundly indifferent to scooping sand and digging holes and wanted only to run to the water, and we had to take turns getting up and chasing him. He ran in an all-out sprint, not looking back, not checking if we were following, not cowed by the huge waves, and my husband said that some toddlers had a short rubber band, that invisible elastic that pulls them back to their parents, and that Jordan clearly had a long one. Or maybe no rubber band at all. Jordan was blond and dimpled and chubby and wore a chunky gray knit sweater with a blue house and a red roof on the front, and everyone who saw him said, *Awww, cute baby.* I turned cartwheels where the sand was firm because my body still moved in ways unconstrained by fear or age. When we returned home and I took the overalls off before bed, sand poured out of the cuffs.

That day, David took a picture of me lying in the sand, propped up on an elbow, my skin golden, my hair tousled, smiling in that unguarded way you smile when you're young and the world is full of possibility and promise. Less than a year later, Jordan will be diagnosed with autism, and we will have two more children, and I will give the overalls away. My smiles will become tighter, more guarded as the years pass.

The overalls are our holy grail. The golden fleece. The one ring. The sorcerer's stone. If we find them, we will be beautiful, powerful, immortal. But they elude us.

I tell Tracy that our quest for overalls reminds me of when I worked at summer camp in Palo Alto in the late '80s. One of my campers was a smart, funny, snarky, skinny, utterly unselfconscious 10-year-old girl who lived in a T-shirt and a pair of shortalls. Another counselor and I decided that we needed shortalls like Amy's and we headed to the mall.

We tried on every possible size and configuration of shortalls, only to find that we looked, best-case scenario, comical, and worst-case scenario, stupid. At last, it occurred to us that the shortalls didn't work because we were in our 20s and had breasts and hips and fleshy knees. The truth of it stung, and we went to La Petite Boulangerie to console ourselves with chocolate chip cookies.

"Yeah," says Tracy when I finish the story, "but the overalls we're looking for aren't shorts. They cover your legs."

Our quest continues. We go to Savers, a second-hand store in Redwood City, and grab coffee nearby. The barista—tall, slim, her hair in a messy knot at the nape of her neck—is wearing a white undershirt and a pair of wide-legged, perfectly distressed slouchy overalls, because of course she is. They hang on her with careless, casual grace. "Where did you get them?" we ask. She shrugs and says, "Oh, a thrift store somewhere."

Not Savers. Or Plato's Closet. Or the Goodwill in San Mateo, or Menlo Park, or Palo Alto, or Sunnyvale.

One day, as we're walking, Tracy says, "You know, I feel like it's not really the overalls. It's that we're chasing our lost youth."

Of course we're chasing our lost youth. We're two suburban middle-aged women who fret over the state of the world and lie awake at night worrying about our children and spend too much time on Poshmark and Zillow, imagining lives we can't have. It's not about the overalls at all. The overalls are not the holy grail. The holy grail is having a friend who will text you a link to a Poshmark listing that no longer fits who you've become, and you both know this, and you both understand why it's sad and funny at the same time.

MY BEST FRIEND

Christy Piszkiewicz

I will never forget the blonde-braided girl who seemed to be my age jumping in and out of two tan cardboard barrels full of grass clippings.

I was riding my bike in our alley when I spotted her.

In Chicago in the 1960s, these two-foot-tall, metal-rimmed heavy cardboard cylinders were used for storage. My mother stored her sewing scraps in them, and people used them when moving. Yet, to my astonishment, someone I had never seen before was springing and leaping in the grass-filled cans. I was drawn to her immediately.

Anne was born in Norway and lived with her divorced mother and two small brothers until her aunt and uncle adopted her when she was ten.

With no children of their own, they wanted to raise Anne in Chicago, where they lived. With Anne's mother's approval, Anne came to live in the United States with little conversation. In the 1960s, most parents didn't discuss family issues with their children. You just listened to your parents and did as you were told, not questioning the whys of arrangements. With my pre-adolescent mind, it never occurred to me to ask how she felt. As an adult, she worked to overcome her feelings of abandonment.

My parents were second-generation Polish immigrants who, just five years ago, moved from the Catholic Polish church and neighborhood, which had helped them thrive in this new country. The house on the northwest side of Chicago where my family of five lived was a significant step up in the American dream.

I longed for a good friend in this neighborhood full of younger children. She and her aunt and uncle magically moved across the alley from my house. Anne became my best friend when we were both ten. We spent every waking moment we could together.

We loved to read. Once a week, we'd bike down to the public library, bringing back stacks of books to devour and discuss. How did other girls and women overcome their dreary, simple lives, like ours, and become strong, intelligent, and famous? We just had to find out. We just had to find out the secrets.

Our shared love for reading and TV shows sparked our imagination. We would spend hours crafting elaborate stories inspired by our favorite shows, Man from U.N.C.L.E. and Hawaii Five-O. We would be the heroes, saving our country in our little world. We talked into "phone pens," dropped secret messages in our neighborhood, and sat next to fellow spies on the Chicago buses. In our minds, we'd use our brains, looks, and wisdom to save our world. With us as the main characters, these narratives gave us a sense of power in our lives. Anne would be the President, using her skills to prevent a nuclear war, while I would be the White House doctor, helping the staff keep it all together. We didn't think we had much control or influence over who we were, but we hoped we'd find the strength to become successful women.

In the 1960s, the term "stress" was not in our vocabulary, but the fear of Russia bombing the United States was a constant worry. We had drills in school to go under the desks and put our hands on our heads. It was a genuine threat to our lives. Anne and I could understand disappointing our parents with poor report cards or telling a fib; we could do something about that. But big worldly things that were out of our control scared us. We grew up together, hoping we could make a difference.

I attended a Catholic school and Anne, a Lutheran school, from elementary to high school. Living right across the alley from each other, we spent most of our free time with each other. Sharing each other's cultures enriched us as we grew up. I learned to love *krumkake*—a delicious, rolled cookie—and freshly made *lefse*, a kind of crepe with sugar and butter. Every year on May 17th, Norwegian Independence Day, you could find me celebrating with my best friend, often riding on the back of a flowery float. I even attended Vacation Bible School (VBS) with her for one week in the summer. My mother was very open-minded, as it would be years before Catholics had VBS sessions.

Our growing-up years were a time of innocence. The 1960s brought talk about the mysteries of sexual freedom, the supernatural, and how women were gaining a voice in society. We spent time trying to understand these complexities, searching for clues in books, overhearing private conversations, and attempting to understand jokes on the Laugh-In TV show. We were best friends who could share worries about body changes (will we ever have breasts?) and strange, frightening moods (I just screamed at my mother).

Our friendship taught us what to do when our peers snubbed us or did not invite us to an event. We also helped one another deal with the "My Parents Don't Understand Me" feelings that often crept into our lives.

Our friendship was magical.

I missed my best friend when her family traveled. They often spent Spring Break in Texas or Florida and sometimes went to Norway for the summer, which seemed like a fairytale existence so far from my life.

Going to different high schools meant we had less time to spend together. Even though our lives were busy with many new activities, we were instantly connected when given the opportunity.

After graduating from high school, I attended Wilbur Wright Junior College. Chicago offered free college for the first two years to residents.

Anne's uncle worked at Loyola University, giving Anne a free college education there. I was jealous of her attending this outstanding school, but I did well at my school and met many new friends of both genders. In college, I had a chance to make my own choices. Making my own plans was so freeing. Working in the college's AV (audiovisual) department, I was the only girl scheduling 40 or so male workers where to set up slide projectors, movie reels, and record players in the school building. Working 20 hours a week helped me learn how to talk to guys and save money. My newfound freedom was terrific. I planned to finish my degree in biology, and I could do that after completing my AA degree at Wright and transferring to a state school.

When I was a sophomore in college, Anne mentioned backpacking in Europe—staying in youth hostels and riding on trains with a Eurail Pass—with me; I jumped at the chance. No one I knew was planning such an adventure. It was very cheap to do this sort of traveling. The two months, including airfare, were under $2000, which I could afford.

We did a great deal of growing on that trip. During our travels, we met many friends from different cultures and mostly ate great food (did you know that a can of Spanish stew called tripe was garbage food?). Some of our Europe/UK adventures helped us realize the consequences of our actions. Deciding to take the last ferry in the dark from Dover (UK) to Calais (France) because the captain looked so handsome, the lights of the ship sparkled on the ocean water, and we loved the night crossing seemed like a beautiful idea until we landed in Calais at midnight when the youth hostels were closed for the night. Our guardian angels were working overtime, for we found a lovely lady who ran a pension and took us in. From then on, we checked into a hostel, the first thing we did when we came to a new city.

Sometimes, it seemed we escaped trouble with pure dumb luck. We left Rome the day before a cholera epidemic started. We ran a bit of the course just before the bulls came charging down at the Running of the Bulls Festival in Spain.

Learning to trust ourselves and each other made our time together so rich and life-assuring. Lifelong friendships can build you and stretch you to be greater than you would be if you had not met.

It is knowing and sharing life with that little blonde braided girl at ten that opened new worlds to me. I will always cherish my best friend.

GEORGIA

Merimee Moffitt

I didn't fixate on her at first. She was in my living room adjusting her shawl, rusty red hair cascading out and down. She wasn't petite or starved looking but stood there solid as a bull. "Hello," I must've said. "I'm Merimee." She said her name was Georgia and I indicated we should move out to my shady yard where poets were gathering to sit in rows of patio chairs. A giant wisteria acted as an outdoor cooling shrub. The grape arbor held an old chandelier to offset the darkening dusk. We were fed and comfortable, and I could tolerate Eleanor bringing a box of wine to my sober house, the yard sometimes an exception. A mic stand and amplifier faced the chairs in the lavender hues and longish old lawn green evening.

Georgia had brought her 20-something son, and they sat together. He was a bit standoffish when she introduced him to me. I wondered if he was there to hear her read or what?

Various poets were called off the sign-up list, mostly people whose work I knew. When Georgia read, my spirits jumped up: a woman who could really write. I understood my nervousness about meeting her. This happening was a divine setup, a gift. She gave care and respect to the depth of every word she read. Her material was stunningly personal whether the New Mexico mesa "Out back of Rayado" or to-die-for humor about the depreciating value of women, like cars, as they age. There were locals whose work also had had an instantaneous and forever effect on me, but Georgia was the first woman whose poetry resonated so deeply. I fell into a serious platonic swoon. You might call it love at first sound. She knows how to read with the nuance of a full and interesting life in her images and rhythms.

I didn't know then that she'd be a BFF, a bestie to me for 15 years now, but I knew I wanted to reach out and offer her a ride on my pony.

"Hey, wow," I said when the crowd took a break. "Are you busy Tuesday night? Come to Winnings Coffee Company on Harvard. I'll be reading something. 7 pm. Bring poems."

At Winnings she showed up with a different son and his wife and baby, and we started the first of years of telling and comparing our life stories. It was insane how many of our individual plots and paths had run parallel without crossing: numbers of kids, their same schools as my three, number of husbands, northern NM years in ramshackle cabins or *ranchitos,* hauling water, cooking on woodstoves, returning to UNM to complete our educations, both of us studying poetry for fun in alternate years with different teachers. Back then, we lived just blocks from each other.

We spent eons talking about our alcoholic mothers, our years in Al-Anon for the addicts we loved. We attended ACA (Adult Children of Alcoholics) together. Sharing rides and going to meetings and writing groups, we'd sit in our cars discussing endlessly our addicted loved ones.

She invited me to her salon-style writing group at the HOOKAH lounge in Belen, 30 miles south of Albuquerque, where she lived when I met her. We traveled to Europe meeting in Germany to visit my daughter then wrote a book together, *Berlin Poems and Photographs,* which won state and national awards. She has idioms that make a dark mood sunny. "Uh oh," she once said, "You look like you been drug through a knothole backwards." We both love the peaks and valleys of our semi-arid state, and those of our long-term drought-resistant friendship.

Our first holiday meal together we called the Bad Boy Thanksgiving. Her oldest child with whom she'd had a falling out, hadn't come over for years. My first-born son and troubled one, had been estranged via his struggles with drugs, but these two eldest kids were available, and they both seemed willing, even eager, to call a truce, no questions asked. It went so well for us and it's been going well since: the food was great—they knew it would be, and we got to spend time with my son's new girlfriend, her son's new wife, and her kids and his kids. Bonds were reasserted and love was appreciated by all. It took a bit of effort and time to walk Georgia out of her stereotypes and labeling regarding drug addicts, but she was willing once she met them. I'm still battling my judgment about her husband's deep dive. He was a nice guy before his decline. But Georgia and I hash it over with time limits on her repetitive astonishment about his behavior. Fortunately, she can laugh and dust herself off. At our age, there's so many reasons, good ones, to stick it out. Besides coddling her husband, she has a small child her youngest son came home with seeking shelter from an adventuress marriage gone bad. Her house has a lovely tiny apartment that she gave to the baby and his father. I grieved over being displaced but knew it was up to me to manage. All of us, everyone everywhere during the pandemic, were faced with existential threat, and my friend would face it all in her new position of Granny-nanny.

At the same time, my daughter on the East Coast was having a pandemic baby, followed by another, three years later. My fear of germ-sharing was foremost, vaccinations required, so I would be able to travel to see my kids and grandkids.

I begged Georgia to get an iPhone so we could FaceTime through the walls and barriers of Covid. It worked! One time she called with her screen on video and I, in a sleep state, couldn't tell right if I was looking at her or myself. The pandemic gave us both full heads of fluffy long silver-white hair. We met on our porches and in the parks to keep in touch. Supporting each other in vaccinations for all—toddlers and teenagers coming and going—she finally got Covid and had what she called her Covid Vacation.

We've traveled everywhere in Albuquerque, appeared at poetry venues on and off stage, performed together in Taos, Santa Fe, Burque, and Berlin. We encourage each other's writing and living. We are often called by each other's name even though we don't have similar faces. We have similar souls. She's a soul mate who lives a mile away. We used to walk to each other's houses. Now we walk halfway, meet in the middle and rest on a wall under a tree. We have our phones if one of us craps out with bad knees, bad breathing, old age issues, but after the heat waves pass, we'll be at it again. When her house burned down 12 years ago, she and her husband bought in our neighborhood just a mile away, intentional community.

Georgia is many generations New Mexican, grew up in Albuquerque. I've been here since 1980. When I get the urge to flee the desert and the looming heat and droughts, she asks me not to leave her. I've got the instinct of a salmon to return to where I am from.

She has buried a husband and divorced another. She's estranged from long lost half-siblings, just as I have lost besties and siblings to death and madness. We're getting old together. We love each other's families. We are close and comforting to each other. She shows up with her homemade *calabacitas* or fabulous made-up pies. We can count on each other, count our blessings and laugh at losses. We are poets. We grieve, love, and admire in well-turned phrases. We praise and study our favorites (oh Tony Hoagland!) Parallel lives unparalleled!

My Three L's
Kathie Arcide

For the last forty-five years, I've had three "Best Friends".

Delightfully, their names sound like those siblings whose parents chose names for their children all starting with the same letter. Lee, Linda and Lenore could not be more different from each other. They've brought an abundance of logic, loyalty, and love to my life. Their support of me all these years saved me again and again.

I met Lee in 1978 when he was a professor teaching child psychology at the university where I had been working and taking a few last classes as I started my psychotherapy practice. He was brilliant but slightly pompous about it. I was a smart ass and had no problem pointing that out to him. We became instant friends.

...

In our years together, Lee and I experienced just about every form of relationship two people can have. Friends, teacher/student (in both directions), romantic partners (a short stretch we just had to try), "siblings" (his parents adopted me as one of their own), Psychotherapy Community leaders, co-therapists and business partners.

He retired before me and in the last 13 years, Lee and his wife Patty, I call her my "best-friend-in-law", have lived in Madrid. They have returned to Washington state for 6 to 8 weeks a year to stay with us. Because that worked so well, we all built a huge addition to James's original mountain home where he and I live part time. This fall, Lee and Patty will move here from Spain, and as we've always dreamed, the four of us will wind down at our Casa Esmeralda, finishing our "final rides" together.

...

I met Lenore in a professional support group for new therapists doing their personal work. It brought out the worst competition and the best ethics in budding young practitioners. It was intimidating to clear out the issues left in our own psychological "basements" in front of several others who were scanning for newly learned diagnoses. Lenore and I bonded, drawn to each other in our determination to be in the healthy, ethical, loving therapist category.

We decided early on that our relationship was much more sister-like than just being friends, so we made a deal to be connected to each other, like family, for life. Sometimes we don't even like each other but we love each other in that permanent sister way. Here we are, 47 years later, having shared all of life's ups and downs. I had the honor of standing up for her at her wedding, being at the birth of her only child, living through the long dying process of her husband, and the joy of watching her finally find, and marry, her sweet husband now of 20 years, a match made in heaven. I claim John as my "brother-in-law" whether he likes it or not.

The real fun started 18 years ago when our two men met each other. James and John discovered so many parallels in their lives, not the least of which was they had both built unique homes from scratch, in amazingly similar ways, using found, reclaimed and repurposed materials. They both still work on their masterpiece homesteads, but now, have additional expertise from each other. James helped them build a lovely green house, and John expertly tiled the beautiful master bathroom in the Casa.

Lenore and John live an idyllic life on their beautiful Bamboo Farm in the San Juan Islands north of Seattle. Their place has a huge pond, with an entertaining variety of wildlife. They also have gorgeous gardens full of flowers and vegetables; people travel distances to tour the Farm. Lenore is a Master Gardener, and I am so proud of her expertise, not to mention her fantastic cooking!

On a good day, it's a three-hour drive and ferry ride for us to visit them in person. These days we mostly see them when James and I housesit their paradise while they take their yearly sailing trip all around the Islands. Sometimes in the summer they make the long trek to visit us in Spokane.

Lenore recently retired from her community leader roles and from her long-time therapy practice, in which I had the privilege of participating. We have always worked well together, and I was her Monday night group co-therapist for a time.

We still fight like sisters, and love like sisters, and she is often my most trusted human.

...

I met Linda first, before my other two L's. With our then husbands, we randomly crossed paths in a campground in Biloxi, Mississippi in 1971. Both couples were camping all over the country, looking for the place where we wanted to settle down. Linda was a conservative Jewish girl from Ohio. I was a full-blown Peacenik/Flower Child. But somehow it worked instantly! Within a couple of hours, Linda and her husband had given us the keys to their flat in New York city so we would have a place to sleep on that leg of our journey.

We all chose to live in the Pacific Northwest. Turns out, Portland, Oregon, and Bellevue, Washington are the perfect distance from each other to maintain a wonderful, lifelong, best-friendship.

In our early married lives, Linda and I would cut the three-hour drive in half and meet weekly in Centralia, WA, for conversation-packed lunch visits while our kids were in school.

We have that rare relationship that needs no regular feeding to keep it alive and thriving. We developed a shorthand language and were able to use the telephone as our lifeline, sometimes daily, sometimes not for months, but we'd always start right where we left off, as if no time had lapsed.

We've laughed at how often over these 53 years, we've been in the exact opposite place in our lives. That freed us to be unconditionally supportive of each other, with no competition, ever. It was almost like taking turns with life's inevitable challenges. I'd go through a divorce, but she'd be solid in her marriage. She'd have trouble with one of her babies, but I'd been through that stage successfully. I'd be in love, and she'd be single. She'd be discovering herself as a woman in a new relationship, and I'd be in a long stretch of chosen celibacy. I'd have an empty nest, and she'd still be immersed in the activities of her three children.

Linda was moved early in our friendship when she was having problems breastfeeding. Without a thought, I simply climbed in the car and drove the three hours, so I could share my expertise as a La Leche Leader with her in person.

And later, I can't describe how loved I felt when she surprised me, not once but twice, by hopping on planes to be with me at the memorials for my father-in-law, and just two months later, my dad.

Linda still holds the title in my heart of "*Best* Best Friend."

. . .

I've shared about each of them individually. Let me tell you something about them collectively. One time I read a book called *Still Loved by the Sun; a Rape Survivor's Journal* by Migael Scherer. Unexpectedly, I found myself thrown into a tough round of PTSD remembering my own sexual assault survival.

Guess what they did? They didn't often interact with each other, but in this circumstance, they each read that book too, so they could understand more of what I had been through. And then, in a gesture formerly reserved just for my biggest birthdays, they got together. They planned how to "triple-team" me, and then loaded me up with amazing love and support.

I mean, who does that? My Three L's, that's who!

And I am forever grateful!

Author's note:
More gratitude for my wonderful Flash Writing Group. Eight of us have been through several classes together now and have become dear friends. My Writing Sisters were so gracious in helping me edit this piece. We have bravely shared our most private, precious and experimental writing with each other, and received loving, supportive feedback, given in Story Circle Network's wonderful tradition of unconditional encouragement for women to tell their stories.

FRIENDS: A KISS, A HUG, AND A DANCE

Carol J. Wechsler Blatter

I'm thinking about our survivors. Our daughters. And our granddaughters. Will they be fortunate enough to have lifelong friendships like ours? I remember the look on Pat's face when we met recently after many years apart. Her eyes widened. Her joyful tears flowed. Her smile illuminated. Her lips, perfectly applied with frosted pink lipstick, formed a treasured kiss on my right cheek. I returned the kiss on her left cheek. We hugged. We danced up and down free of embarrassment from any onlookers.

...

Serendipity brought us together, two two-year-olds, Pat and me. My family lived next door to Pat's aunt and uncle and when she and her mom visited our mothers brought us together.

I'm imagining what it was like meeting each other. The scene is set in my family's apartment's kitchen. Pat greeted me carrying a fuzzy faux brown bear she held onto tightly. I greeted her by showing her my small rubber doll wearing a tattered, faded pink dress that must have been handed down from my sister. Despite its condition, I loved her. Talking between us may have been limited to a few words, "My bear." "My doll." "My mommy," pointing to mine. "My mommy," pointing to her mommy. I picture us standing and looking at each other making eye contact, maybe staring at first, then sharing smiles. Slowly, gaining more confidence, we dropped our lovies and took tiny steps holding hands marching in place, then bigger steps, and getting more creative we walked in circles around each other. Seeing a blanket on a green linoleum-covered floor we plopped down. We eyed the toys. We rolled over and each one of us found something to play with. What kind? Maybe we played with Mom's pots, pans, and wooden spoons to pretend to be drummers. With short attention spans we wanted something else to do. Mom noticed. She went to the closet and took out some funny brightly colored papier mâché hats. With excitement, we danced around wearing them. Then we ate tiny half-peanut butter sandwiches with a little strawberry jelly inside. Messy faces of course! Our mothers did the cleanup.

...

Years elapsed. We lived far enough apart that we went to different elementary schools. After completing fourth grade at age nine, we went to sleep away camp. Going together offset any fears of being away from home for three weeks at University Settlement Camp in Beacon, NY. Here Pat and I shared the joy of singing together. We followed the lead from a then-young folk singer, Peter Seeger, who lived in Beacon and came to our camp to entertain us. We sang "Everybody Loves Saturday Night" in several languages, like in Spanish, "A Todo El Mundo Le Encanta El Sábado Por La Noche." "She'll Be Coming 'Round the Mountain When She Comes," and a variety of this song, "She'll Be Wearing Pink Pajamas When She Comes," then "The Sloop John B," and "Michael Row the Boat Ashore." We sang a song about the Titanic. It was fun to us; we were oblivious to the meaning of this tragedy. As kids, we never thought about death.

...

There were two summers we spent together at Girl Scout camp. Billed as "rustic," we can agree this was true. The other camp was luxurious compared to Camp Brady and Camp Andree Clark. Here we slept on army cots in tents. I didn't mind the tent, and neither did she. We agreed the food was terrible. We dreaded those meals. Welsh Rarebit, often served as a topping on bread, and by itself, originally named Welsh Rabbit, had nothing to do with rabbits. The back story was about the English snubbing their noses at the Welsh who could not afford to eat rabbit. Only those waxy, dry, tasteless lima beans were worse than eating Welsh Rarebit.

...

I remember those long wintry walks from the train station to the Henry Street Playhouse where we took dance and drama lessons. Our cheeks red, our steamy breaths emitted, bundled in heavy winter coats, scarves, wool gloves, and warm wool-lined boots, we were briefly rescued from winter weather's wrath by eating irresistibly hot, freshly fried crinkle-cut French fries from a street vendor using our allowance money for these purchases. Barely waiting even a minute, we began to devour them, leaving just a few for the rest of the walk.

...

Although neither of us have become professional actresses and dancers we grew with knowledge of the arts and an expanded view of the world beyond our little sheltered places with our families in Brooklyn. Now we realize how lucky we were to learn from many teachers at the Henry Street Playhouse who made significant national and international contributions to the arts as successful actors and dancers, our drama teacher, Archie Smith, and our dance teachers, Gladys Bailin Stern and Phyllis Lamhut, with the newly formed Alwin Nikolais Dance Company.

...

1953. Columbia University's theater was then named the McMillan Theater, now the Kathryn Bache Miller Theater. Some Columbia and Barnard students, part of the drama club, decided to perform the play, "The Enchanted," by Jean Giraudoux. In addition to the adult actors, they needed young girls who could be Eumenides. Where to find them? The Henry Street Playhouse. Once asked to act in this play, Pat and I happily agreed. A few other girls from our drama class were also picked for these parts. Together, we all went to their school where they made costumes for us, black below-the-knee dreary, nondescript dresses, devoid of any design except for small white Peter Pan collars.

...

Years passed. We never forgot each other even as life's happenings sent us in different directions. She graduated from Brooklyn College. I graduated from Upsala College in New Jersey. She was an elementary school teacher; I was a clinical social worker in private practice.

...

Now in retirement, I have become a published writer. My favorite genre is creative nonfiction, and I have a budding interest in writing memoir. Pat tells me that she has a very busy life in retirement which includes aerobics, so she is very fit. Dancing is her passion. She said that dancing creates endorphins that help her feel euphoric. We are both fortunate. Age isn't preventing us from living full and exciting lives.

FRIENDSHIP, COLLABORATION, AND MAGIC

Sue Boggio

I was ten years old in 1963 when President Kennedy was assassinated. All of the adults were distracted and sad. The TV sets in Iowa began to show a war brewing in southeast Asia. My parents sold the house I had come to consciousness in, a lovely little green cottage with a grove of pine trees perfect for forts and secret gardens. We moved a few miles northwest into a new subdivision where all the trees were so spindly they were tied by ropes attached to stakes pounded into the earth so they wouldn't blow away.

The new neighborhood was lonely. My little sister was only six and, therefore, boring. I decided to walk two blocks to the new grade school I'd be attending in the fall. I thought about The Beatles—the only interesting thing in my life. When I saw them on Ed Sullivan, my breath caught in my chest, and I felt something I'd never experienced before: elation pierced by sadness. On the commercial break, I found I had squeezed my fists so tightly my fingernails had made little half-moon cuts in the tender flesh of my palms.

Near the school there was a house with a girl in the yard who looked about my age. She had wavy long dark hair, and she held the collar of her mean-looking dog so it wouldn't attack me. We knew each other at first sight.

Mare was short and round and I was tall and skinny. Mare was Lennon and I was McCartney. Jewish and WASP. Brash and funny, reserved and serious. Mare taught me how to giggle and I taught Mare how to think deep thoughts. We played Beatles music nonstop and spent every minute we could together. We started our sentences with "What if" and let our imaginations run wild with scenarios in which we would meet John and Paul and impress them with our sarcastic wit and beyond-our-years maturity. These "what ifs" became stories with dialogue, twisty plots, and surprise endings. We harmonized to Beatle songs while Mare learned guitar.

We were the Beatles for Halloween, even though the girl who was supposed to be George dropped out at the last minute to be a ventriloquist with her Chatty Cathy doll. Mare quipped we should still include her as our opening act and go as the Ed Sullivan show. We performed Love Me Do and were the hit of the neighborhood.

Mare and I became teenagers in 1967. John and Paul were still our muses for our creative collaboration. We would brainstorm for hours, astounding our families, peers, and teachers that we never ran out of things to talk about. Our words overflowed into long rambling notes, stories, poems, and essays. We kept all of this in a fat notebook hidden in Mare's footlocker.

The war in Vietnam raged and older kids we knew were drafted. The Beatles' music became dark and psychedelic, changing as we were. Mare and I wrote about other things now, but still found our inspiration in the partnership of Lennon and McCartney.

The Beatles broke up in 1970, but we understood. They just needed to explore their individuality. They still loved each other, deep down.

When high school graduation loomed in 1972, I made plans to attend nursing school. Mare would go to New York City to study musical theater. It hurt like hell, but we understood. It was time to give up childish things.

Living over a thousand miles away from each other, we drifted apart because it was easier than keeping the feelings fresh. We sacrificed our friendship to be able to forge these adult lives we were supposed to be leading.

By 1980, eight years had gone by without significant contact. I had a precious two-year-old daughter and a failing marriage I didn't want to admit to. Meanwhile, Mare was miserable in Pennsylvania living with her husband and his parents. Each of us privately wrote sad poetry we showed to no one, especially each other.

On December 8, 1980, John Lennon was murdered. Mare heard first and grabbed the phone, desperate to reach me. She called my parents in Iowa to get the phone number where I was working as an RN on the evening shift at an inpatient adolescent psychiatric center. The kids were in bed. It was quiet. Time to chart and look forward to going home. The desk phone rang, and I answered it—worried it might be an emergency admission that would require me to stay late. Mare was crying, John Lennon was dead.

I called Mare back when I got home and we talked all night, pouring out our grief, our rage, and the truth about our lives. That next summer, Mare came to New Mexico to visit. We began writing again, long letters requiring extra postage containing stories we would add onto and pass back and forth across the country. We visited each other two or three times a year and ran up huge phone bills in between. We cursed each postage increase, stuffing ten- or twenty-page letters with our stories into envelopes. On her visits, Mare fell in love with New Mexico and vowed to live here someday.

I found the courage to end my dysfunctional marriage. Life was too short to live without happiness, John Lennon's untimely death had awakened me to that. I became a single mom, poor but contented. I found my forever love and remarried in 1986. Mare was struggling with her own marriage but not ready to leave it yet.

The most pivotal event occurred when Mare moved to Albuquerque in 1988. We sat in her new living room, 34 years old, marveling at the power of our friendship. Now that we were finally living in the same city again, we would create something together, something big. We tossed around ideas. It would be fun to own a funky vintage clothing and antique store together but had no start up cash. Writing was in our blood and free to pursue. We would learn how to write novels.

Mare joined the staff at the psychiatric center, finding the work as rewarding as I did. Due to our experiences there, we decided the guiding theme in all of our books would be: although it is the human condition to be wounded in relationships, it is only through the alchemy of relationships that we heal and fully evolve as human beings.

After 14 years of dogged determination, we had completed four unpublished novels and a screenplay, enjoyed encouraging successes and survived heartbreaking rejections. Now, in 2004, we were finally celebrating our first published novel: *Sunlight and Shadow,* a book about friendship and hope. We wrote two more to complete our Esperanza, New Mexico trilogy: *A Growing Season* and *Long Night Moon.* All three have won awards, including each winning the Tony Hillerman Award for Best Fiction in 2013, 2014, and 2017, making us the first three-time winners in the history of the prestigious award. In 2019, *Long Night Moon* also won the Zia Book Award from the New Mexico Press Women. All of our literary accomplishments have sprung from our mutual dedication to our creative partnership that was born from (and is sustained by) our abiding friendship.

In 2023, our fiction collaboration continued with the publication of our novel *Hungry Shoes,* inspired by our long careers at the inpatient adolescent psychiatric center, an uplifting story about two teen girls, and how their friendship helped them heal from their trauma.

We're both retired now and thoroughly astonished that we turned 70 this year. When we look at each other, we don't see the obvious evidence of our aging. Instead, we see timeless souls who have been traveling together for over 60 unbelievably quick years. Together, we've been young, old, and everything in between as age and time itself becomes another absurdity to share.

Magic happens in the alchemy of collaboration—taking the best each has to offer and combining it to make something neither of us could have created alone, in our books, in our lives, in our very selves.

Friendship isn't a big enough word for all that we've shared. We have so much yet to talk about. So much still to say. One lifetime will not be enough.

Best Friends for Life

Charlotte Wlodkowski

Where would I be without my best friend—lost. I'd be sitting in a corner, allowing someone else to control my life. I would have no thoughts of my own, nor would I be who I am today, an independent person.

Some so-called friends linger too long, while others leave too soon. Many work their way into our lives with deceit only to gain something for themselves. A true friend follows us on our road through life. They are always there, inspiring, giving encouragement, and silently sitting with us in our moment of sadness. All is done in a gentle and mindful way.

She was a member of an organization I joined. It's been so long ago that I don't remember how we began a 25-plus-year friendship. I do recall the first time an offer of help came from her. I was on a committee and watched committee leaders give reports at the podium. I admired these women and said so. Without a second thought, she offered to teach me the art of public speaking. She supported my endeavors with, "You can do this." She patiently critiqued my words, my stance, and my eye contact. It was the whole deal. At one point, we travelled together and spoke at schools and businesses about the benefits of our organization.

A complete trust grew between us. We gave each other permission to speak our minds, without the loss of friendship. The two of us enjoyed sharing ideas and planning events. We attended numerous seminars and conventions, always knowing we would discuss the day's activities.

There were times when I called, and she listened to me rant and rave about something I deemed unfair. She gave me courage to elevate my career path. My best friend held my hand during the breakup of my marriage.

I knew she was only a phone call away. On one such occasion, my manager assigned me to set up a communications room for an off-site training session. Of course, I agreed without knowing what was needed in a communications room. I immediately called my best friend, and she walked me through it.

Throughout our friendship, she taught me the importance of listening. This definitely aided my career. We became a duo, a two-for-one in our organization which advanced our chapter efforts. Our life has slowed as we no longer are involved in the organization. However, we still try to make a difference in whatever we do.

At this point in our lives, it is my turn to be there for my best friend. Her beloved spouse passed away after many years of illness. He was the only man she ever knew. I can hear the pain in her voice and see the tears erupting at the mention of his name. She is falling apart, and I want to convince her she remains relevant to this world. I know she still has much to teach others.

Although I am retired and she continues to work, we talk on a regular basis. We both know we will always be there for each other with love and understanding.

STRING BEAN JEAN AND CLARA COMMODE

Claire Butler

Not the most flattering of nicknames for two best friends, but somehow, we rose above them. Jean and I met on one of the hottest summer days of 1960. I was walking home from the neighborhood market with a popsicle, and she was hanging on the wrought iron railing of her small porch in a sleepy little suburb called North Riverdale, north of downtown Dayton, Ohio. I later learned that we were both five years old and heading to kindergarten the coming fall.

We stared at each other without a word between us, and I can't imagine what her first impression was of me, but she was so skinny that her legs resembled two long sticks topped by baggy-legged shorts, and her hair was the color and style of the Little Dutch Boy. She interrupted my thoughts…"I dare you to eat this." I looked at what she had pulled from one of her pockets.

"That's a *dog* biscuit," I said, wondering if she made a habit of eating dog food. She laughed.

"Yep, it is!" She giggled again.

"You first," I challenged. And to my astonishment, she took a bite, chewed it and swallowed it. Then she pulled another biscuit from her pocket, and said, "Your turn."

It would have been just plain unfriendly not to follow through with her request at that point. I inspected the biscuit, took one bite, chewed it and instinctively spit it into the grass. Jean fell into laughter. And that was the beginning of a 65-year-long friendship between us to this day.

Jean and I got our nicknames from one of the more inventive kids that hung around on Addison Avenue, which is where I lived. Jean lived two streets down on Wampler, the main drag near our homes, at the corner of FerDon. Somehow, Jean and I, forever inseparable, were tagged with "String Bean Jean" and "Clara Commode." Jean was tall and thin, so her nickname made sense, but they hijacked my name, Claire, and sang a little ditty, "Put another nickel in the Clara Commode," which offended me to no end because my name is "Claire," not Clara. And although we never knew just who in the neighborhood invented those nicknames, I had my suspicions.

The kids on Addison met each night in the street to play games and dance to rock and roll, which at the time was Elvis Presley and, later, the Beatles. Everyone gathered across from my house in Tommy's driveway and when we had enough kids, we formed teams for either kick-the-can or kickball. For the latter, the Clark boys had authentic baseball bases, so we placed them and played until dark on most nights. As word spread about how much fun our street was, kids from nearby streets wandered over to play. And, of course, Jean joined in because she already knew me, and a mutual friend of ours from kindergarten, Judy, who lived next door to me, joined us as well.

. . .

Jean had an older sister, Suzanne, and an older brother, Bob. I held a fascination for Bob as he rode a motorcycle, collected animal skeletons that had been professionally preserved, and his bedroom was in the loft of Jean's house. Unknown to him, when Bob was gone, Jean and I hung out in his room and played his 45 rpm records. Suzanne, who was ten years older than us two girls, shared a bedroom with Jean. They had twin beds, and when I spent the night with Jean, she and I shared her tiny bed. Pillow fights ensued.

By the time we were eight, Suzanne was in college, and it seemed to me that she did little else than study and wear her hair in big brush rollers. When I asked Suzanne how she slept with those rollers in her hair, Jean's mom, Betty, remarked that all three of us girls could use a good haircut. She called my mom and the next thing was Suzanne, Jean and I were on the Number 7 bus to downtown for haircuts at the beauty college.

This was not the first time I'd had my hair professionally cut, but it was the first time I saw women getting manicures. The odors of nail polish remover and ammonia from perm chemicals combined to intoxicate me, in a positive way. If that was what college was like, I was all for it because everyone was having fun.

We didn't have appointments, so we were called one-by-one to different beauticians (which is what they were called back then). Suzanne went first, and I was last. We were silent after our haircuts; we each paid three dollars for them and left a one-dollar tip, as Betty had instructed us. Mom had given me five dollars and two bus tokens. As soon as we got into the salon hallway to leave, we looked at each other, not knowing whether to laugh or cry. We had been scalped!

We marched single-file across Main Street to the Metropolitan department store and bought scarves for our bus ride home. I reported what my grandmother always said, "A bad haircut is temporary." It didn't comfort me nor did it comfort Jean, and Suzanne was horrified because she was dating boys.

...

Jean and I spent hours exploring the creeks that were situated down the middle of a boulevard just halfway between our two homes. We walked in them a quarter mile or so from one end to the other. The creeks were rarely dry, so we balanced rock to rock making our way. Needless to say, we often got wet feet! We marveled at frogs, crawdads, and the tiny minnows that would one day grow and swim in the Great Miami River, which is where the creek water ended its journey. We were fascinated by and unafraid of snakes. We turned over some of the bigger rocks—many were fossils thousands of years old—looking for them, and at times we'd catch one.

Betty was a believer in studying nature. During the summer, she enrolled Jean in rocks and minerals classes, nature walks, and other classes involving our natural world at the Museum of Natural History. I went with her and, while she was in class, I embarked on my own journeys inside the museum. We spent so much time there, that one day a staffer asked us to volunteer. So, every day, after Jean's classes, we worked in the baby wild animal wing of the museum. We cleaned snake cages, fed live mice to them, and did odd jobs that were asked of us by the museum staff. We walked or rode our bikes home through DeWeese Park, which was about two miles from Jean's house. We were never bored, but when Jean went to camp for two weeks every summer, I was so unhappy. We hated being separated, but Jean wrote to me every other day, and I lived the camp experience vicariously through her.

And so it was until 1967—we were twelve—when my family moved from Addison to a neighborhood about four miles west. I was sad to leave Jean, but unlike many moms at the time, Betty knew how to drive, and she made certain that our friendship held fast. I discovered that a four-mile walk to Jean's was very doable, and Betty always drove me home.

...

Jean and I attended different high schools but, on the bright side, I became fast friends with some of her new schoolmates; our circle of tight friends was growing. I didn't date much through high school, but Jean had a steady boyfriend. They married after Jean completed community college, and her husband enlisted in the Navy; they moved to San Diego. When Jean returned to Dayton two years later, our friendship picked up right where it had been before her move.

Over the years our friendship grew into a sisterhood. We shared memories, tragedies and joys, and many, many secrets. We laugh at so many things we recall from our days on Addison, we cry over our losses, and we support each other in ways that most people only experience with family. We chat by phone nearly every day and despite now living 60 miles apart, we work to see each other as often as possible.

We are sisters now, and forever.

AUDREY

MaryAnn Easley

When Audrey, my sophomore college roommate, got a summer job at Knott's Berry Farm, she encouraged me to do the same. Being best friends, it would be difficult to be apart. I lived in Los Angeles, and she suggested I stay at my Aunt Till's house in Long Beach, not far from where she lived. She thought my Aunt Till, a divorcee with a flirtatious eye for fun was less strict than my parents, I could save money, and we could shop and ride to work together since she had access to her fiancé's car while he was away at officer's candidate school.

It was an easy decision. Aunt Till enjoyed my company and cleared space for me, setting out a jar for my tip money to guarantee savings.

I interviewed and got the job even though I'd never waited tables in my life. By the time I received my official Knott's Berry Farm badge and bought my official uniform—a plaid shirt and a denim skirt from the employee's shop—Audrey had been on the job long enough at the Steak House to show me how to sneak ice cream cake from the freezer and buttery rolls from the bun warmer so we wouldn't be forced to buy the discounted employee's salad. She introduced me to the boy cooks who assigned us nicknames they yelled to waitresses through a narrow window when orders were ready.

For example, a boy cook would shout "Blackie, pick up!"—Blackie because my last name was Black—the sobriquet not as cute as Blondie or Toots, Lulu or Daisy Mae.

My tips were scarce due to my inability to multitask delivering trays of food in a timely manner and remembering to refill coffee cups. Audrey, far more adept at service, doubled her tips, but I had to rely on the hourly wage.

Famous for its Chicken House—specializing in fried chicken, mashed potatoes and gravy, biscuits, and boysenberry pie—Knott's hired only pink-cheeked grandmothers in white aprons; younger applicants were relegated to the Steak House. A perfect fit for Audrey who knew medium from rare. My parents didn't have money for meat. The first steak I ever ate was that summer at Audrey's house, a slab of sirloin that overflowed my plate, so thick it had to be cut with a special knife my family didn't own.

Audrey gave me driving lessons. She taught me about plucked eyebrows, shaved legs, tampon use, and insisted on breast-growing exercises. She'd taken modeling lessons in high school and knew about posture, walking properly, and swaying her hips.

I met her during freshman orientation in the living room of what had once been the lobby of an historic hotel that was now our dorm. Eighteen-year-old girls half-listened to a recitation of rules, curfews, dining room etiquette, expectations on room upkeep, rooftop sunbathing safety, and signing in and out at the front desk whenever we left the premises.

From where I sat on a sagging sofa, I could see a cluster of girls— residents of what had once been the hotel's bridal suite—shining like starlets on the artful curving stairs that accessed rooms above.

And there was Audrey in a red plaid dress with a curved neckline, her arched eyebrows perfectly plucked, hazel eyes bright, smiling directly at me! Her posture spoke volumes, daring others to challenge her status. Confidence haloed around her. I guessed that she once owned a horse, a dog named Laddy, and had a boyfriend named Jimmy. Didn't all my storybook heroines?

I thought to myself "Now there's a wild sort of girl," which both terrified and fascinated me; I had no wild streak at all. She was a risk taker, a free spirit. Rules were meant to be broken. If the dining room was closed, she'd know how to get into the kitchen to steal snacks. If a date kept her out past curfew, she'd find an open window to crawl through. No one in authority was going to tell her what to do.

Near the end of our freshman year, she passed me in the empty hall. "The weather's great," she confided. "Want to study in the park?"

Was she speaking to me? Was such a thing allowed? "Me? Uh, now?"

A roll of her shoulder shrugged off any argument.

Was it a dare? Weren't the rules clear enough? Still, it made sense since I took detailed notes, and she possessed a scintillating personality. At Sylvan Park, we debated Hemingway. If I suggested his brilliant conciseness, she held up his history with women. When our writing instructor commented I wrote like Hemingway, I thought it a compliment; she rolled her eyes.

Sometimes we took a beach pose on the grass; other times we sat at a picnic table. Our fervor to discuss F. Scott Fitzgerald and D.H. Lawrence escalated. To have such a friend enrolled in the same courses made studying more enticing. She critiqued my creative writing efforts, correcting grammar and verb tense. I interpreted

Plato's *Republic* and philosophy assignments. We each thought the other brilliant and studied on Saturdays until the sun set. "See? Isn't this place better than those stuffy old library stacks where everyone else studies?"

We'd often skip dinner in the dining hall to have spaghetti in Ontario or a chocolate malt in Loma Linda or take a break to drive around town to see the old mansions hidden behind ancient trees. I tried to retrace ancestral steps since it was the very town my parents had chosen as young lovers. Audrey said, "There's a story there. And you will write it."

We began studying together all the time, escaping downtown to the park or to the Smiley Public Library where we could perch in windowsills wide enough for two.

We were given more choices sophomore year and decided to room together at Fairmont Hall on campus. We chose a first-floor room with an escape window, which increased our popularity. She decided what sorority we should rush: Alpha Theta Phi since we'd already taken up residence in the Theta Wing. Also, Audrey pointed out that all the coolest most popular girls belonged.

We went through Rush Week together.

I got in; she didn't.

A turning point.

I wanted to back out; she wouldn't let me. Had her popularity with upperclassmen threatened senior Thetas? Being blackballed was the ultimate shock since Audrey was the coolest girl I'd ever known—like main characters in my favorite novels. She'd never been rejected for anything. She knew how to walk, stand, and pose in the most photogenic provocative way. She possessed status, poise, and finances.

Would Greek life divide us? Would I lose the only friend I'd ever really had? No one had Audrey's independence or appeal. Sorority girls dressed alike and thought alike. Lockstep. I went through the motions of Pledge Week, I dutifully obeyed every command and attended weekly meetings. During hours of exclusion, Audrey resorted to studying in the library stacks. There, she encountered an upperclassman, a town boy who was a handsome fraternity man and drama student, the best dancer in school. She fell in love, becoming engaged before any of the rest of us.

Our college was a Christian sort of school with religion a required subject. We scored points by attending church on Sundays; buses arrived to take us downtown to the First Baptist where professors were deacons or sang in the choir.

"Church is such a waste of clothes," Audrey complained one Sunday as she tore off another cashmere. "Our coats will cover everything. Let's wear only a bra and panties." Another dare? With our hats adjusted, gloves pulled on, and high heels in place, we appeared proper enough. However, I hesitated.

"Don't be such a goody two-shoes," she scolded.

The idea of being half-naked before deacons and God and the whole congregation made me giggle. Would she shock boys on the bus? Would her coat fall open as we rose—like good girls—with our hymnals in hand?

Chosen to be her maid of honor the following June, she promised I could borrow her wedding dress whenever I got married. And I did.

Now 70 years later, I'm grateful she's still my BFF. We meet to shop together, and she still challenges me to be my better self, to risk and feel life in all its intensity.

UNBROKEN BOND

Sara Etgen-Baker

through trials and triumphs, we've stood side by side
  in whispered secrets and shared dreams
    in each other we confide
      our souls entwined like rivers and streams

I hear echoes of laughter, echoes of memories, echoes of tears
  in your eyes I see reflections of my soul
    and a friendship timeless, slaying dragons of fear
      with one another we console and frequently praise and extol

in the silence between words, our hearts converse
  in your presence I find peace and serenity
    no need to pretend, no need to rehearse
      for we share a bond, a kinship deep with authenticity

with hearts grateful our friendship continues to bloom
  in a bountiful garden where faith and hope flourish
    patience, mindfulness, and careful tending we consume
      our friendship is perennial like forget-me-nots, never will it perish

THE COFFEE BREAK

Kathryn Haueisen

A neighbor introduced Jean to me back in 1976 when she and I were both home raising young children and trying to fit in a little writing during their elusive naps. The neighbor thought we needed to know one another so she invited us and our four children over for coffee. My daughters, Carol and Karen, were five and three. Jean's sons, Nick and Pete, were three and eight months. Karen and Nick became great playmates. Carol loved being a junior mom to baby Pete. At that coffee break we started a friendship that has seen us through multiple phases of life for nearly 50 years.

Initially we watched each other's children once a week so each of us had a child-free day to write or manage whatever else life might require of us. Whenever we had four healthy children, sufficient funds, and enough maternal energy, we'd put the kids in the back of one of our cars and head off on a child-friendly adventure. In summer months Delaware State Park, some 30 miles from our Columbus, Ohio neighborhood, was a popular destination. There the little ones splashed in the lake while we enjoyed a little adult conversation.

Realizing how worn-out young children and long car trips often result in meltdowns and fights, we planned ahead with a bag of marshmallows for the trip home. For every ten minutes that passed with no crying, complaining, or conflicts, whichever mother wasn't driving passed out a round of marshmallows. I doubt Dr. Spock would have approved; but then I doubt he ever had to transport cranky kids in wet bathing suits.

At other times we might pack picnic lunches for trips to a park with a playground or go to a museum together. In December we braved the elements and the crowds to take them downtown to see the holiday decorations and visit the red-suited jolly fellow who inquired what they wanted for Christmas.

When we weren't up to the challenge of car outings, we'd give the kids water-filled plastic bottles and let them chase each other around the yard. From the dry zone of Jean's porch swing we planned events for the "Mom Olympics" we thought someone should sponsor. Events would include "Fastest diaper changer," "Most food *in* rather than *on* the baby," and "Fastest time to get a child dressed in boots, jacket, mittens, and scarf."

Eventually we got our husbands involved. Eating out proved too expensive for our tight family budgets, but we could afford to split the cost of a babysitter. Several times a year we'd park all four children at one home with the sitter, plenty of snacks, and a pile of kid-appropriate books and movies. Then we adults enjoyed a long, leisurely home-cooked meal at the other house.

As Nick and Karen approached kindergarten age, we decided it was time to explore options to re-enter into the world of income-earning adults. We each applied for a variety of editorial positions. Much to our surprise and delight, we discovered we'd both applied for the same position at a state agency. The job consisted of writing press releases, brochures and updating an agency calendar of events.

When we discovered we'd both made it to the list of finalists for the same job, we hatched what we thought was a brilliant plan. We'd share the job. While we were both eager to spend more time around people who could cut their own meat, we weren't really sold on the idea of being gone from home forty or more hours a week.

We made an appointment to talk with the man in charge of filling the position. For 15 or so minutes we did our best to convince him of the numerous advantages of our plan. We'd watch each other's children while the other one was at work. We already knew this was a workable arrangement. We could split the job mornings and afternoons, or Monday through lunch Wednesday and after lunch Wednesday through Friday. Or every other week. We could easily cover for each other for vacations or should one have to stay home with a sick child. The agency would save money because both our husbands had jobs with insurance, so we could waive the agency health insurance plans. We thought it was a great idea.

He did not agree. He sat in stunned silence for what seemed like an hour but was probably only a half minute or so. Then he told us, "That won't work. I'm going to hire one of you. You decide which one."

I took the job. Jean took another job. I worked at the agency a year before my husband's job took us out of town. I no longer remember the name of the man who hired me. But to this day, whenever Jean and I talk about our brilliant job-sharing plan we conclude we were just too ahead of the times for a state agency.

Jean and her family stayed in Columbus. My family started a series of moves that ended our regular moms-united child rearing collaborations. Years later a move took us to Houston where Jean's son Nick decided to go to college at Rice University. That facilitated a few reunions since Nick married and settled in Houston.

After years in Texas, our daughter Karen chose to go to college back in Columbus. When she graduated, she got a job that intersected with Jean's husband Bill's work, allowing us to connect vicariously through that connection. With some family in Ohio, we visited Ohio often, usually managing to visit Jean and Bill when we did.

I can still picture our family room in LaGrange, Texas, the year I opened Jean's Christmas card and read that she and Bill were divorcing. I was shocked. The four of us had been friends for decades. A few years later she married Al, a friend she'd known in college. After Al's wife died, he contacted Jean. They now live in Michigan, where they've recently celebrated their 25th anniversary. My brother and sister-in-law live near them, so I've managed to reconnect with Jean occasionally in person when I've visited my Michigan family.

Back in 2002 it was my turn to shock Jean with the news that Jim and I were divorcing. We were still in Texas, but with family in Ohio and Michigan, I made regular visits to the area. Two years ago I decided to retire in Ohio where some of my family still lives. Though we're living closer to each other than we have in years, we're also closer to 80 than 70. That means we have to sometimes account for assorted health issues in making plans. Nonetheless, between email, snail mail, and phone calls, we manage to stay in touch.

A lifetime has passed since that coffee break at a mutual neighbor's home. Our children's children are now all out of high school and settling into their young adult years. The men who made us mothers have moved on without us. Yet, the bond we forged as a mom team of two has kept us linked through the decades. I am forever grateful to that neighbor who decided Jean and I should meet one another. Jean's friendship has been an anchor through the assorted storms of life.

FRIENDSHIP IS LOVE

Linda Healy

Friendship is a view into someone else's mind.
It is kind and thoughtful.
Friendship is beautiful and bountiful.
Friendship is trust and intimacy.
It is to be devoured and relished.
Friendship is love.

Friendship is for cherishing.
It is alive and joyous like a blossoming flower.
Friendship memories are to savor for always.
Friendship is respect.
It is an opportunity to know and be known.
Friendship is love.

Friendship is a blessing and a privilege.
It might mean late night phone calls or interventions.
Friendship is a juicy, sweet, sweet peach.
Friendship is having someone to sing and dance with.
It is a miracle that might end when you least expect it.
Friendship is love.

Friendship is someone to jump over puddles with.
It is tender and sometimes fragile.
Friendship may be long distance.
Friendship may take back up where it left off years before.
It is to be held tenderly in the palm of your hand.
Friendship is love.

Friendship may be a joy beyond belief.
It just happens.
Friendship cannot be expected.
Friendship may sometimes be bittersweet.
If you are lucky someday your memories may be just sweet.
Friendship is love.

Friendship takes courage to stare down the wounds life bestows.
It requires holding a hand and finally holding nothing.
Friendship is to be surrendered; someday it must end.
Friendship is to be understood.
Even when we can't, we must.
Friendship is love.

HOLY RIVALRY

Joy Packard-Higgins

As she hurried toward the ringing telephone, Lucille dried her hands on a dishtowel. "I'm comin'. Hold your horses." She picked up the receiver, slightly out of breath. "Hello?"

"Hi, it's Mildred. Hot enough for you today?"

"Hi, Mildred. I've got the AC running. It's nice in the living room."

"Did you get the Baptist Messenger article I sent you?"

Lucille frowned as she dug through the pile of bills, advertising flyers, and magazines on the telephone table. Finding the heavily underlined newspaper clipping, she sighed. "Yes, Mildred. I got it."

"Well, did you read it?" Mildred's tone was expectant, almost pressing.

"Of course I read it." *I knew you'd be calling.*

"Well?"

Lucille sighed. Mildred loved to cut edifying articles from newspapers and newsletters and send them to people she felt needed the message. No one was exempt from her scissors and red pen.

"I don't see how an article on dressing modestly applies to me. My skirts have been the same mid-calf length for over 40 years. I always wear stockings. What's your point?"

"I'm not one to gossip, but some of the skirts the girls wear to church are pretty short." Mildred's voice dropped to a whisper. "I swear, I don't think they wear slips, either."

"And?"

"Lucille, we've been friends for 20 years. I'm telling you this out of the goodness of my heart. Maybe you should take a look at the length of your granddaughter's skirts. You don't want her sending the wrong message. You know how boys are. My Donita's skirts are always below her knees."

Lucille heard the crunch of tires on gravel. Someone was pulling into her driveway. Clutching the telephone receiver, she peered out her living room window.

"Mildred, I need to let you go. The preacher is here."

"You didn't tell me Brother Atwood was coming to see you."

"I didn't tell you because I didn't know. Bye." Lucille hung up and scurried around the living room, picking up newspapers, straightening the white crocheted doily on the console TV, and removing a used glass from the maple end table.

She glanced into the tiny hallway mirror, smoothing back a few errant strands of short, salt-and-pepper hair. *And here's me wearing an old house dress—no time to change. Thank heaven, I'm wearing a brassiere!*

She opened the door to reveal a tall, gaunt man in a blue seersucker suit, white shirt, and blue tie.

"Brother Atwood, what a nice surprise!"

"Miz Benton, how are you on this fine summer day?" The preacher's voice was silky smooth.

"Come on in out of this heat. I've got the window air conditioner goin', and it's cool in the front room." Lucille led him into the small living room. "Would you like a glass of iced tea? I made some fresh this mornin'."

"I would, thank you." Brother Atwood folded his lanky frame onto Lucille's sofa, moving the coffee table to avoid bumping his knees.

Lucille bustled into the kitchen. She slid a metal ice tray from the small freezer compartment of her elderly GE refrigerator and grabbed a pitcher of iced tea. She set these items on the countertop and pulled the lever of the ice tray, sending shards of ice flying. She selected two tall glasses from the cupboard and filled them with ice and tea. After placing a slice of peach pie on a glass dessert plate with a fork, she carried the refreshments to her visitor and set them on the coffee table. She quickly returned with her glass and several paper napkins.

The preacher eyed his plate appreciatively. "Miz Benton, aren't you having any pie?"

"No sir, I had a piece with my lunch. I couldn't eat another bite. But you go ahead and dig in." Lucille sipped her tea. *I wonder what the preacher wants besides some refreshments.*

"Miz Benton, that was one fine peach pie! I can't remember the last time I tasted one as good," Brother Atwood said, setting his fork-topped plate on the coffee table.

"Thank you, sir. How's Miz Atwood feelin' now? We prayed for her arthritis at our Women's Missionary Union meeting." *Even though she thinks she's better than the rest of us.*

"What would the church do without the good ladies of the WMU? Marnella's feeling much better, thank you for asking. I'm sure the prayers helped. As the Book of James says, 'The effectual fervent prayer of a righteous man availeth much.' I reckon that applies to women, too," he nodded sagely.

"Can I get you some more iced tea, Brother Atwood?"

"Thank you, Miz Benton, but no. I do have something I'd like to discuss with you."

What can it be? Cecil and I tithe and are at church every time the doors open. I haven't had a spat with anyone in over six weeks.

"As you know, Miz Robinson has moved to Twilight Meadows since she broke her hip," the preacher shook his head sadly. "That leaves us without a coordinator for the Bereavement Committee. When I learned of this need, I immediately thought of you, Miz Benton. You're a natural leader," he beamed, proud of his clever idea. "Would you consider filling this essential position?"

I knew it! More work for me. I already work in the church nursery on Wednesday and Sunday nights. I'm in charge of refreshments for Vacation Bible School next month and serve on the Clothing Closet Committee. I've made my famous potato salad for every funeral meal for the past 20 years.

"What about Miz Hobart? She's very organized." *Someone else needs to do this.*

"Miz Hobart has a part-time job in Star School's cafeteria, so she won't be available during the day. Also, you've served faithfully on the Bereavement Committee for years. You are the logical choice."

If I'm in charge of the committee, I can put Bea Cavanaugh on set-up instead of making her awful tuna casserole. Nobody ever eats it.

Oh, won't Mildred be pea-green jealous when she finds out the preacher asked me and not her? She thinks she's so high and mighty since she was picked for the Baptism Committee. Maybe now she'll think twice before calling me again to complain about my granddaughter's short skirts.

"I'll do it. With the good Lord's help, I'll lead the Bereavement Committee."

"God bless you, Miz Benton! Thank you!" The preacher looked relieved and sighed as he stood, towering over Lucille.

"No need to rush off, Brother Atwood."

"I have a few other visits to make. Mr. Chandler is in the hospital again."

"I'm mighty sorry to hear that. He sure has had a lot of sickness this year." *I bet the first thing the nurses did was give that man a bath. He always gives off a powerful stink!*

"Might we have a word of prayer before I leave?"

"I'd be honored, Brother Atwood." Lucille bowed her head and waited.

He cleared his throat and clasped his hands. "Lord, I thank you for your faithful servant, Lucille. May her service in this leadership position bless those who have lost loved ones. In Jesus' name, Amen."

"Amen," Lucille echoed. She accompanied the preacher to the door.

"Please tell Mr. Benton I'm sorry to have missed him."

"I'll do that, Brother Atwood. He's usually home from work by now, but he's gettin' a new tire put on the Chevy over at Oklahoma Tire and Supply this afternoon.

After closing and locking the door, she sat in her favorite upholstered chair next to the telephone table. She picked up the receiver and dialed the familiar number. *Mildred will just die when she hears this!* Lucille smiled slyly as she waited for her friend to answer.

A LIFELONG FRIENDSHIP

Patricia Roop Hollinger

It was destiny. Lois was born on February 16th, and I was born February 28th, 1939, just a mile from where she was born. Our families had enlisted the help of a local nurse, who was then stolen from Lois to be present for my birth. However, that did not hinder our friendship that began in the nursery at the local Church of the Brethren where both families attended regularly.

We began our school day at Elmer Wolfe High School, Union Bridge, Maryland. Ms. Riser was our teacher and was known for "shaking" students who talked too much or were out of line for any reason. My older sister reported that she had been shaken by her, so I was determined to be "good" to avoid the Ms. Riser shaking; thus, Lois and I did not talk during class.

We were a class of 22 and together from grades one to twelve. We were a family away from home. We shared secrets, our joys and then the death of Lois's mother. I could not imagine losing my mother, so Lois was welcome any time at our home. I recall while watching a film about the last days of Pompeii, Italy in grade school and being struck by the death and destruction, wondering how this impacted Lois who was sitting beside me. Just recently while visiting Lois she was recalling how I comforted her while watching that movie.

Lois's father was our math teacher in high school. We always sat beside each other during any class and of course we always had so much to talk about (the new boy in class, what we had for supper the night before, what team do we play in basketball next week, etc.) Finally, Lois's father said for all to hear, "Lois and Pat you must stop talking." Of course, we did with that scolding in front of the whole class.

On Sundays we attended the same Sunday School class at the Union Bridge Church of the Brethren, Union Bridge, Maryland, where her father was a preacher. We were both steeped in the traditions of wearing the prayer covering after we were baptized. However, I was the one who had so many questions when no one had the answer to who Cain and Abel married. Since more people showed up in the Bible, I wanted to know where they came from. Also, the Immaculate Conception did not make sense to me. I knew how babies came into being. However, Lois bought the teaching "hook line and sinker" and she just wanted to head for the nursery to be with the babies while I wanted answers to my questions.

Sunday afternoons were boring. We needed to get together. Thus, began the Sunday ritual of me asking my mother if I could visit Lois. "You have to ask your father first." she responded.

When I asked my father he said, "You have to ask your mother first."

"But Dad, I have already asked; and she referred me to you." The answer was always "yes" but this ritual happened every Sunday.

We both lived on farms so there was always something to do outside, like watching the watercress grow, milking the goats, or just soaking in the goodness of nature. We played the piano and sang. We played Monopoly while in another room her father was busily typing his weekly letter to family. On Sunday afternoon, he was just Lois' father. Not the math teacher or the preacher.

When Lois' father re-married a woman who had never had any children, we were both worried how she would cope with our need for being together 24/7. One evening, we arrived at her home after a basketball game, and we had the answer to that question—on the kitchen table was a plate of fudge that she had made for us. "AH!" Our friendship was validated.

Upon graduation we both enrolled at Bridgewater College, Bridgewater, Virginia; a Church of the Brethren affiliated college. Of course, we were roommates. However, my college days ended with a hospitalization for major depression. Lois married her college sweetheart and moved to Elizabethtown, Pennsylvania. My college sweetheart and I did not survive such a major disruption. I was bereft and married a man that my younger sister introduced me to. I had no idea what I wanted to be when I grew up other than being a mother. My first child, Michael, was a delight. However, his brother Stephen was born with multiple birth defects. Our marriage did not survive his never-ending care. Once again, I was bereft. Wondering what to do with my life led me to finish my aborted college education.

During this process, I attended events sponsored by Parents Without Partners where I met my second husband. I made it clear that I was in pursuit of my college degree, and he proposed that I also obtain a master's degree. This led to me obtaining a BS in Sociology at Towson State University, MS in Pastoral Counseling and Licensed Clinical Professional Counselor in the state of Maryland where many of my questions were being answered. My articles about mental illness were published in the *Messenger,* which is a Church of the Brethren publication. During a speaking engagement at the Elizabethtown Church of the Brethren, Lois was in the nursery taking care of babies while I was in the pulpit. This spoke volumes about our childhood interests and the Church of the Brethren years ago.

In December 2023, I received the news that Lois' husband Joe had died. I attended his memorial service on April 20th at the Elizabethtown Church of the Brethren as we continue to share significant events in our lives.

MOON OVER MALIBU

Helen (Len) Leatherwood

When Sophie came over that afternoon back in 2015, I was feeling like a complete loser. Jake had walked out on me again, and I, feeling like a dumbass, was sitting in a dark room sipping a gin and tonic.

"Where are you?" Sophie called out from the kitchen, knowing full well what she was walking into after my tearful phone call just a half hour before. "I'm in the den," I said, knowing I should at least switch on one light so she didn't break her neck tripping over the hassock. Before I could get up, she was standing there, her slim frame illuminated by the hall light, and she said, "Girlfriend, I know you're hurting, but just remind me of where the lamp is."

We sat for four hours that afternoon, me crying for at least two of them and spending the other two lambasting myself for letting that sorry excuse for a human back into my life to do this to me AGAIN. Finally, Sophie stood up and said, "Okay, enough of that, let's get our shoes on. We're going for a drive."

"I don't want to," I protested, but she went into the bedroom and found my sandals. "Sorry, honey, you owe me at least 30 minutes outside with the top down on that sweet convertible of yours. But, one rule: I'm driving."

Again, I protested, but this time about not wanting her to drive my car. "You've had four gin and tonics too many," she said matter-of-factly, "and you know I am always the designated driver since I have a five-year chip I'm hoping to earn by the first of next month."

It wasn't long before we were off on the open road with the top down, and I will admit that seeing that full moon rising on the horizon was good for my heart and my soul.

"I have an idea," Sophie said as she turned on her signal and entered the on-ramp for the freeway. "Let's go on a little adventure. Neither of us has anyone waiting up for us, so let's go up the coast road and look at the ocean."

"But, it's too late. We're two women alone, and you know that can be—"

"Yes, dangerous," Sophie said. "But guess what? We're two grown-up women and we can handle a drive up Pacific Coast Highway, just the two of us. Somehow, I think we'll be okay."

I sank back in my seat. She was right. I was always the one who brought fear into every picture. We could drive up the coast and enjoy the moon reflecting on the calm waves of the Pacific. I took a deep breath of the salt air and felt glad to be able to lean back and see the sky full of stars.

We drove through the business district of Malibu, past Pepperdine, and then on up past Zuma Beach. There were cars on the road, but not too many. We came down a tall hill and saw Neptune's Net off to the right. Sophie slowed down and put on her turn signal. "Let's grab something quick to eat," she said. "They close at nine on Friday nights, so we'll have at least an hour."

Neptune's Net was not my first choice of prime entertainment. There would be a lot of bikers there since it was the weekend, and by this time of the evening, many would be feeling a bit "too happy" after an afternoon and evening of drinking. "Do we have to?" I said. "We could just turn back around and head back into town."

"Sorry, but I need a pee stop, too," Sophie said as she made the turn into the crowded parking lot and found a spot near the back.

"Okay," I said, "but let's not spend too much time here. These bikers can get a little rowdy, and I'm not in the mood."

"Agreed," she said as she hopped out of the car. "Meet you inside."

As I made my way through the crowded outdoor sitting area full of a wide range of people, from bikers to families to chic Hollywood types, I went to the end of the line to order. Fairly sober by now, I realized I was hungry, and getting some food in my stomach was probably a good idea. I was standing there glancing at my watch, 7:55, when I heard a voice behind me say with a tinge of flirtation, "Fancy meeting you here." I looked up, and there stood one of my old friends from a job at a restaurant I'd had a few years back. "Danny!" I said. "What a surprise. What are you doing here?"

"Drinking in the atmosphere," he said with a grin. "Just like everyone else."

I looked around at the crowd and saw that everyone did, in fact, look happy they were at this place tonight, with a full moon glinting on the ocean for all to see.

Sophie arrived about this time, and I introduced her to Danny, one of the few non-biker types around us.

"How do you two know each other?" she asked.

"We were both poor college students back in the day trying to make ends meet. We met at a restaurant in Westwood," Danny said.

"Danny's a chef now," I tossed out. "At a Michelin-ranked restaurant in downtown."

Sophie smiled. "Impressive. And you are here? Why? Surely not the food."

"Fresh fish, big portions, the ocean smiling at me from right over there," Danny said, pointing west. "Hard to beat that combo for a guy who almost never gets a Friday night off."

"Can you join us then?" I said, already sensing a possible love connection between my best friend and my long-lost college buddy.

"I can if you give me a second," Danny said. "I just have to let my buddies know that I am going to sit with you two for a while."

"Buddies?" I said.

"Those two guys over there are my friends, Josh and Terry. You could join us if you like. We have space for two more."

Sophie glanced at me and gave an almost imperceptible nod.

"That'd be great," I said, happy not to be the third wheel at a table with these two who could hardly keep their eyes off each other.

As it turned out, Josh was another chef, and Terry was a food critic. "Is Neptune's Net getting a write-up?" I asked.

Terry shrugged. "They've been reviewed lots of times. I'm off tonight, just hanging out. The last thing I want to do is work." Josh raised his beer, "I'll drink to that."

As it turned out, that drive up PCH proved to be a fateful choice. Sophie and Danny started dating and were married within a year; Terry and I hung out together at first as another couple for Sophie and Danny and then followed them to the altar a year later. Josh was the best man for both Danny and Terry and the honorary uncle to the four kids we've had between us, two and two.

Now that I look back on that afternoon in 2015, I am struck by just how lucky I was that Sophie came over that day. She knew the balance between grieving and then letting it go, and it was her idea to be done with the former and embrace the latter.

They say a good man is hard to find, which I can wholeheartedly agree with. But I would also add that a good girlfriend can be equally hard to find, especially one who has kept me on the straight and narrow, drinking-wise, over all these years and who also is single-handedly responsible for pushing me out of my house to meet the man who truly would be better than good.

Sophie and I have pledged to stay best friends until we die. Since our husbands are close friends and our kids are near the same ages and go to the same schools, we may actually have a real shot at making good on that promise. In the meantime, I'm just happy every day that I have her in my life. She is like that moon on our drive up PCH: full, glowing, and shining bright. I am grateful to have her to help light my path: then, now, and always.

Dear Teenage Friend

Amy J. Bostelman
(for Amber)

Swimming and shenanigans
"sisters" shopping the Neiman Marcus clearance racks
with your mom

Learning to be classy while
being sassy

We became friends when my lunch table rejected me
because girls can just be plain right mean

We only had one thwarted physical scuffle that
Jennifer broke up that summer we were inseparable

I remember standing under your drunk neighbor's eave during a rain
pour shimmering drops brought to earth by gravity

It was truly an in the "Now" moment

Summer days swimming and sunbathing at the "Island,"
That first time we shared a bottle of Strawberry Hill atop
that cute little red bridge swans used to swim by

The Ouija board we created with notebook paper and a planchette made from a keyring summoning answers of who would be our future husbands

Hanging out with Tami and you
smoking cigarettes passed between us

That year I went to high school and you were still in junior high
we kind of drifted away and no longer talked
I think it was because of a boy

Now we have our husbands
Now we have our daughters
Now we're in our forties

So many memories of yesterdays
Many of which I experienced with you in the state of the "Now"

"A friend may be waiting
behind a stranger's face."

— MAYA ANGELO

"Lots of people want to ride with you in
the limo, but what you want is someone
who will take the bus with you when the
limo breaks down."

— OPRAH WINFREY

BOOKS PUBLISHED BY STORY CIRCLE NETWORK

Inside and Out: Women's Truths, Women's Stories
edited by Susan Schoch

Kitchen Table Stories
edited by Jane Ross

Kitchen Table Stories 2022
edited by Susan Schoch

Starting Points
by Susan Wittig Albert

True Words from Real Women, the SCN Anthology 2009-2014
edited by Amber Lea Starfire, Mary Jo Doig, Susan Schoch

Real Women Write: Sharing Our Stories, Sharing Our Lives,
the SCN Anthology, 2015-2023
edited by Susan Schoch

What Wildness Is This: Women Write About the Southwest
edited by Susan Wittig Albert, Susan Hanson,
Jan Epton Seale, Paula Stallings Yost

With Courage and Common Sense:
Memoirs from the Older Women's Legacy Circle
edited by Susan Wittig Albert and Dayna Finet

Writing From Life
by Susan Wittig Albert

Story Circle
N E T W O R K

...by, for, and about women.

"Sometimes it's not the book.
It's where the reader is on her journey."

— Susan Wittig Albert

This book was designed using
Proxima Nova, Eccentric, and Adobe Garamond.
Designed and typeset by Sherry Wachter:
sherry@sherrywachter.com

www.ingramcontent.com/pod-product-compliance
Lightning Source LLC
Chambersburg PA
CBHW060449280326
41933CB00014B/2706